THE COMPLETE
DAIRY
FOODS
COOKBOOK

THE COMPLETE
DAIRY FOODS COOKBOOK

HOW TO MAKE EVERYTHING FROM CHEESE TO CUSTARD IN YOUR OWN KITCHEN

by
E. Annie Proulx
and
Lew Nichols

Editor: Charles Gerras

Book Design: Jerry O'Brien

Original Art: Jean Gardner and Jerry O'Brien

 Rodale Press, Emmaus, Pa.

Special Contributions:

    Test Kitchen Personnel: Anita Hirsch and Rhonda Diehl

    Editorial Assistant: Camille Bucci

    Copy Editor: Judith S. Camarda

    Additional Visual Material: State Historical Society of Wisconsin;
       The Ron Yablon Graphic Archives; Dover Publications, Inc.;
       Morgan & Morgan, Inc.; Hoegger Supply Company

Printed in the United States of America on recycled paper, containing a high percentage of de-inked fiber.

Library of Congress Cataloging in Publication Data

Proulx, Annie.
    The complete dairy foods cookbook.

    Includes index.
    1. Cookery (Dairy products) I. Nichols, Lew.
II. Title.
TX759.P76   641.6'7   81-23396
ISBN 0-87857-388-7   hardcover   AACR2

2 4 6 8 10 9 7 5 3 1 hardcover

Contents

This book is dedicated to the milch animals of the world—the kindly cows, ewes, does, reindeer, camels and mares who have given so generously to mankind's welfare and pleasure.

1 YESTERDAY'S DAIRIES

Not so long ago the family cow was a commonplace in rural life, and so was the home dairy with its pans of rising golden cream for hand-churned butter or for pouring over baked apples and blueberry pie. In the cool springhouse crocks of butter stamped with a decorative mold waited to be spread on warm bread. Milk puddings, flips and milk custards were part of every cook's repertoire. Protein-rich cheeses, from sweet fresh cottage to mellow aged oldsters, were so prized they were used for money or trade in rural early America.

In those days it was possible to taste cheeses with tang and snap, pleasantly acid buttermilk freckled with golden spots, and hand-cranked ice cream mingled with the fragrant flesh of ripe peaches. This book is written for people who long to enjoy again the delicious flavors of homemade dairy products; for people who keep a milk cow or goat (or who have neighbors who do) and want to make their own cheeses, butter and yogurt; for people who like to know what's in the food they eat; for people who know the satisfactions and values of homestead self-sufficiency; and for those of us who delight in good food and whose happiest hours are spent pottering in the kitchen.

ANCIENT DAYS

Thousands of years ago when humans began to domesticate cattle, they discovered that milk has complex and unusual properties which allow it to be made into dozens of tasty, life-sustaining foods, from fermented milk to dried milk powder, from sweet butter to powerful-smelling cheeses. Perforated clay jars for making cheese have been found in the excavations of the Swiss Lake Dwellers' towns, and butter was celebrated in the ancient Hindu *Veda* nearly 4,000 years ago. A stone relief from the city of Ur shows dairy workers milking cows and straining the fresh milk into large jars. Marco Polo, in his thirteenth century travels with Kublai Khan, described in detail how the Khan's soldiers made dried milk powder and used it as a basic soup and gruel ingredient in their harsh nomadic existence. Medieval manuscripts show peasants loading cheeses into carts for shipment to town markets, and Charlemagne learned to like green-mold Roquefort — after a little

initial hesitation — at the monastery of St. Gall. Gourmets have elevated certain cheeses to the rank of nobility, and one of the world's most curious occupations — that of Professional Cheese Rapper — is practiced in Holland by people who can determine a cheese's ripeness and value simply by knocking on it smartly.

FROM ASS TO ZEBU

Humans have experimented with the milk of ewes, cows, goats, camels, mares, asses, water buffalo, reindeer, llamas and zebu to make a bewildering variety of cheeses; fermented milk products like yogurt, koumiss, kefir (the fermented mare's milk of southern Russia), Scandinavian *kaeldermaelk, filbunke* and *taette* milk, Armenian *matzoon*, Egyptian *leben*; buttermilk, acidophilus milk; dried milk; butters ranging from gilt-edge to grease in quality; creams in different weights and acidities; and, in modern times, sherbets and ice creams flavored with nuts, fruits and spices.

Certain regions have become household words through the fame of their dairy products. The Emmenthal Valley in Switzerland is famous for its *Emmenthaler* Swiss cheese; Devonshire, for its cream; the towns of Roquefort, Camembert, Cheshire, Cheddar and Stilton were put on the map by their cheeses; Bulgaria has been known as the source of the world's finest yogurt since Nobel Prize-winning Russian biologist Ilya Metchnikoff attributed the amazing longevity of some Bulgarian tribespeople to their large daily consumption of yogurt carrying the benign bacterium *Lactobacillus bulgaricus*.

Other places have gained fame through special breeds of stock which produced superior milk, butter or cheese — breeds like the Jersey and Guernsey cows from the Channel Islands of the same names, and goats like the Toggenburg and Saanen of Switzerland or the La Mancha of Spain.

Cheeses alone, whose names and varieties fill specialized dictionaries, have inspired turophiles, or cheese lovers, to some of the most ecstatic prose written in their attempts to describe the tangy, crumbly goat cheeses, the noble blues veined with rich mold, the flower cheeses scented with rose, violet or marigold petals, and the French *fromage au foin*, a delicate skim milk cheese ripened on new-mown hay.

MODERN "FLOOR WAX"

Yet in the United States, where almost all dairy products come out of the factories of the mass production food industries, fine aged cheeses made from superior quality milk are rare and expensive, forced off the market by the bland processed horrors one cheese lover has aptly described as "solidified floor wax," and the so-called Cheese Foods, those highly spiced, additive-crammed chemical mixtures with mere traces of cheese, gluey concoctions which bear as much resemblance to their noble cheese cousins as a plastic flamingo does to a real one. The "natural" cheeses, those familiar plastic-wrapped rectangles in the supermarket, are rushed through the factory and onto the shelf when they have barely had time to coagulate, much less ripen and mature through slow aging. Nearly all commercial butter is made from sour cream with coloring and salt added; few consumers know the delicate, fresh taste of unsalted sweet cream butter made from high-quality Jersey milk. Our commercial ice cream is loaded with stabilizers, gelatin,

sugar, neon-strength colorings and high-powered flavorings to mask the inferior quality of the raw material. Commercial yogurts — mostly thin, runny soups — are disguised with sugar and artificial fruit flavors. The scarce high-quality dairy products seldom available anywhere but in natural foods stores command prices that can only be characterized as extravagant.

How did we get from the home dairy of the last century to the prepackaged, tasteless stuff that crams the coolers in every supermarket from Maine to Arizona? Why have we lost the ability to make our own good, nutritional dairy products?

THE COLONIAL GOAT

Most people feel that a homestead isn't a home unless it has a milch cow or a few goats. This is the continuation of a small farm tradition that goes back to our nation's beginnings. Although cattle came to the New World with Columbus on his second voyage, the history of neat stock (animals with cloven hooves) in North America is linked directly with that of the struggling early settlements. Three heifers and a bull were brought to Plymouth Colony as early as 1624 by Edward Wilson. Governor William Bradford, however, yearned for a taste of goats' milk, and in 1626 the Colony, anxious for more livestock, sent out a ship on a trading voyage. At Monhegan Island, off the coast of Maine, the crew swapped corn for various goods with the temporary inhabitants of the fishing and trading settlement there, including "a parcell of goats" to Bradford's pleasure. Captain John Smith and Lord Delaware had brought goats to the southern settlements early on, and for decades these sprightly, pale-eyed creatures were the dominant milk stock in America.

Goats were favored over cows in the young colonies because not only did these vigorous, hardy animals need less care than cows, but they acted as self-propelled brush cutters, clearing the land as they browsed. In 1629 a shipment of 42 milch goats arrived at Salem, and a few years later another 80 came from Virginia Colony where the animals were rapidly multiplying. By 1639 a contemporary observer, William Wood, estimated that there were 4,000 goats in Massachusetts Bay Colony. The Indians rather soon developed a taste for goat flesh, the Narragansetts reputedly killing 200 of Governor Winthrop's goats from his large herd.

Goats did very well in the rich new country — too well, for within 30 years of their introduction to the colonies they had acquired an evil reputation as unstoppable garden raiders in a land where fences could not be built fast enough to keep them out. In the mid-seventeenth century their numbers began to decline, and they were replaced by more docile kine, the red cows of Devonshire, which offered an important service that was beyond the powers of goats — they could pull plows.

THE FAMILY FARM

In 1626 in Plymouth Colony the tillable land was divided into individual shares, and the livestock was apportioned out also, an important break away from the traditional communal farm customs of the Old World past. This was the beginning of the American family farm where the farm value, the well-being and sustenance of the farm owner, were based on the number of individually owned livestock. In 1626 each family was allotted one cow and two goats for every six shares of land they held to supply them with cheese, butter and milk as well as pulling power and, in the end, meat and tanned leather. This ideal characterized small farming in America for another two centuries. When Timothy Dwight, president of Yale from 1795 to 1817, toured the rough back country of New England 'he wrote in his *Travels*:

> Even a poor man has usually a comfortable house, a little land, a cow, swine, poultry, a few sheep.

From the colonial period into the nineteenth century, milk production, butter and cheese making were only sidelines on the farm, the exclusive province of the women in the household during the few pasture months that cows yielded milk. Winter milk production was unusual until the advent of the silo in the late nineteenth century. More important for our ancestors was the cow's ability to provide beef, leather and plough pulling power. Selective breeding for milk or beef production was virtually unpracticed until a century ago, and agricultural historians have traced a gradual decline in the quality of the original Devonshire red cow stock brought to this country thanks to indiscriminate and careless breeding. An English cattle authority touring North America in the 1840s visited one of New York state's outstanding stock farms and described it disapprovingly:

> His stock comprehends about 400 cattle. . . . and I could not but regret seeing land so valuable covered with stock of so inferior a description.
>
> The red breed of cattle which I had seen all over the State of New York . . . are considered to be Devons. If so, they are much degenerated, being of diminutive size, coarse, and evidently bad feeders. . . .
>
> . . . They seem starved and stunted in their growth, and as miserable as the worst stock on the bleak sides of our Grampian hills.

These wretched native cows, known familiarly as common stock, rarely gave more than six quarts of milk a day. The editor of *The Cultivator*, one of the best agricultural journals of its time, also disparaged the American common cow.

This mixed breed are not celebrated for anything; some of them are good milkers as far as quantity is concerned, but as to quality of the milk and aptitude to fatten they generally fail. . . . They are small, short-bodied, thin and coarse-haired, steep-rumped, slab-sided, having little aptitude to fatten or lay on the fat at the right places.

It was the wealthy gentleman farmer, breeding cattle as a hobby in the late eighteenth and early nineteenth centuries, who began to perk up the common stock by importing the improved English and Channel Islands breeds. The Durham, also known as the Shorthorn, was brought into Maryland and Virginia in 1783, praised as a dual-purpose milk and beef cow. In 1809 the first livestock improvement association in the country was formed in Pennsylvania—the Pennsylvania Society for Improving the Breed of Cattle. It was familiarly called The Cattle Society and offered good purses for bettering the native stock.

By 1820 imported pure-bred English cows were the rage among the gentlemen farmers who vied with each other for the ribbons and prizes at county fairs and livestock shows. Although some of their efforts were misdirected, particularly the brief but bizarre craze for monstrously oversized cattle—like one New Jersey bovine that weighed in at more than 3,000 pounds—or the stubborn attempts to

Briarcliff Farm, Sing Sing, New York, property of James Stillman, is typical of farms where wealthy owners could afford to "improve the breed" as a hobby.

breed cattle for the threefold purpose of "the yoke, the pail, and the knife," within several decades the benefits of improved breeding began to catch the attention of the small farmholder. At the same time, the demand for farm-fresh butter and cheese in the major metropolitan areas — New York, Philadelphia and Boston — opened people's eyes to the fact that money could be made from dairying. Although the transformation of the dairy room into the factory took another century, from that moment the home dairy started its slow but inexorable decline into near-extinction.

Home dairies were small. In New England, writes agricultural historian Howard Russell:

> Nearly every farm, even those of village tradesmen, had at least a family cow for milk and perhaps butter or cheese. Seldom were herds large, often four to eight plus young stock. . . . In old, settled, eastern Massachusetts there were, in 1767, about two cows for each five persons.

These cows were left to their own devices in the matter of feed; they browsed in the forests and along roadsides. Milk production was often scanty and the cow was dry for most of the year except during the lush summer months. Some of the poor beasts made it through the winter by eating the tips of evergreens. Others survived on corn husks, poplar leaves, straw and poor-quality hay, reviving and plumping out again on spring clover. They gave enough milk for the cornmeal mush with some left over for butter and cheese. The quality of the butter and cheese was uneven, often with peculiar off-flavors related to the animal's wild diet, and frequently heavily salted to keep it longer in those days of no refrigeration. The dairy woman sometimes had enough milk

to make extra cheese and butter in the summer which she would literally salt away to sell during the winter months when most cows were dry.

Yet many skillful dairyists gained a reputation for a fine product, and certain regions became well known for the richness and excellence of their dairy products — almost exclusively butter and cheese, since fresh milk for drinking and cooking was not common until after the Civil War when the serious business of making money with milk got underway. Rhode Island, with its lush meadow grasses, was a famous dairy region in the mid-eighteenth century. An English traveler marveled that the whole of Rhode Island seemed laid out in rich pasture lands and pronounced the butter and cheese excellent. The best New England cheeses, whether they came from Vermont or Maine, when shipped to southern markets were called "Rhode Island cheese," the mark of a superior product in that time. Some of these dairy farms in Rhode Island were enormous by the standards of the day; "College Tom" Hazard made 3,627 pounds of quality cheese in 1754. A few dairies kept over 100 cows and made more than 10,000 pounds of cheese a year. These were the famous Quaker dairy farms that ran on slave labor. One Rhode Island dairy had 24 slave women working up cheese in this period.

In New York state, Herkimer County was well known for the excellence of its cheese and is considered the cradle of the American cheese industry, while Orange County made outstanding butter. Contemporary explanations as to why these particular regions made the best dairy products were laid at the doors of rich pasture or pure water; others claimed the quality of the salt used made the difference; some cited the local breed of cows as the reason, and still others swore that the area's deft and skillful dairy women were the secret source of the delicious products. U. P. Hedrick in his *A History of Agriculture in the State of New York* comments wryly:

> . . . but reading the articles now with a better knowledge of sanitation than those old writers had it is certain that Herkimer made better cheese and Orange made better butter by reason of the fact that cleanliness was better observed.

In Pennsylvania, the other leading dairy region, Lancaster and Delaware counties were renowned for cheese and butter. In the nineteenth century, when the best butter brought 20 to 30 cents a pound, Pennsylvania "gilt-edge" butter fetched one dollar a pound! Wrote P. H. Nichlin in his *Pleasant Peregrinations Through the Prettiest Part of Pennsylvania Performed by Peregrine Prolix* in 1836:

> The butter and cream-cheese to be found in the Philadelphia market in the spring and summer are such dainties as are found in no other place. They are produced on dairy farms near the city whose energies have for several generations been directed to this one useful end and who now work with an art made perfect by the experience of a century.

THE OLD HOME DAIRY

The dairy, as well as the kitchen, was strictly woman's business in the days before large market demands. She supplied the family needs for fresh milk, butter and cheese, and often made a respectable income from surplus dairy products, either selling for cash, or taking trade credit at the general store. Running a dairy operation took considerable time, skill and labor, and the work had to be done twice a day every day of the milking season.

A separate dairy house was usually built over a spring, and the cold running water, stone flooring and good ventilation made a cool, fresh atmosphere well suited to making cream, butter and cheese except during the hottest weather. On some large farms a tenant house was built over the spring and a hired couple installed. The man did farm chores while his wife ran the dairy on shares, getting a few cents a pound for the butter and cheese she made. The farmer marketed the dairy produce. An 1871 writer in *The Practical Farmer* reported enthusiastically:

> The owner of the farm has only to back his Dearborn up to the springhouse once or twice a week to take the butter, already packed in tubs with a receptacle for ice at each end, to the railroad station.

The fresh milk was lugged into the dairy twice a day, and poured into crocks or milk pans to let the cream rise. Before 1840 heavy earthenware crocks about 9 inches wide at the base and 12 to 14 inches wide at the top, with no handles, glazed on the interior but not the outside, were standard in Pennsylvania. These cream crocks were known as Dutch potteries, and after 1850 were generally replaced by lighter 8-quart tinned pans and a tin skimmer. After 1875 dairyists were divided on the merits of shallow cream pans versus deep cans, proponents of each type acrimoniously savaging the rival containers while extolling the virtues of their own.

The deep-can procedure was commonly known as the Swedish system and consisted of large tinned cans submerged in water kept at the low temperature of 44°F by ice cooling; there was a greater recovery of the butterfat than when the

☞ Every experiment that will take from the wives and daughters of farmers a part of the heavy drudgery of the farm-house should receive the hearty approbation of the "men folks." In the matter of butter-making, for example: Why should not "creameries" be established in all dairy regions, so as to relieve the women of the vast amount of hard work, care and anxiety incident to butter-making? It is stated that the farmers of Franklin county, Mass., sent to market, during 1880, 490 tons of butter, which fetched on the average about three cents a pound less than creamery butter from factories in the vicinity. Thus, besides the drudgery imposed on the women of their households—the cost of which cannot be expressed in figures—the farmers lost in money nearly $30,000 that year by making their butter at home.

In the late nineteenth century, newspapers were at odds with the romantic idyll of farm women contentedly churning butter on the back porch as a respite from in-house drudgery.

air-temperature shallow-pan method was used. Mr. L. S. Hardin, a Kentucky butter maker from Louisville, exhorted Vermont farmers to adopt this Swedish method of setting milk and described a number of butter-making competitions in which he had triumphed over shallow-pan competitors. Economics won the game. Not only was more butterfat recovered from the milk with the deep-can method, but the initial investment in containers was about one-third that of a shallow-pan setup.

The shallow-pan method took up a lot of space, also; scores of pans about 13 inches across were filled with milk to a depth of about 2 inches. The milk stood from 24 to 60 hours until the cream rose to the surface. The cream was then skimmed off and ladled into a stone crock where it "ripened" until enough was gathered to make butter. The cream, usually sour by this time, was churned; then, after the butter "came" it was washed to get out all the buttermilk. Finally the butter was salted and "put down" in crocks or wooden firkins. It was a matter of pride with the skillful dairy woman to make butter that would stay sweet for a year if stored in a cool place. Contemporary reports indicate that these master butter makers were far and few between.

The deep-can method offered another advantage. The chilled water kept the milk and cream fresh and sweet much longer, and was well suited to the making of gilt-edge sweet cream butter, a period delicacy.

Dairyists who had no cold spring-house but had to depend on well water, put their milk in the cellar—the coolest place on the farm—for the cream to rise. It was important to have a well-ventilated, sweet cellar, for milk is notoriously subject to picking up musty off-flavors.

A third cream-setting method of the late nineteenth century which was warmly defended was the practice of heating the milk to 130°F, and then setting it in either deep or shallow pans for the cream to rise. The arguments of the proponents of these rival cream-procuring methods fill the agricultural papers of the nineteenth century, until they are all swept away by the revolutionary invention of the cream separator.

Cheese making was more difficult than butter, largely because additional equipment and space were needed— especially curing rooms that could be kept at a steady 70° to 75°F with few fluctuations in temperature and constant humidity to prevent the ripening cheeses from drying out. Most dairyists specialized in either butter or cheese, but some managed both.

There were numerous styles of churns. The two most common were the *dasher* churn, an upright hand churn, and the *barrel* churn, often worked by dog or horse power in large dairies where human time and labor were in short supply. The

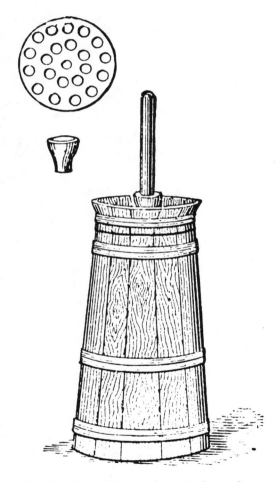

The old-fashioned butter churn, dasher style, whose hollow thunk, thunk, thunk once echoed in every rural community.

At the turn of the century, a better butter churn was a big seller in the mail-order catalogs.

dasher churn was replaced in the final quarter of the nineteenth century by an oscillating churn that saved many weary hours of labor.

Although delicious gilt-edge butter was made and sold at a premium, most farm butter was not very good according to contemporary accounts, especially the stuff made in the summer dog days, which was heavily salted to keep it barely edible. The worst of this butter was sold as "grease" for a few cents a pound, and was a wretched product in which the grain of the butter had broken down into a greasy glob. Much country butter came to the country store in trade for goods that couldn't be made on the farm. The storekeeper mixed all of this variable, different-colored butter into one lot and sold it to the traveling butter agent as "marbled butter."

Home dairy butter production peaked around 1880, when, in Pennsylvania alone, it is estimated that 79,336,000 pounds of farm butter were made. Home butter making then began to disappear as creameries and cheese factories replaced this ancient farm occupation.

GIANT CHEESES

The nineteenth century was given to excesses in both directions: poverty was abject while wealth was ostentatious; butter was inedible grease or sky-high gilt edge; cheeses were modest in size or, in an odd dairy fad, of gargantuan and staggering dimensions. Of the many huge exhibition and celebration cheeses made, one of the most remarkable was the giant cheese of Cheshire, Massachusetts.

Western Massachusetts's Berkshire country was confirmed as an outstanding cheese-making center after its turophilic triumph in 1801. The town of Cheshire was made up of ardent Jeffersonian Democrat farmers who followed the lead of Elder John Leland, the Baptist pastor. When Thomas Jefferson of Virginia was elected president, beating out Massachusetts's John Adams, the apostate Cheshire Democrats celebrated the victory in one of American dairying's finest hours by making a huge and awesome cheese. Elder Leland persuaded every farmer with milk cows to bring in the whole day's milking on July 20, 1801. The record shows that 1,200 cows contributed to the cause. The milk was curded, salted and spiced with choice herbs. An oversize cider press squeezed out the whey for over two weeks. When the ripened cheese was later shipped by horse team and water to President Jefferson in Washington, it weighed 1,235 pounds. A six-horse team drew the great cheese through the Washington streets and Cheshire's name went down in cheese history.

BIG BUSINESS

As city dwellers packed in closer and closer together, and the cow became identified more definitely as a creature of the rural hinterlands, astute farmers and middlemen began to recognize that there was money in butter, cheese and milk. Improved breeds, vigorous marketing and a number of outstanding dairying inventions led to the infant dairy industry.

The 1856 invention of a practical vacuum milk condenser by Gail Borden, a New York-born surveyor and inventor, meant that milk could be kept for long periods of time without turning. The extensive use of this condensed milk in Union Army supplies during the Civil War gave people a taste for the product.

Louis Pasteur's revolutionary work demonstrating that bacteria could be destroyed at a temperature of about 140°F without destroying the flavor and food value of milk, revolutionized American food habits and made us a nation of milk drinkers. Entrepreneurs quickly discovered that the cities represented a vast market for liquid fresh milk.

De Laval's continuous cream separator, invented in 1878, meant that the tedious business of raising cream in crocks and pans was a thing of the past. Now, swift, efficient separation of the cream from the milk was possible. Because the early equipment was bulky and expensive, local creamery centers, many of them co-ops, became points for milk collection, cream separation and butter making. The creamery movement was underway, and butter making, once the occupation and income of hundreds of farm women in a county or region, became the profitable business of the commercial creamery. Farmers hauled their whole milk to the creamery where the cream was separated out and bought by the creamery; the skim milk was returned to the farmer, who hauled it back home to fatten pigs and calves or for the home manufacture of skim milk cheese. In 1890 the small hand separator which could be used on the farm meant the farmer only had to haul cream to the creamery.

1890 was a great year for dairy farmers; not only did the hand separator appear, but Dr. S. M. Babcock invented a testing *(continued on page 16)*

An early cream separator worked by sheep power.

The Iowa hand separator. Although the early separators were inefficient and made inferior cream for butter, they were immediately popular on the farm. The farmer no longer had to haul his whole milk to the creamery, wait until it was separated, then drag the skim milk — usually in poor condition — back to the farm, but could separate it on the spot at once. Even better, it reduced daily trips to the creamery to once or twice a week.

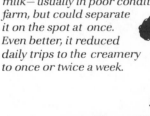

The biggest selling hand separator after 1890 was the De Laval "Baby No. 1." Hundreds of thousands of farmers and farmers' wives were free of cooling the milk, skimming the cream, traveling daily to the creamery, and washing the dozens of cream pans and cans when the Baby came into the dairy room.

There was a time when a sidewalk sale of cream separators did not draw undue attention.

Advertisers were aware long ago that the right images could suggest spotless efficiency.

A simple machine could insure magical results.

device which accurately and easily measured the butterfat content of whole milk. Now dairyists could know which cows in their herds were "boarders" and which were producing the money-making cream. Low-butterfat cows were culled from farm herds and high-butterfat milkers were bred. A saying began to make the rounds that "the Babcock test can beat the Bible in making a man honest."

Finally, the practice of selling milk in sparkling glass bottles instead of an open 5- or 10-gallon can with a dipper in a traveling wagon, was introduced by a smart milk seller in Brooklyn, New York, in 1878. The milk bottle was an overnight consumer success, and the Brooklyn milk distributor's competition had to follow suit or close down. Within a few years the milk bottle was the common container for cow juice.

The first commercial creamery was set up in Wallkill, New York, in Orange County, heart of the butter belt, by Alanson Slaughter in 1861. Seven years earlier the first cheese factory had been built in Rome, New York, in Oneida County, swiftly followed by a number of cheese factories in Herkimer County cheese country. But the Eastern cheese and butter interests, both farm and commercial, had only a few decades of dairy supremacy left before they were eclipsed by the new dairy state in the mid-West—Wisconsin.

Early Wisconsin butter and cheese were generally wretched products. The small amounts that were shipped into Eastern markets were contemptuously labeled "Western grease." Most Wisconsin farmers had bought cheap land for growing wheat, and they clung to their grain-growing notions despite the decline in the fertility of the soil over the decades. Yet several New York farmers who had

An early milk bottle, perhaps the most popular food-packaging innovation of all time to consumers.

With the introduction of the milk bottle, the traveling milk wagon, selling milk from an open can by the dipper, became obsolete.

come to Wisconsin on the tail end of the wheat boom, saw the possibilities of dairying as a money-making alternative. Chester Hazen, ex-New Yorker and leader of the Wisconsin dairy movement ("trade your plow for a cow") built the first cheese factory in the state in Fond du Lac County in 1864. Though it was called "Hazen's Folly" it was a success, and by 1870 there were nearly 50 cheese factories in the state. A strong dairymen's association,

the famous University of Wisconsin Agricultural College "short courses," and vigorous marketing as well as a lack of agricultural alternatives made Wisconsin farmers into dairymen. Although there were more than 2,000 cheese factories alone in Wisconsin during the 1940s, giant food industries and mass production conglomerates have taken over most of them and now dominate dairying, not only in Wisconsin but in the whole country.

WHISKEY-MASH COWS AND OTHER SHARP PRACTICES

When dairying left the farm springhouses for the factories, some unscrupulous profit makers tried to milk the last penny out of every quart the cow gave. The most common abuse was the adulteration of milk, so widespread that even reputable agricultural papers often published information on how to make the milk go farther, offering such advice as "a little salt or other ingredient, may be added to watered milk to bring the density up to the pure milk mark" and "the blueness of milk, produced either by skimming or watering, may be removed by the use of burnt sugar which will give it a rich color, or annatto may be used for the same purpose." Much of the "blue milk" was already skimmed of its cream before the milkman watered it down with copious infusions from the water pump. The distributor was not the only villain in the milk adulteration scam — many

farmers succumbed to the lure of gold and "married the cow to the pump." The Shakers had a simple test for detecting adulterated milk:

> A well-polished knitting needle is to be dipped into a deep vessel of milk, and immediately withdrawn in an upright position. If the milk is pure, some of the fluid will hang to the needle, but if water has been added to the milk, even in small proportions, the fluid will not adhere to the needle.

The most noxious practice of all was the whiskey-mash milk factory, large "dairies" of permanently stabled cows situated outside large cities like New York and Philadelphia. These unfortunate beasts were fed the warm, wet whiskey mash that was a by-product of the distilleries. The drunken animals rapidly became addicted to the diet and gave plenty of milk, but, as reported in one contemporary account, the cows

> . . . soon become diseased; their gums ulcerate, their teeth drop out, and their breath becomes fetid . . . [they] puff up and bloat;

The treatment of cows by some uncaring mass producers is vividly depicted by an artist of the day.

their joints become stiff, so that they cannot lie down.

The copious but inferior milk these wretched animals gave was doctored up with "molasses, water and whiting" and sold for pure milk. The profit was considerable, one writer computing that 6 cents' worth of whiskey mash resulted in 80 cents' worth of milk.

These cows were hand milked in the days before milking machines, and the normal hazards of hand milking — caked manure on the udder falling into the milk along with a rain of loose hairs, dust, bits of chaff and straw, or, if the cow was milked outside in the rain, the filthy drippings from the animal's back and sides — were multiplied in the whiskey-mash barns. Writes an outraged reporter of the day:

> The milker has to raise the cow from the filth in which she has been lying and with which she is covered . . . . The hands of the milkers seldom or never are washed before milking and if they were they would soon be soiled by the cow's udder. It occasionally happens that a lump of filth falls into the milk; then the hand of the milker follows it and brings it out. . . . When a cow becomes diseased it is milked up to within one or two days of its death, even though two men may be required to hold her upright. . . . The cattle seldom or never are allowed to leave the stable; they are constantly breathing the fetid air of their prison. Their teeth rot out, their hoofs grow to an un-natural length and turn up and may be so sore that the animals are quite lame and unable to stand. . . . It is a melancholy sight to see some of the poor creatures, when they are so fortunate as to get out of their pens for an hour or so, attempting to walk.

Dairy products also received shots of powdered chalk or flour, formaldehyde or boric acid (milk preservatives); cheese and butter were colored up with dyes and different color agents, as well as preserved with large amounts of salt; and *filled milk*, where cheaper fats such as coconut oil replaced butterfat, was common in evaporated milk. Although ice cream was made in some quantity by 1850, S. W. Fletcher in his classic study *Pennsylvania Agriculture and Country Life*, remarked:

> Part of the reason for the slowness with which the American people adopted ice cream as the national refreshment was said to be the fact that so much of it was made with oleo and artificial flavors.

In the 1870s oleomargarine, a cheap imitation butter made out of skim milk and animal fats, originally for use in the French army, began to appear on the American market. In this country, but not in France, it was colored and often passed off as butter by unscrupulous dealers. Within two decades oleo had captured the low-income consumer market and butter manufacturers were feeling the pinch of competition, especially when the stuff was sold as butter at a price which undercut the real thing. One report described

> half a ton of oleo in the Quaker City, fresh from New York and labeled "Philadelphia Best Print." It looked exactly like the best locally-made butter but tasted more like lard. . . . There is at least one tallow candle in every pound. It is sold for about ten cents a pound less than the best genuine butter.

GOOD-BYE TO ALL THAT

Consumer outrage, as well as muckraking reportage of food adulteration and unsanitary food producing facilities, gradually led to municipal, state and Federal legislation to stop flagrant abuses and regulate the standards of what was to become one of the largest industries in the country—food. Ironically, while the consumer was saved from the worst evils, the small farm dairy was forced out of existence, unable to afford the sophisticated equipment and sanitary processes now required by law. Today inspectors oversee fulfillment of the rigid requirements for ventilation, light, manure disposal, screening, cooling facilities, bulk tanks, even the placement of light bulbs and the materials of which dairy utensils are made. Wrote Wendell Berry in his important book, *The Unsettling of America*:

> And nowhere now is there a market for minor produce: a bucket of cream, a hen, a few dozen eggs. One cannot sell milk from a few cows anymore; the law-required equipment is too expensive. Those markets were done away with in the name of sanitation—but, of course, to the enrichment of the large producers. . . . Future historians will no doubt remark upon the inevitable association, with us, between sanitation and filthy lucre. And it is one of the miracles of science and hygiene that the germs that used to be in our food have been replaced by poisons.

THE BEST OF THE HOME DAIRY

Not all butter, cheese and milk in the last century were doctored up by scalawags. There were thousands of small-scale, conscientious home dairyists who took pride in making superb cheese and delicate "gilt-edge" butter, and whose sleek, carefully bred and well-cared-for cows gave quantities of rich, good milk. One of them was Mrs. John T. Ellsworth of Barre, Massachusetts. In 1876 Mrs. Ellsworth wrote a prize-winning essay entitled "Management of the Butter Dairy" which was presented at the seventh annual meeting of the Vermont Dairymen's Association. In her essay this skilled butter maker outlined every step of her careful procedure in detail, stressing immaculate cleanliness. She commented, matter-of-factly, "If you would attain to eminence as butter-makers, all these minute particulars must be carefully attended to."

Today almost the only source of the prized fresh, sweet cream butter like Mrs. Ellsworth made, or of thick yellow cream, or firm, tangy goats' milk pot cheese, and a dozen other dairy delicacies, is at home. You can make unusual and savory dairy products that most supermarket shoppers have never heard of, and you can make them in your kitchen with the minimum of equipment. As you grow more skillful and practiced you can equip a small dairy room or set up a corner of your kitchen as a dairy center. Hand separators can be bought cheaply at auctions and barn sales in dairy areas, and retinned for many years of additional use. Small churns, cheese presses, butter molds, rennets and cultures may be ordered from home dairy supply dealers by mail. Cheese-making classes in some parts of the country can start you down the path of tyro turophilism. The Jersey cow and the Guernsey are coming back in popularity, esteemed for their fine rich milk and suitability to the home dairy. The dairy goat population has soared in the past decade as homesteaders discover the value and usefulness of these animals. Half a dozen yogurt and dairy cookbooks are on the market, all of them pointing out that the best yogurt of all is that made at home.

The family cow, a few milch goats, some basic dairy skills and a little kitchen space will keep you healthy, make you self-reliant, and allow you to dine superbly on the world's most perfect food in many forms. With a little practice, you may even "attain to eminence" in your home dairy.

2 THE RAW MATERIAL OF DAIRY FOODS

The cow has been the favorite dairy
animal in America for nearly three
centuries and continues to be
despite the growing popularity
of goats.

Various breeds of cattle have quite different milk characteristics, each with its own champions and defenders. But it's a hard fact of life that federally subsidized commercial dairy farmers who sell the largest quantities of milk (much of which goes to fill warehouses with dried milk powder) make the most money. Therefore, it stands to reason that a fiscal-minded farmer will try to build up a dairy herd from the breeds that give the most milk. Holsteins are the leading breed in quantity milk production. Yet the voluminous milk these big cows give is more watery, less rich and flavorful than the milk of the butter and cheese breeds, the Jersey, the Guernsey, and that increasingly rare breed, the Gloucestershire.

> Little drops of water poured into the milk
> Give the milkman's daughter lovely gowns of silk.
>
> Anonymous

The nineteenth century author of a classic study on Jerseys, *Jersey Cattle in America*, wrote scathingly on the differences between the two breeds:

> Between the rich milk secretions of the best strain of Jerseys and the excessively watery secretion of the Dutch or Holstein breed, there is the greatest possible difference. It is much easier to draw water from a hydrant by the force of gravity than to laboriously pull it from the teats of a Dutch cow.

The pretty little Jersey cow and her golden milk remains a home dairy favorite, yielding plenty of milk for the average family and lots of thick yellow cream that makes the best butter of all.

Good vs. Poor Cows.

As a general thing, farmers are not sufficiently circumspect in the selection of their dairy stock.—There may be animals which scarcely pay their way, and others we have no doubt run their owners in debt. The expense of keeping an 'extra' cow that will afford daily, from nine to ten quarts of milk, is not greater than is required to keep one that will average only five or six, and the difference in the amount would, in the course of a year, be a handsome profit.

"If," says a late author, "we estimate the cost of keeping a cow at twenty-five dollars, we shall find that if a cow gives six quarts of milk a day, the *loss* in keeping her will be $4.75. If the yield per day be eight quarts, then the *profit* will be about $5. If the milk is ten quarts a day, the profit will be $11.75."

This is an important branch of husbandry, and one which demands the serious and candid attention of every one who has the management either of a dairy or a farm.—*Maine Cultivator.*

Newspaper editors knew that the economics of dairying was always a topic of interest to farmers.

Beautiful Jerseys

The poetic names that devoted owners of Jersey cows gave their animals in the nineteenth century indicate the esteem and affection these fine milkers enjoyed. Here are a few names of pedigreed Jerseys from the past.

Old Noble	Satin Bird
Chrome Skin	Gilt Edge
Footstep	Milky Way
Deerfoot Maid	Silver Rose
Baby Buttercup	White Frost

In the last decade, goat keeping has increased dramatically, especially on homesteads and smaller farms, and in rugged, brushy terrain where cows can't make a living. *The Journal of Dairy Science*, usually more concerned with scientific articles on bovine milk and its related dairy products, responded to this growing interest recently with an entire issue (vol. 63, No. 10, 1980) given over to papers from all over the world on dairy goats.

Although goats cannot begin to compete with cows in the large-scale commercial production of milk, goats' milk can be made more economically for the household or kitchen dairy than cows' milk. Keeping goats means more efficient use of the land since these friendly animals thrive on brush and coarse vegetation that cows cannot eat, which grows in places where cows cannot go.

In Europe, the Caribbean, the Middle East, India and Africa, goats' milk is highly esteemed. In this country, after a slow start, goats' milk has finally earned a solid place in the dairy cases of natural foods stores, if not in supermarkets. In Los Ange-

Alice Hooper of the Barnyard Chorus in Brookfield, Vermont, poses with some of her goats. The Hoopers sell their goats' milk all over the state.

les alone people buy more than $1.5 million worth of goats' milk annually. A goats' milk processing plant that was set up recently in Yellville, Arkansas, has already attracted many dairy goat herd owners to the area. Research herds of dairy goats include that of the Winrock International Livestock Training and Research Center in Morrilton, Arkansas. At the University of Georgia in Athens and at the Southern Agriculture Corporation in Atlanta, exhaustive studies on making and marketing goats' milk dairy products are underway. The California Goat Dairyman's Association markets goats' milk nationally and has the equipment to produce evaporated goats' milk.

David MacKenzie, internationally known goat authority and author of the goat keeper's bible, *Goat Husbandry*, observed that goat populations increase in periods of economic hardship and social instability.

> While few Durham miners could buy or graze a cow, in the days when they were grossly underpaid, many of them were keen goat-keepers. The same principle holds good the world over, goats exist to cut the cost of living for many millions of hard-pressed families in cow-dairying country.

In North America the major breeds of dairy goats are the Toggenburg, Saanen, French Alpine and Anglo-Nubian. The Swiss breeds give more milk than do the Nubians, but the milk of the Nubians is richer in butterfat; Nubians are therefore known as the Jerseys of the goat world.

In other parts of the world — the Near East, the Mediterranean, and many European countries, especially Norway and France — special breeds of sheep are raised for their milk. Creamy, sweet ewes' milk is the raw stuff for some of the world's great cheeses, with Roquefort as the queen of them all. However, as widespread as milk sheep are globally, and as important as their milk is to the production of quality cheeses, in this country ewes' milk is, for all practical purposes, non-existent.

Though it would be nice to be able to make ewes' milk cheeses at home, there are formidable problems. One is the expense and difficulty of bringing new sheep breeds into the United States. Although wool breeds were imported all through the nineteenth century, long before the stringent sheep quarantine laws were enacted, interest in woolly milkers was negligible. The cow reigned queen of the dairy room, and sheep were tedious and unrewarding to milk. Who would choose a few cups of ewes' milk, laboriously gained, when he could have gallons of easy cow milk? Milking breeds were not brought in, and today they are virtually unrepresented here. There is presently a seven-year quarantine on sheep imports into the United States (a more relaxed rule holds in Canada) out of fear of a virulent disease called scrapie, a slow virus that affects the central nervous system and often takes years before any symptoms show. So, although sheep-milking machines have existed ever since they were invented in Roquefort decades ago, there is no source and no demand for them in this country. Sheep-raising readers seriously interested in milker ewes may want to embark on their own program of selective breeding with wool breeds that have decent milk characteristics, such as Dorsets.

THE GENERAL PROPERTIES OF MILK

Milk is truly a unique and amazing substance, and although the composition and characteristics of it vary among breeds and individual animals, all milk has certain general similarities, be it milk from whales or milk from mice.

FLAVOR

Fresh milk has an agreeable but ephemeral milky fragrance which rapidly disappears when exposed to air. All milk absorbs odors very easily, and if allowed to stand in the barn, quickly takes on a "barny" flavor, or, if stored open and warm in a refrigerator, will pick up the odors of whatever else is stored there—fish, curried lamb, celery, apples or cucumbers. Animals feeding on turnips, wild onions or garlic will give milk flavored by their diets—not always pleasant. However, butter made from milkers fed on apples is esteemed for a particularly rich, nutty flavor. Never feed milking goats or cows strong-flavored foods such as onions, cabbage or silage within four hours before milking time.

Most goats' milk is bland and pleasantly neutral in taste, but occasionally it will have a "goaty" flavor. Some cheeses are the better for this goaty flavor, but liquid milk is not esteemed for it. Research has shown that to some degree goaty-flavored milk is an inherited trait, and dairyists are advised that milkers who give strong-flavored milk be culled from the herd. Moreover, the fat globule membranes in goats' milk are less stable than those in cows' milk, and this is thought to make goats' milk more susceptible to adverse flavor changes. Goats' milk has a slightly lower lactose content than cows' milk, and a greater chloride level—both factors contribute to a very faintly saltier taste in the milk of goats. Buck goats should never be kept near the milking parlor or milk room, nor should the goat owner go near the buck or handle him in any way before milking time—the pungent odor of the buck will cling to garments and eventually taint the milk.

pH

When milk is tested with litmus paper, it displays an *amphoteric reaction*—blue litmus paper turns red and red litmus paper turns blue—apparently indicating that milk has a neutral pH. Actually, fresh milk tests out with a pH from 6.6 to 6.7, slightly on the acid side of the neutral 7. As milk ages, the acid increases through the multiplication of lactobacilli, a phenomenon which gives us many delicious dairy products, from sour cream to yogurt. Milk is a buffer; that is, it can absorb a certain amount of acid or alkali without registering a change in pH. Goats' milk has a higher buffering action than cows' milk, in part because of a greater amount and a different arrangement of phosphates in its composition. Goats' milk is therefore often prescribed for people with ulcers, since it can absorb good amounts of acid before turning acid itself.

Apple Pomace — Milkers' Delight

Both cows and goats enjoy leftover pomace or apple pulp from the cider press. This can be mixed with other feeds, 1 part pomace to 4 parts other feed. Apple pulp in the diet adds very fine flavor to both the milk and the meat of livestock.

CURD

If acid is added to milk the solids precipitate into a soft mass known as curd, and a nearly clear liquid called whey, a reaction which is the basis of cheese making. If fresh milk is allowed to stand undisturbed at room temperature for 24 hours or longer, it will develop a definite acidity, and eventually coagulate into curds and whey of itself. In cheese making this period is called "ripening the milk," and ripening stages occur in the preparation of most dairy products.

The softer the curd the more easily it is digested. The milk of Holstein cows has the softest curd, while the milk of Jerseys has the hardest. Goats' milk curd is very much softer than any cows' milk curd.

The size of the curd has some bearing on the dairy products made from it. Cows' milk curd has been described by a goat fancier as a "rubbery mass" in comparison to the very fine particle size of goats' milk curd. Dairy products made from goats' milk have a creamier, softer texture.

CREAM LINE

When fresh cows' milk stands undisturbed for several hours, the fat globules in it begin to rise to the top in a distinct layer, the so-called cream line. This is gravity creaming. The cream can be simply skimmed off, leaving behind the skim milk. If the separated milk and cream are vigorously agitated after the cream line has formed, the cream will remix with the milk to form whole milk once more. The mechanical process of homogenization breaks up the fat globules into such tiny particles that they cannot reform and rise to the top as cream again.

Most of the fat globules in goats' milk are far smaller than those in cows' milk

cream line

skim milk

and do not rise readily to the surface. It takes several days of standing before the cream line in goats' milk forms. Most goat dairies prefer the rapidity of a separator to get the cream. Goat advocates often claim that goats' milk is more digestible than cows' milk because of the relative smallness of the fat globules. However, if this were so, homogenization, which breaks cows' milk fat globules into even tinier sizes than those in goats' milk, should theoretically render homogenized cows' milk as digestible, which is not the case.

BUTTER

If the cream that has been separated or skimmed from the milk is shaken and agitated, the fat globules mass together as butter, leaving behind buttermilk. Both cows' and goats' milks make excellent butter, though goats' butter sometimes takes a little longer to come.

COLOR

The rich yellow of the milk of Jerseys and Guernseys comes from carotene, a pigment found in such feed plants as green grass, green alfalfa hay, green corn fodder, green silage and, of course, carrots. Hay which has lost its green color, dry corn fodder, straw, corn, wheat, oats, beet pulp, bran and oil meals are all low in carotene, and even a Jersey on winter feed gives milk that is less yellow than in summer when she is pastured on green grass. For unknown physiological reasons, carotene is greatly absorbed by Jerseys and Guernseys and passes into their body fat and milk. Holstein and Ayrshire breeds absorb the least carotene and their milk and cream is consequently very pale. Commercial dairy products, such as butter and cheese, that are traditionally yellow in color (from the days when Jerseys were responsible for most of those products), now usually have color added when made from Holstein milk, to match consumers' expectations.

The thyroid systems of goats and sheep are extremely efficient in converting the carotene in plants to vitamin A in their bodies and milk, so that the milk and cream of goats and ewes is snowy white. Butter made from goats' milk is also white unless coloring is added to suit our conception of what butter should look like.

MILK COWS

Heifers usually have their first lactation at around 2½ years of age, following the birth of the first calf. The heifer begins to secrete colostrum several days before the calf is born, and normal milk appears 4 to 5 days later. The period of lactation lasts about 300 days. During this time the cow may be bred again, and as the new calf grows *in utero*, the cow keeps on producing milk, though in diminishing quantity. Finally, about two months before the new calf is born, milking is eased off and the cow dries up — for a while. Another cycle of lactation begins with the birth of the calf. The cow keeps up this cyclical rythym for about five years, peaking in milk production with the third lactation. Many home dairy cows have even longer productive lives.

MILKING TIME

Before the actual milking process can begin, the let-down of milk in the cow's udder is triggered by a hormone, oxytocin, which is released into the bloodstream by the pituitary gland through certain

Strip Cup

The first milk from both cows and goats should be drawn into a strip cup with a black background which enables the milker to see any flocculence or abnormal separation or clumping in the milk that might indicate mastitis or other diseases and problems. Also, the first squirts of milk are laden with bacteria present in the teat channels, so discarding the first few ounces of milk lowers the total bacteria count.

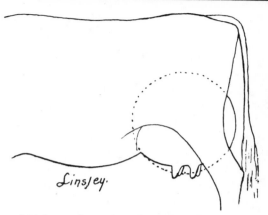

Interior and exterior of a cow's milk reservoir are outlined.

The let-down reflex time is fairly brief— 4 to 7 minutes, and in that time the cow should be completely milked out, for after the reflex fades, she is an unwilling participant in the milking game, and attempts to strip her may irritate her udder and eventually result in a bad-tempered "poor milker."

stimuli that say "it's milking time" to her: all the familiar sounds and sensations she associates with milking. If she's hand-milked as cows have been since the dawn of history, the clanking of the pail, the sound of the milker's voice talking or singing, and the massaging effect of hands on her bag and teats all give the cow the signal to let go—and she does.

L. B. Arnold says the best dairy products he has ever seen have been produced on small farms, as the result of skill in managing the milk of a few cows. The milking has been regular, and the spaces of time between milking. Much depends on this. Milking at four o'clock in the morning and at eight at night never makes the finest butter or cheese. Sixteen hours, or approximation to it, is too long a time for the milk to remain in the udder, for the good of the milk or the cows, especially when the flow is large. By crowding and straining the bag it becomes painful and feverish, and the butter-fat, and other elements of milk, become altered in consequence. There is nothing like a sound and healthy udder for secreting good milk.

Farmers looked to the papers for tips on getting the highest quality milk from their herds.

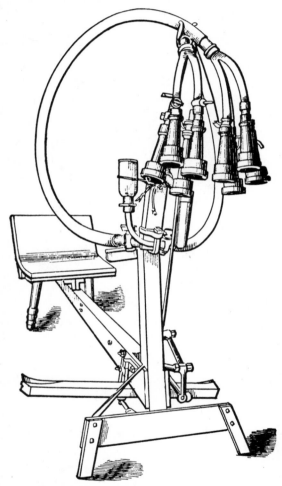

This odd contraption is a foot-powered milking machine. Few farmers found it easier to milk with their feet than their hands, and this oddity disappeared from the ranks of milking machines in a few years.

14: Milking Time, Good Friends
in Wisconsin.
(Scenes along the country roads.)

*A postcard exemplified Wisconsin's pride in
its dairy industry.*

*Like early cars, many of the most popular
brands of milking machines when they first
came out have faded from the scene. This is
the Globe, one of the leading sellers in its day.
Others were the Sharpless, the Hinman and
the Hazelwood.*

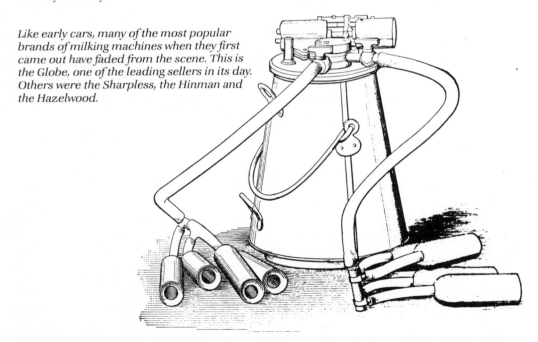

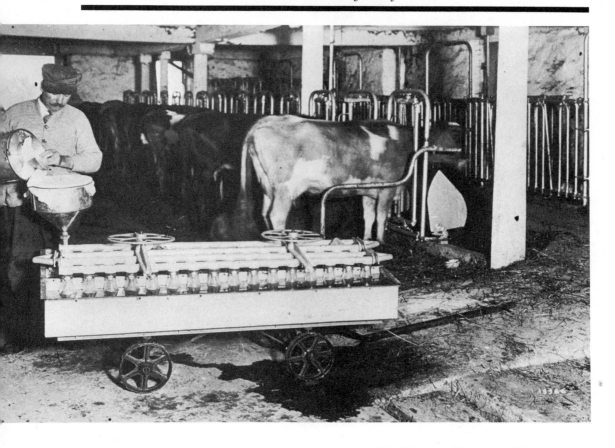

Not all milking machines were this complicated.

The milk is usually collected in pails and cooled *at once*. Milk comes out of the cow at 98.6°F which is an ideal temperature and medium for bacterial growth. It should be chilled as rapidly as possible to the ideal low temperature of 40°F which almost completely halts the growth of bacteria. At this point the milk is out of the cow, out of the barn, and into the home dairy.

MILK GOATS

Goats mature early. A doe is ready to breed at 10 months of age, and these fecund animals are also prolific, with multiple births common. In lush tropical climates goats can breed all year round and normally have two annual pregnancies with short lactations since there is plenty of food available for early weaning. In the northern hemisphere, things are different. Here goats are seasonal breeders, seldom coming into heat in the spring and early summer, but instead having late summer and early autumn heats.

A diminishing amount of sunlight seems to trigger heats in the north. Most northern does, then, are bred in September, October and November, producing kids in five months — February, March and April — after a gestation period of 150 days. This means that most yearly bred goats have a lactation period of from 3 to 7 months and dry up in late winter. Much is made of this lactation cycle which reduces the milk supply to nothing in the winter, but MacKenzie suggests the problem is easily solved. The lactation period of a goat can be extended to 22 months by breeding her alternate years and allowing her to skip through one annual autumn heat without being bred, for the sake of the winter milk. This is known as letting the goat *run through*. In North America, however, running through is not the common practice, and 75 percent of the annual yield of goats' milk is collected between April and September.

Hormonal secretions in the goat, still not entirely understood, have a great effect on lactation. There are common examples of barren does producing significant amounts of milk at the triggering of hormonal secretions. These are the so-called maiden milkers. An occasional goat has a lactation period that lasts for years.

MILKING TIME

Goats are easier to milk by hand than cows. The process, somewhat different from hand-milking the bovine, takes 6 to 7 minutes per animal. Goats should be milked at very regular intervals 12 hours apart. If the time is longer the butterfat level will be lower than normal. Goats like a rigid, orderly milking routine — the same person, the same tune whistled, the same succession of goats, always with the queen of the group first. Cleaning the udder of the first goat is enough stimulus to trigger

> ### How Much Milk?
>
> A poor goat in her first lactation will give only a couple of cups of milk a day.
>
> A prime goat at the peak of production will give as much as 5 quarts a day.
>
> A small Jersey cow will give 2 to 4 gallons of milk a day.
>
> A big Holstein will give 4 to 7 gallons of milk a day.

the milk let-down reflex, and the subsequent goats are all ready to go by the time they climb onto the milking platform. Goats are milked out but not stripped dry, for this distorts their udders and can cause permanent damage. As with cows' milk, the freshly drawn milk should be cooled immediately and rapidly to prevent bacterial growth.

MILK IS MILK

The composition of milk varies considerably from animal to animal, breed to breed and species to species. For decades there has been a subtle rivalry between the promoters of cows' milk and those who favor goats' milk. Although there are real differences between cows' and goats' milks, far more striking are the similarities. For the home dairyist this means that although there will be variations in the time it takes for cultured dairy products to mature, differences in flavor and texture, and differences in making butter come, cheeses set or cream separate, the same range of dairy products is available to goat milkers as to cow keepers.

The milk of both animals is delicious to drink cold or hot; both milks produce cream from light to heavy weights; both

This old photograph was captioned "The Wrong Way to Milk a Cow." The bearded farmer with his little milking stool and pail is amazed to see a greedy pig helping itself to milk straight from the udder.

milks make excellent butter, yogurt, sour cream, acidophilus milk, whipped cream, ice cream, cream cheese, cottage cheese and hundreds of other cheeses. Nor is the culinary range of the goat-owning dairyist restricted in any way; cream soups, desserts, sauces, puddings, gravies, beverages, whey dishes, breads and dips are easy to make and as delicious as if they were made with cows' milk, if not more so. All the recipes and directions in this book, unless otherwise noted, apply equally to cows' milk and goats' milk.

A look at the basic composition of milk, its behavior and structure helps us understand precisely what happens in the home dairy room and what causes things to sometimes go wrong. Milk is a complex liquid, and much is still unknown about why it acts and reacts as it does.

Antibiotic Caution

Milk from animals treated with antibiotics cannot be used for making cultured dairy products. The antibiotics speedily kill off the essential bacterial cultures.

WHAT'S IN A DROP OF MILK?

BUTTERFAT

	Goat	Cow
% butterfat	3.8	3.67

Butterfat is tremendously important in determining the food value, nutritional content and flavor quality of milk. It is estimated that a single drop of cows' milk contains about 100 million fat globules. The size of these tiny spheroids varies from breed to breed. In cows, Jersey milk contains the largest globules and Holstein the smallest. Goats' milk has a greater number of very small fat globules. Large butterfat globules mean quicker, easier churning of cream into butter, and small globules mean a long session with the dasher at lower temperatures, and even then sometimes the butter fails to come. Large globules can break away from the skim milk more easily and form butter, and big globules also give higher butter yields.

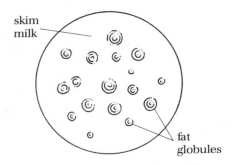

Butter-making success is surer when the cream of Jersey or Guernsey cows or Nubian goats is used, rather than that of Holstein cows or Swiss goats. Individual animals also have noticeable differences in their fat levels and the diameter of the butterfat spheres in their milk, but it's a well-known dairy fact that the fat globules are relatively large in all breeds during the first months of lactation, shrinking smaller and smaller as the lactation period lengthens.

For home dairies where there is no cream separator, the size of the fat globules is important; the bigger they are, the faster they rise. A globule which has a diameter twice the size of another—as Jersey fat does compared to Holstein—has four times the surface and eight times the volume, so that the surface tension which keeps a fat globule in suspension in the whole milk is easier to overcome in the agitation of churning; the result is easy butter. This same propensity meant, in the old days when milk was shipped long distances by wagon and rail, that Jersey milk tended to "butter up" in transit.

At milking time the first milk the animal lets down is low in fat while the last milk contains much more butterfat. Failure to get all the milk from your dairy animal at each milking means a noticeable decrease in the butterfat over time.

A long-lived dairy myth is the belief that the amount of butterfat in an animal's milk depends on what she eats. Actually, the percentage of butterfat in milk is related to the breed and individual heredity. A cow or goat on starvation rations will go dry before the butterfat level in her milk drops much. However, the *consistency* of the butterfat is very much affected by feed differences. Fresh grass and pasture means softer milk fat, and butter made from such milk will melt at relatively low temperatures. There are wide seasonal variations in the consistency of the butterfat in goats' milk. Goats' milk fat contains more of the simple *short chain*

FAT CONTENT OF MILK

	Breed	% Fat
Cow	Holstein	3.55
	Jersey	5.18
Goat	Saanen	3.5
	Nubian	5.6

fatty acids than cows' milk, which some authorities feel contribute to the superior digestibility of goats' milk, since the lipases attack and break down such short chains more efficiently, making them susceptible to rapid digestion.

Butterfat is one of the most complex natural fats known, a triglyceride containing various fatty acids, including butyric, capric, caproic, caprylic, lauric, myristic, oleic, palmitic and stearic acids as well as traces of half a dozen others. For the home dairy maker, two of these—butyric and oleic acids—are important. Butyric acid gives butter much of its characteristic taste. The rancid flavor which sometimes occurs in old dairy products comes from liberated butyric acid produced when the chemical bonds break down. Oleic acid, which is liquid at room temperature, largely controls the hardness or softness of the butterfat, and the amount in an animal's butterfat varies with her diet. Generally, Jersey butterfat is lower in oleic

acid than Holstein. This means that the melting point of Jersey butterfat is high, that the butter is firmer and keeps longer.

PROTEINS

	Goat	Cow
% total protein	2.90	3.23

Proteins, which are indispensable to life, are extraordinarily complex organic substances whose mysteries are still far from completely explored. Most of us know only that we need protein for life and health. Milk is an excellent and cheap source of protein. One quart supplies half an adult's daily protein requirements, and cheese is one of the most concentrated forms of protein in existence. Milk protein contains all the essential amino acids known, in amounts exceeding other major protein sources such as eggs and most meats. Milk with a butterfat content of 3.8 percent will have a protein level of about 3 percent. Although goats' milk has a slightly lower protein content than cows' milk, it is apparently digested more readily and its amino acids absorbed by the human body more efficiently.

Milk contains two major proteins—casein, about 80 percent of the total protein, and albumin, about 18 percent. A third protein found in tiny amounts is globulin.

Casein

	Goat	Cow
% casein	2.47	2.63
% albumin & globulin	0.43	0.60

Casein—found only in milk—is like no other natural protein known. Because it is sometimes found in combination with calcium in milk it is also called *calcium caseinate*. Casein is dispersed through milk in such minute particles that it can only be isolated in a laboratory by straining the milk through a porcelain filter. Casein can also be precipitated or forced out of the milk solution by heating or adding alcohol, weak acids or enzymes to the milk. When an unwatched pot of milk boils on the stove, the "skin" that forms — the bane of all hot milk drink devotees — is a fine layer of heat-precipitated casein plus some fat and other milk parts. Most of us have also noted that when lemon juice or tomatoes are added to milk it curdles — an acid precipitation of the casein.

Hundreds of cheeses are made by adding enzymes, particularly in the form of animal rennet — natural enzymes collected from the stomachs of newborn calves — to the milk. This coagulates the casein which is the major stuff of cheese. The casein proteins are what make cheeses such rich protein foods. Cheddar contains an amazing 33 percent protein, Swiss cheese about 30 percent. The soft cheeses have more moisture and are therefore less concentrated, with lower protein levels for their density. The smooth texture of ice cream comes in part from the large proportion of protein in the non-fat milk solids.

Casein has hundreds of industrial uses — making plastics, sizing paper, making glue and paints, as a filler or binder in processed foods, as a textile fiber and even as synthetic rubber. In the home dairy, however, casein can sometimes be a problem. When milk utensils are scalded with hot water before all the milk residue has been flushed away, an invisible but hard, resistant film forms which can affect the flavor, taste and quality of later milk if not removed. This deposit, called *milk stone*, must be chemically dissolved.

Albumin

The other major milk protein is a mild-tasting substance that can be coagulated by heat, but not by rennet. When a rennet-precipitated cheese, such as cheddar, is made, the albumin protein passes into the whey along with the milk sugar, milk ash and small amounts of butterfat. This is why albumin is sometimes called *whey protein*. The familiar ricotta cheese is made from whey by heating it until the albumin precipitates out, boosted by the addition of a little acid in the form of vinegar or lemon juice.

Tooth Decay and Cheese

Research on tooth decay at the National Institute of Dental Research in Bethesda, Maryland, has turned up some intriguing new material. A preliminary finding of one study, by W. M. Edgar et al, of the National Caries Program, is that cheddar cheese may inhibit the process of tooth decay. If so, it would be the first food discovered to have this important property.

The study involved feeding rats frequent meals (22 a day) of a high sucrose diet. In one group of rats 12 of those sugary meals were followed within 10 minutes with powdered cheddar cheese. Caries were significantly lower in the group that got the cheese. Although the study is preliminary, as Dr. W. H. Bowen, Chief of the Caries Prevention and Research Branch of the NIDR stresses, an abstract of the report concludes:

The results suggest that a) cheese after cariogenic food may reduce caries incidence especially in smooth surfaces. . . .

Some individuals who are allergic to the proteins in cows' milk benefit greatly from a switch to goats' milk—but others react adversely to both milks.

LACTOSE

	Goat	Cow
% lactose	4.08	4.78

Lactose is a unique sugar found only in milk. Although it is a disaccharide like sucrose (ordinary cane sugar), its molecules are not one each of fructose and glucose, but one each of glucose and galactose. Sucrose is 30 times sweeter than lactose. But lactose breaks down more easily under heat — the brown, caramelized mess familiar to anyone who has ever scorched milk.

The lactose content of milk is important in making home dairy products, since it is the fermentation action of certain enzymes in the lactose that converts lactose to lactic acid. This acid fermentation is vital to cheese and butter making, and gives both their distinctive flavors. The lactic acid formed in the fermentation process checks the growth of undesirable bacteria by making a medium unfavorable for the expansion of these microorganisms. Without the protective action of lactic acid, most dairy products would break down into objectionable messes.

Because lactose is water soluble, a good deal of it passes into the whey during the cheese-making process. Dried milk also contains a very high proportion of lactose, and can "brown" if it is not stored in a cool place in air-tight containers.

In the last two decades we have become aware of a widespread condition that affects a majority of the world's adults—lactose intolerance. Humans possess two different lactose-digesting enzymes in their gastric secretions; the first is present in every normal human infant for the first few years of life. The other, apparently genetically determined, is present in some adults. The white populations of northern European descent and certain Nigerian tribes are the minority among the world's populations who can tolerate and digest milk as adults. Researchers generally agree that lactose tolerance seems to be a genetic trait conditioned by environment. Most non-white populations and a certain percentage of whites cannot take lactose into their systems without suffering unpleasant symptoms ranging from abdominal pain and bloating to severe diarrhea and gastrointestinal difficulties. One well-known study in 1966 showed that lactose intolerance affected about 70 percent of blacks and 6 to 12 percent of whites in the United States. An interesting sidelight of this problem is that most mammals follow the same pattern of adult lactose intolerance. It is ironic in view of this widespread inability to digest the lactose in milk that this country has been shipping tons of milk to native American populations and abroad to so-called third world countries and underdeveloped nations where lactose intolerance is the norm. Some Navajo Indians threw such donated milk out, while others fed it to livestock. A Central American people who received such dry milk shipments used it to whitewash their houses because they couldn't drink it. Comments David MacKenzie in *Goat Husbandry*:

> The charitable distribution of dried cows' milk to protein starved Africans and Asians has brought rewards to western dairy farmers and nausea to many of the intended beneficiaries.

Fortunately, delicious, nutritious and beneficial dairy products can be and are enjoyed by lactose-intolerant people, for lactose intolerance does not mean milk intolerance. Fermented dairy foods, such as yogurt, cheeses and many regional drinks are made by the fermentation of the lactose content into lactic acid and other products; such foods play an important part in the diets of lactose-intolerant people.

Goats' milk has a slightly lower lactose content than cows' milk. This shows up in some dairy products, such as yogurt. Goats' yogurt is less acidic and more digestible because there is less lactose to be converted into lactic acid. The taste is softer and the texture creamier than yogurt made from cows' milk.

ASH (MINERAL SALTS OF MILK)

	Goat	Cow
% ash	0.79	0.73

Liquid milk can be dried and then burnt up. The fine, pale powder which is left is the ash, or mineral content, about 0.7 percent of the whole milk. This little heap of ashes contains a complex mix of metallic elements, the same ones found in animal bodies: iodine, potassium, sodium, magnesium, calcium, chlorine, phosphorus and sulfur, as well as minute amounts of silicon, titanium, boron, vanadium, rubidium, lithium and strontium. Milk is an extremely important source of minerals in the human diet. Milk and cheese along with green, leafy vegetables are major sources of calcium, which cereal and grain products lack, and which is one of the main constituents of bones and teeth, is necessary for the proper clotting of blood, and is beneficial to muscle and nerve

tissue. Cows' and goats' milk has four times as much calcium as human milk. It is thought that the calcium in goats' milk is slightly more easily absorbed than that in cows' milk. However, milk is low in iron, an essential nutrient which has to come from other sources.

Ash helps milk keep its stability under heat. When butter is made, most of the ash passes into the buttermilk, and in cheese making a good deal of it goes into the whey. This is why buttermilk, skim milk and whey, aside from being delicious and nutritious for humans, are excellent for livestock and hens to supplement the low mineral content of grain feeds.

LECITHIN

Thousands of commercial food products on the supermarket shelves contain lecithin as an ingredient. Lecithin not only fills and plumps out these products, but gives them a more substantial, richer taste. Lecithin, a fat-like substance containing nitrogen and phosphorus, is found in milk in small amounts as part of the colloidal, gelatin-like layer around each microscopic fat globule. When cream is separated from milk, most of the lecithin comes along with it. But if the cream is churned for butter, the lecithin is rubbed off the fat globules by friction and remains in the buttermilk while the fat globules themselves coalesce into butter. It's thought that the concentrated lecithin in buttermilk (real buttermilk from the butter churn, not the cultured buttermilk from the supermarket dairy case) gives it its full, rich taste, far richer than the small amount of butterfat remaining in it can account for.

CHOLESTEROL

Milk contains cholesterol in direct proportion to the amount of butterfat — roughly 105 to 176 parts per million. Goats' milk has slightly higher cholesterol levels than does cows' milk. Some milk products have very high amounts of cholesterol and saturated fats, such as butter and many cheeses. In the last two decades cholesterol has become a sinister substance with an evil reputation, and the debate about whether or not cholesterol in the average diet should be sharply curtailed has raged back and forth.

In 1965, 1968 and 1973 the American Heart Association officially recommended that *all* Americans reduce cholesterol and saturated fats (as well as simple sugars and excessive salt) in their diets. The recommendation was based on the postulate that excess lipids in the diet raise serum cholesterol, which leads to deposits of the cholesterol in the blood on the walls of arteries — which in turn leads to atherosclerosis, increasing the chances of heart attacks and cardiovascular disease. This broad recommendation was both supported and questioned by various scientists, nutritionists, health professionals, as well as official and unofficial health care and research associations.

In the spring of 1980, the Food and Nutrition Board of the National Academy of Sciences made the statement that healthy Americans who exercise regularly need not reduce their intake of cholesterol and saturated fats in the diet. Many health professionals and scientists now agree with this more moderate view. There is also considerable agreement that adjusting the diet along the lines suggested by the AHA is proper for high-risk individuals with raised blood lipid levels, and that blood lipid profiles should be a routine part of any physical examination.

Dr. Richard B. Shekelle, preventive medicine specialist at Rush-Presbyterian-St. Luke's Medical Center in Chicago prepared the recent report, "Diet, Serum Cholesterol, and Death from Coronary Heart Disease, the Western Electric Study" (*New England Journal of Medicine*, January 8, 1981). This report covers one of the longest and largest studies made on the links among dietary lipids, cholesterol levels in the blood and the risk of premature heart attacks, and though it finds that indeed the composition of the diet does affect blood lipid levels and the risk of heart disease, Dr. Shekelle comments in a letter:

> I do not think that these results indicate that people should abstain from eating and drinking dairy products. I subscribe to the recommendations of the U.S. Department of Agriculture as indicated in the recent publication, "Nutrition and Your Health — Dietary Guidelines for Americans."

The USDA takes a reasonable, Socratic stance on the question in this 1980 publication.

> Most foods contain more than one nutrient. Milk, for example, provides proteins, fats, sugars, riboflavin and other B-vitamins,

vitamin A, calcium, and phosphorus — among other nutrients.

No single food supplies all the essential nutrients in the amounts that you need. Milk, for instance, contains very little iron or vitamin C. You should, therefore, eat a variety of foods to assure an adequate diet.

The adequate diet recommended includes selections of fruits, vegetables, whole grain and enriched breads, cereals, and grain products, milk, cheese, and yogurt, meats, poultry, fish, eggs and legumes. In the section on fats and cholesterol, the key words are *avoid too much*. Specifically, "Nutrition and Your Health" states:

Some people can consume diets high in saturated fats and cholesterol and still keep normal blood cholesterol levels. Other people, unfortunately, have high blood cholesterol levels even if they eat low-fat, low-cholesterol diets. . . .

There is controversy about what recommendations are appropriate for healthy Americans. But for the U.S. population *as a whole*, reduction in our current intake of total fat, saturated fat, and cholesterol is sensible. This suggestion is especially appropriate for people who have high blood pressure or who smoke.

The recommendations are not meant to prohibit the use of any specific food item or to prevent you from eating a variety of foods. For example, eggs and organ meats (such as liver) contain cholesterol, but they also contain many essential vitamins and minerals, as well as protein. Such items can be eaten in moderation, as long as your overall cholesterol intake is not excessive. If you prefer whole milk to skim milk, you can reduce your intake of fats from food other than milk.

Many dairy products are not the high cholesterol foods they are reputed to be. A glass of whole milk, for example, has

CHOLESTEROL CONTENT OF SOME FOODS

	mg/100g	mg/usual portion
Whole milk	14	32 (1 glass: 240 g)
Low-fat milk	4	9 (1 glass: 240 g)
Skim milk	2	4 (1 glass: 240 g)
Butter	227	32 (1 tsp: 14 g)
Cheddar cheese	103	30 (1 cube: 28 g)
Ice cream, vanilla	45	51 (1 scoop: 114 g)
Yogurt, plain, low-fat	6	14 (1 carton: 240 g)
Whole egg	504	286 (1 egg: 57 g)
Chicken breast, raw, meat only	79	67 (85 g)
Tuna, canned in oil, drained solids	65	55 (85 g)
Halibut, broiled with vegetable shortening, flesh only	60	51 (85 g)

less cholesterol (32 mg) than an average portion of chicken (79 mg) or fish (60 mg). However, it should be noted that whole milk (1 cup) does have 15 to 20 times more saturated fat than chicken, and some researchers hold that such fat tends to enhance cholesterol's undesirable effects in the bloodstream.

If you do not have high lipid levels in your blood, there is little reason to deprive yourself completely of such a bounteous and delicious source of vitamins, minerals and proteins as dairy products provide. Moderation in the use of butter, cheese and creams, or reduction in other sources of fats also makes sense. Such rich foods are, by their very nature, limited in the frequency in which they are served. Heavy cream soups, sauces and desserts are almost synonymous with *occasion*. One such at a festive meal is plenty. Cottage cheese, buttermilk, yogurt and many other dairy products in this book can be made with low-fat skim milk. If you do have problems with high fat levels in your blood or other factors associated with cardiovascular disease, by all means follow the advice and diet recommended by your doctor.

ENZYMES

Milk contains a number of enzymes; these are a group of proteins with the ability to set off chemical reactions in the milk and to influence the rate of these reactions without being affected themselves. These catalysts have an important role in the mellow, controlled ripening of many cheeses. Some of the more important enzymes in cows' milk are catalase, lipase, peroxidase and phosphatase. Goats' milk has lower levels of phosphatase than cows' milk, and completely lacks two other enzymes found in cows' and human milk. The enzymes in milk come from two sources — the animal's udder contains the original enzymes, and bacteria that get into the milk are the source of bacterial enzymes. Enzymes are destroyed by temperatures between 122°F and 248°F.

Lipase is an enzyme that can cause problems for the home dairy maker, for it has the ability to liberate free fatty acids from the fat molecules. Certain levels of free fatty acids give wonderful aroma and tang to cheese, but too many of these acids can produce, especially in butter, an unpleasant rancidity. The goaty flavor in some goat cheeses is linked to free fatty acid content.

VITAMINS

Milk contains vitamins A, B_1 (thiamine), B_2 (riboflavin), niacin, B_6 (pyridoxine), pantothenic acid, folic acid, B_{12}, vitamin C and vitamin D. A milk animal's diet influences the amount of some vitamins in the milk. For example, the vitamin A content of milk rises when the animal is on green pasture.

Both cows' milk and goats' milk are winners in the vitamin sweepstakes. Goats' milk has sufficient supplies of vitamin A and niacin for the human infant and more than sufficient levels of thiamine, riboflavin and pantothenic acid. It is deficient in vitamins C, D, B_{12}, pyridoxine and folic acid. Neither cows' milk nor goats' milk has enough of vitamins C and D to satisfy the needs of infants. Natural vitamin D levels are low and must be augmented in the diet; the vitamin D that nutritionists urge us to get from milk is added to commercial milk. Cows' milk contains levels of pyridoxine, folic acid and B_{12} adequate for human babies' diets.

Infants fed on goats' milk alone in

one classical study of several decades ago, ended up with "goats' milk anemia," and the low level of B_{12} was seen as the problem. This study received a great deal of attention over the years, persuading many health professionals that goats' milk was an inferior food. However, in recent work it has been discovered that the villain is the lack of folic acid in goats' milk, for folic acid is a necessary ingredient in the synthesis of hemoglobin.

Another feeding study sometimes cited in goats' milk literature is one dated 1952 that involved 38 children on the same basic diet for five months, half of whom received daily 0.946 liters of raw goats' milk, while the other half received daily 0.946 liters of raw cows' milk. Both groups made good growth during the study, but the goats' milk drinkers showed statistically significant higher bone density, higher vitamin A in blood plasma, and higher blood serum calcium than the cows' milk group. The goats' milk drinkers also had a slightly higher concentration of blood hemoglobin, the folic acid for hemoglobin synthesis having been provided in another form in their diet.

3

MILK

Warm, raw whole milk fresh from the animal is the beginning of all dairy products. It can be used as it comes, or converted into a variety of milks and cultured or fermented dairy foods. Here are some of the more important forms of liquid milk.

Raw Milk—milk as it comes from the animal, unpasteurized and unhomogenized. Some health food advocates, cooks and cheese makers swear by raw milk for its slightly superior nutritional level, better taste and excellent cooking qualities. The disadvantages of raw milk are the risk of dangerous bacteria which can cause serious illness or overwhelm the benign cultures that make consistently good dairy products.

Whole Milk—fresh milk, either pasteurized or unpasteurized, with a minimum of 4 percent butterfat in it. If whole cows' milk is not homogenized, it shows a cream line. Goats' milk will also show a cream line but must stand several days before the cream rises. Whole milk is the finest milk for cooking purposes.

Pasteurized Milk—milk which has been heated to a mild but critical temperature that kills harmful bacteria that may be in fresh milk from several sources—the teat channels, ailing animals, airborne contamination, foreign objects (which have fallen into the milk) and unclean utensils. If properly done, pasteurization does not affect the flavor of milk, but it does destroy about 10 percent of the vitamin C and inactivates some of the natural enzymes. The reason for pasteurization is to change raw milk from a potentially dangerous

Easy on the Cream and Butter

By its very nature, this book contains dozens of enticing but rich recipes that call for quantities of milk, butter, cream and cheese. They are meant to be *used in moderation* rather than with mad abandon. If you do your own milking and have a surplus of these dairy products, share the cream and butter with your neighbors. To prepare a menu consisting of a cream cheese appetizer followed by an avocado cream soup, a main dish of creamed turkey with carrots in cream as a side dish, and a big salad drenched with a creamy dressing, all topped off with a dessert of Bavarian Cream, is to court physical disaster.

Not only will pounds of lard adhere to your frame with such a diet, but your arteries may clog solid with cholesterol deposits! A century ago farm families lived active, vigorous lives and had little problem with overweight or cholesterol despite great slabs of butter applied generously to their baked potatoes and griddlecakes, and oceans of thick yellow cream poured with a free hand into everything from codfish chowder to sliced peaches. Today's more sedentary people must watch their intakes of high-calorie, high-cholesterol foods—and that means butter or cream in particular.

How Heat Affects Milk

Fats—Fats are not changed by temperatures under 212°F, but cream will not separate from the milk as well when temperatures go above 167°F.

Proteins—Casein loses its calcium when it's heated, and the rate of coagulation of milk by rennet decreases as the heating temperature climbs. At high temperatures the casein can be precipitated out of the milk—albumin starts to precipitate at 158°F. Milk held at 167°F for more than a minute will have a cooked taste and smell.

Enzymes—Enzymes can be destroyed by heat—in fact, the absence of peroxidase in milk is a test of whether a temperature above 176°F has been reached. Unfortunately, lipase, which has an undesirable effect on fat by freeing fatty acids, is very resistant to heat.

Lactose—A reaction between the lactose and protein content of milk occurs above 212°F and gives milk an unpleasant brown color.

Vitamins and Minerals—Vitamin C suffers most from heating—about 10 percent is lost. There is also a loss of about 7 percent of B_1 and a small amount of B_{12}. Other vitamins remain largely unchanged, as does the mineral content of milk under heat.

medium well suited for the growth of lethal microorganisms, to a tasty and safe product entirely free of pathogens. In the past diseases like tuberculosis and typhus were spread by raw milk, and the quality of cultured milk products was hit or miss since the bacterial content of the milk varied, sometimes dangerously, sometimes just enough to convert the cheese or yogurt to a disagreeable off-flavored mess.

Yet the heat treatment of milk can affect it radically. If milk is kept at high temperatures for long periods, the pathogens are killed but the flavor is ruined, the milk scorched, cream separability adversely affected, the enzymes inactivated and the vitamins destroyed. In commercial milk production the high-temperature, short-time flash pasteurization techniques under pressure cause little nutrient loss or noticeable change in flavor. Old-fashioned home pasteurization methods, particularly by the *open kettle* batch process which holds the milk at 145°F for 30 minutes, may mean a cooked flavor as well as the loss of vitamins and enzymes. There are better ways to pasteurize milk at home, including sophisticated automatically controlled home pasteurizers in 1- and 2-gallon sizes (see Index). A pasteurizer is not essential. In this section we give several ways to pasteurize milk without a pasteurizer. The results are good—pathogen-free, tasty milk with little destruction of vitamins or enzymes.

Homogenized Milk—fresh, fluid whole milk which has lost its cream line but not its cream. The fat globules in whole milk are broken up mechanically into particles so fine that they cannot regroup and rise to the surface, but remain suspended throughout the milk. Many cooks prefer non-homogenized whole milk in the kitchen for its superior binding qualities and smoother texture. Commercial milk producers like homogenization because they can mix older stale milk with fresh milk, homogenize and package the mixture without a noticeable loss of flavor.

Fortified Milk—milk to which vitamins A and D have been added, or other constituents including lactose, minerals and non-fat dry solids. Most commercial milk is fortified.

Things are seldom what they seem.
Skim milk masquerades as cream.

Gilbert and Sullivan,
H.M.S. Pinafore, Act II

Skim Milk—the remainder after the cream has been separated out or skimmed off whole milk. A small amount of fat usually remains in skim milk, about 1 percent. Skim milk has the same protein and mineral content of whole milk, a much lower caloric value, and has lost almost all the valuable fat-soluble vitamins A, D, E and K. Commercially, skim milk is frequently made into other dairy products such as cottage cheese, buttermilk and yogurt. Home dairy makers can do the same.

Low-Sodium Milk—a specialty milk pasteurized and homogenized, available in either fresh or canned form. This product is for people who want to limit their sodium intake. The fresh whole milk goes through an ion-exchange process which replaces the sodium with an equal amount of potassium. The B-vitamins and vitamin D are destroyed in the process.

Two-Percent Milk—a mixture of skim and whole milk, pasteurized and homogenized, with a low fat content of 2 percent. It tastes better than skim milk yet has less fat than whole milk.

Certified Milk—raw milk produced under extraordinarily rigid sanitary conditions supervised by the Medical Milk Commission. This specialty milk dates back to the days before pasteurization techniques were perfected. It is available in only a few places in this country.

Acidophilus Milk—a cultured milk product widely used in Europe. It is recognized for its ability to reduce intestinal gas, discourage intestinal pathogens and help to correct intestinal maladies. When antibiotics are given to humans, beneficial lactobacilli as well as harmful bacteria in the gut are killed, a considerable disservice to the patient. Taking in quantities of *Lactobacillus acidophilus*, the primary bacterium in acidophilus milk, regulates the intestinal flora and opens the way to a rapid return to normalcy. *L. acidophilus* is one of the major microorganisms found in the human intestinal tract through our whole lives.

Acidophilus milk, pasteurized skim milk cultured with *L. acidophilus*, is available in some areas of the United States and in a number of natural foods stores, but it is not widely used here despite its beneficial action on the gut because of resistance to its sharp taste. In Europe *L. acidophilus* is added to yogurt cultures and the result is a widely enjoyed product known as *bioyurt*. Home dairy makers who want the beneficial effects of *L. acidophilus* in their diets can make either acidophilus milk or bioyurt easily . The *L. acidophilus* culture is available from several supply houses listed in the Appendix.

Evaporated Milk—whole milk which has had 50 percent of its water removed. The concentrated milk is fortified with vitamin D. and then canned in a heat process which gives it a cooked taste. The process, invented during the Civil War, takes place under vacuum at very precisely controlled temperatures. It is not in the scope of the home dairy to make evaporated milk. The product is largely useful in hot climates where fresh milk won't keep, though many consumers have developed a taste for it in their breakfast beverages instead of cream.

Condensed Milk — whole milk that has been evaporated and then highly sugared as a preservative technique. One 14½-ounce can of condensed milk contains the equivalent of 2½ cups of whole milk and 8 tablespoons of sugar!

Buttermilk — the liquid remaining in the churn after butter has been made. It is sweet buttermilk if sweet cream was churned, or sour cream buttermilk if the butter was made from soured cream. Thicker than whole milk and flecked with butter, this buttermilk was once widely used in cooking and baking, and much enjoyed as a chilled beverage. It is impossible to buy real buttermilk in supermarkets. Home dairy makers, however, have prime access to this delicious and now rare milk.

Commercial buttermilk is skim milk which has been cultured with *Streptococcus lactis, S. cremoris, S. diacetilactis* and *Leuconostoc citrovorum*. Usually salt is added to pick up the flavor. If you like the taste of commercial buttermilk, you can easily make your own. The correct starter culture is available from several suppliers.

Sour Milk — a natural, pleasantly acid milk once widely used in making soft

Headache Remedy, Shaker Style

The Shaker *Manifesto* of 1879 contains a treasure of advice on animal husbandry, housekeeping and cooking, gardening, canning and preserving, smithing, dyeing, wool production and a hundred other practical subjects including simple cures for minor bodily ills. Here is one:

"Simple remedies are frequently the best for headache. A cup of sour milk spread upon a thin cloth and applied to the head will many times give relief."

cheeses and in baking and cooking. The souring process can only occur with very clean, unpasteurized, unheated raw milk. Pasteurized milk will not sour, it will only spoil. Old recipes which call for sour milk can be adapted to modern use by substituting buttermilk for the sour milk. To make sour milk, set fresh raw milk, covered, in a warm place for 24 to 48 hours. As the acidity increases the milk becomes progressively more sour. When it is clabbered — thick and coagulated with very soft, cloudy curd — it has an agreeable tangy aroma and taste, and has become sour milk. Sister Abigail Crossman, a Shaker of the last century wrote:

There is no end to the nice articles of food that may be made by using sour cream, sour milk, and buttermilk, in a judicious way. There are several things in their use about which care should be taken:

1st. Cream that is to be used in cooking should be thoroughly separated from the milk.

2nd. It should be sour.

3rd. If in any recipe milk or buttermilk is to be employed with the cream it should also be entirely sour, as the mixture of sweet and sour milk or cream tends to make the article heavy.

4th. The amount of soda or saleratus should only be just enough to sweeten and lighten the cream, any more than this imparts the green color and soapy flavor which are so disagreeable and unwholesome in articles of food.

Use sour milk in breads, pancakes, flour-thickened gravies, cakes and casseroles.

Dried Milk—both whole milk and skim milk are commercially converted into dry solids by spraying the liquid milk under pressure onto the heated sides of revolving drums. The final product keeps for long periods when stored in air-tight, moisture-proof, opaque containers at cool temperatures. Dried milk is used both as a solid and in reconstituted liquid form in cooking, baking, yogurt making and to enrich other foods. In all of these functions it is inferior to fresh milk, but the convenience and availability of a milk that doesn't need refrigeration can't be denied. So far, drying milk is beyond the capabilities of the home dairy.

STORING MILK

Liquid milk should always be stored in the refrigerator at 40°F, and even then can only be kept about 3 days before the flavor begins to go off. Milk should never be exposed to sunlight.

FREEZING MILK

Milk can be frozen. Allow a 2-inch head-room for expansion in the container. The container must also be quite completely air-tight to avoid freezer odors in the milk. To defrost, put the milk on a refrigerator shelf for several hours of slow melting rather than quickly defrosting at room temperature.

Freezing Milk

Allow about 2 inches headroom.

SCALDING MILK

Many recipes call for scalded milk. This is a tricky point in heating milk, for under no circumstances must it be allowed to boil. Scalding is the point just before milk boils or foams up in the pan. The temperature will be about 180°F and tiny bubbles will ring the edge of the pan in a solid line. These bubbles are smaller than a pinhead. Milk can be scalded over direct heat or in a double boiler over hot water. It should be watched closely. The chances for scorching milk on the bottom of the pan are reduced when the pan is rinsed with cold water just before you pour in the milk.

Scalding Milk

Tiny bubbles will ring the edge of the pan in a solid line.

Pasteurizing Milk I

for whole milk or cream

Equipment

> sterilized half-gallon jars and covers
> canning kettle deep enough to accommodate half-gallon jars
> temperature control bottle
> dairy thermometer

1. Fill the sterile jars with fresh raw milk and screw on the covers. Leave 2 inches headroom.

2. Stand the jars in the kettle on a rack. In the center put the temperature control bottle.

3. Fill the kettle with water until the water line is above the milk line in the jars.

4. Heat the water until the thermometer in the control bottle registers 145°F. Hold 30 minutes.

5. Cool the water rapidly by setting the kettle in very cold water. *Do not put the hot jars of milk in cold water.* Cool the entire kettle instead. As soon as the temperature of the control bottle reaches 80°F you can cool the jars directly in cold water and bring them down to 40°F. Refrigerate at once.

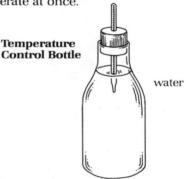

Temperature Control Bottle

water

Bottle is fitted with a cork; cork has a hole drilled large enough to accept the thermometer. Thermometer is inserted so it is immersed in the water inside the bottle.

How to Make a Temperature Control Bottle

1. Select a heavy glass bottle with an opening that will accept the dairy thermometer. The bottle should be tall enough to prevent water in the kettle from seeping inside it. An inverted, empty tuna can in the bottom of the kettle can serve as a handy platform if necessary.
2. Fill the bottle with water.
3. Insert the dairy thermometer so that it is immersed in the water. Wrap the part of the thermometer that protrudes from the bottle with heavy string or yarn if the fit is too loose.

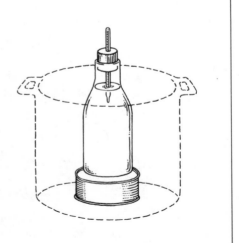

Pasteurizing Milk II

for whole milk

Equipment

> stainless steel pail
> dairy thermometer
> large kettle

1. Pour the milk into the stainless steel pail, then immerse the dairy thermometer.

2. Set the pail in a large kettle of boiling water. Heat until the milk temperature reaches 160°F. Hold 15 seconds, stirring for even heating.

3. Cool rapidly by setting the pail in cold running water. Cool the milk to 40°F, cover and store at this temperature. Stir the milk as it cools to prevent a skin from forming.

Milk Preservation in the Old Days

Before the advent of freezers and refrigeration, most milk was preserved in the form of butter and cheese, but occasionally an enterprising dairyist would try something different. Here are some overly enthusiastic suggestions from a rural New England farm newspaper of March, 1848:

Preservation of Milk

If milk be introduced into bottles, then well-corked, put into a pan of cold water, and gradually raised to a boiling point, and after being allowed to cool, be taken out and set away in a cool place, the milk may be preserved perfectly sweet for upwards of half a year. Or it may be evaporated to dryness by a gentle heat and under constant stirring. A dry mass will thus be obtained, which when dissolved in water is said to possess all the qualities of the best milk—It is called latteina.

Aurora of the Valley
(Newbury, Vt.),
March 4, 1848

MILK RECIPES

Soups

Dried Split Pea Soup

serves four

½ pound dried split peas
1 tablespoon honey
3 cups milk
½ cup whipping cream
3 tablespoons butter
2 thin slices buttered whole grain bread
　　　cut into 1-inch cubes

1. Soak the peas overnight in enough cold water to cover.

2. Next day drain the peas and put them in a heavy saucepan, cover with *cold water* and bring to a boil. Simmer slowly over reduced heat until tender.

3. Puree the peas in a blender, then add the honey.

4. Heat the milk to the scalding point. Set the blender on low speed and then gradually pour the milk into the blender with the peas.

5. Pour the soup back into the saucepan, add the cream and butter, and stir thoroughly as it heats.

6. Fry the bread cubes in a small skillet until they are crispy brown croutons.

7. Serve the hot soup garnished with the croutons.

Endive Milk Soup

serves eight to ten

Gardeners who plant endive always reach a point during the summer when they can't think of another thing to do with it. Here is an unusual and delicious answer to the problem.

6 tablespoons butter
3 medium-size potatoes, peeled and
　　　sliced thin
1 pound endive, washed and chopped
2 leeks (white part only), chopped
2 quarts milk
6 slices whole grain bread

1. In a heavy saucepan heat the butter and saute the potatoes, turning often, until they are *soft* but not brown. Add endive and leeks and continue sauteing until limp.

2. Heat the milk separately to the scalding point. Add the milk to the vegetables and simmer gently 40 minutes.

3. Just before serving, toast the bread, then serve the piping hot soup with the plain toast for dunking.

Pumpkin Soup

serves four

This used to be a staple on New England autumn and winter menus. The pumpkin of yesteryear was a far more versatile vegetable than we give it a chance to be today. The pumpkin has an affinity for milk and cream.

3 cups milk
2 cups cooked, pureed pumpkin
2 tablespoons honey
  pinch powdered ginger
  pinch allspice
4 slices French bread, toasted

1. Heat the milk to the scalding point, then blend it into the pureed pumpkin in a saucepan.

2. Add the honey and seasonings and heat thoroughly, stirring.

3. Arrange the toasted bread in the bottom of a 2-quart tureen, then pour the hot soup over it. Allow it to stand 2 or 3 minutes before serving.

Watercress Soup

serves four

4 medium-size potatoes, peeled and
    diced
2 cups milk
1 bunch watercress (about 2 cups,
    tightly packed)
4 tablespoons butter
4 teaspoons chopped chervil (parsley
    may be substituted)

1. Put the potatoes in a saucepan and cover with cold water. Bring to a boil and cook until tender. Do not drain them.

2. Transfer the potatoes and the potato water from the saucepan to a blender; process and return this to the saucepan.

3. Wash and coarsely chop the watercress and then combine it with the milk. Heat the watercress-milk mixture to the scalding point and then slowly stir it into the pureed potatoes. Gently heat the soup 10 minutes.

4. Just before serving add the butter, stirring until it melts, and the chervil.

Main Dishes

The Classic French Toast

serves four

Serve French toast hot with lashings of honey butter. An alternate way of preparing this is to combine the egg and milk mixtures and dip the bread slices only once. Use a bread loaf with a firm crumb. We find that homemade bread that has ½ cup or more of soy flour added makes wonderful French toast that doesn't disintegrate during the dipping process.

1 vanilla bean (or 2 teaspoons vanilla extract)
2 cups milk
3 teaspoons honey
2 eggs
4 tablespoons butter
8 slices dry or stale whole grain bread

1. Split the vanilla bean in half and put it in a saucepan with the milk (if using vanilla extract, add later) and 2 teaspoons of the honey. Heat to the simmering point and hold this temperature 1 minute. Remove from the heat and cool. Remove the vanilla bean. (If substituting vanilla extract, add it now.)

2. Beat the eggs with the remaining honey until light.

3. Heat the butter on a griddle or in a large skillet over moderate heat.

4. Dip a bread slice first into the milk, hold it up and let it drain a moment, then dip it into the eggs and saute in the butter until golden brown on both sides. Serve on heated plates at once.

Creamed Turkey

serves four

Chicken or rabbit can be substituted for turkey in this day-after-Thanksgiving recipe.

2 cups cooked, diced turkey
2 tablespoons turkey gravy
2 tablespoons chopped parsley
1 teaspoon grated onions
2 tablespoons butter
2 tablespoons chopped almonds or
      walnuts
¼ cup chopped celery
1 tablespoon whole wheat flour
1 teaspoon wine vinegar
1 cup milk
2 eggs
4 slices hot buttered whole wheat toast

1. Put the turkey in a mixing bowl, then add the gravy, parsley and onions. Toss thoroughly.

2. In the top of a double boiler over hot water, melt the butter and cook the almonds and celery in it 2 or 3 minutes. Stir in the flour, mixing well. Add the vinegar. Gradually stir in the milk and cook until smooth and slightly thickened.

3. Beat the eggs until light, then stir in the milk mixture. Cook several minutes, then fold in the turkey mixture. Heat through and serve on hot toast.

Poached Eggs Indienne

serves six

These are very good with lots of buttered toast, and make an excellent lunch or late supper dish.

4 tablespoons raisins
2 tablespoons butter
2 tablespoons whole wheat flour
3 tablespoons curry powder
2 cups milk
¼ cup cider vinegar
12 eggs

1. Simmer the raisins in a little hot water until they plump out and become soft. Set aside.

2. Heat the butter in a saucepan, then stir in the flour and curry powder until smooth. Add the milk gradually, stirring all the while. Cook and stir until the sauce thickens. Keep it warm.

3. Put the vinegar in a large skillet and add the eggs and enough water to make a 3-inch depth of liquid in the pan. Bring to a gentle boil and poach until the yolks are loosely set and veiled with the white.

4. Remove the eggs with a skimmer and drain a moment on paper towels. Put the eggs on a heated platter, cover with the curry sauce and sprinkle the raisins over the surface.

Fish Baked in Milk

serves six

When the fisherman of the family brings home that prize bass or other freshwater fish, try this delicate way of preparing it.

1 or 2 firm-fleshed fish, about 4 pounds, cleaned, scaled and rinsed
2 tablespoons butter
  dash freshly ground pepper
  dash freshly grated nutmeg
  milk to cover
2 *Beurre Manie* Balls (see Index)
3 egg yolks
3 tablespoons grated cheese
1 tablespoon chopped parsley
1 teaspoon chopped tarragon

Preheat oven to 350°F.

1. Arrange the fish in a buttered baking dish and sprinkle lightly with the pepper and nutmeg. Dot with butter, then add the milk to cover.

2. Cover loosely with a sheet of foil and bake 30 minutes. Remove the fish to a heated platter and keep hot.

3. Strain the milk from the baking dish into a saucepan, then work in the *beurre manie*, breaking off little bits and stirring until smooth. Cook over low heat 5 minutes or until the sauce is smooth and slightly thickened. Remove from the heat.

4. Beat the egg yolks until light, then gradually beat them into the sauce. Cook over low heat several minutes, stirring constantly.

5. Put the fish back into the baking dish, pour the sauce over it, sprinkle with the grated cheese, parsley and tarragon. Return to the oven and bake until the cheese is melted and browned and the sauce bubbles. Serve at once.

Onion Tart

serves six

This subtle and beautiful dish is perfectly complemented by a green endive salad. The tart should be baked in a quiche pan, and the dough made several hours before the filling so that it has time to chill in the refrigerator.

Crust
1⅔ cups whole grain flour
  6 tablespoons butter, at room
      temperature
  about 4 tablespoons cold water

Filling
  5 tablespoons butter
  2 pounds onions, peeled and sliced
      thin
  1 egg
  1 tablespoon whole grain flour
  ¾ cup milk
  12 to 16 tiny white onions, peeled
      freshly ground pepper

1. Sift the flour into a mixing bowl.

2. Break the butter into small pieces and add to the flour, then work in with your fingers, adding a few drops of water as necessary until the dough holds together.

3. Gather into a ball, cover and chill several hours before proceeding.

4. Preheat oven to 400°F. Roll pastry and line a 9-inch quiche or pie pan with it.

5. Prick the pastry with a fork and bake 12 minutes or until lightly browned.

6. Meanwhile, make filling. In a heavy skillet melt 4 tablespoons of the butter and saute the onions until golden. Remove the skillet from the heat.

7. In a bowl mix the egg, flour and milk, then add the cooked, sliced onions. Stir well.

8. Pour the onion mixture into the baked tart shell, sprinkle with pepper and bake 15 minutes or until set.

9. While the tart is baking, boil the tiny onions until they are tender. Do not overcook. Drain and saute them in the remaining butter.

10. Arrange the tiny glazed onions around the edge of the tart and serve.

Milk Toast

serves one

This is a traditional easily digested, soothing supper for children and invalids. If upset stomachs are the problem, use goats' milk.

 1 slice whole grain bread
   butter
½ cup milk

1. Toast the bread while heating the milk until it is hot but not scalded.

2. Butter the toast generously and place it on a warm plate. Pour the hot milk over the toast and serve at once.

   The flavor may be perked up with a slight dusting of cinnamon or a few twists of the pepper mill, but small children seem to prefer it unseasoned.

Sour Milk Griddlecakes

serves four to six

An Old Yankee recipe that uses sour milk, this is best when the batter is made the night before. Grated apple adds texture and interest, or add to the batter just before cooking a few tablespoons of applesauce, ¼ cup wild blueberries, strawberries or blackberries. Serve these fine cakes with butter and maple syrup and whipped cream for something ineffable.

 3 eggs
 2 cups Sour Milk (see Index)
½ teaspoon baking soda
 2 tablespoons molasses
 2 cups whole wheat flour
¼ cup vegetable oil

1. The night before beat the eggs in a bowl until light and fluffy. Stir in the sour milk, baking soda and molasses.

2. Add in the flour alternately with the oil, beating well for a smooth batter.

3. Pour the batter into a pitcher, cover and let stand at room temperature overnight.

4. Next morning, pour the batter to form pancakes on an oiled griddle or skillet. Brown cakes lightly on both sides and serve.

Vegetables

Baked Herb Rice

serves four

1 egg
1 cup milk
½ cup chopped parsley
2 tablespoons chopped mixed herbs
    (thyme, rosemary, summer
    savory, mint and the like)
2 cups cooked brown rice
1 medium-size onion, chopped
½ cup cottage cheese
2 teaspoons Clarified Butter (see Index)

Preheat oven to 325°F.

1. Beat the egg lightly, then gradually beat in the milk. Stir in remaining ingredients except butter and mix thoroughly.

2. Butter a 1-quart casserole, turn in the rice mixture and bake until set, about 30 minutes. Serve at once.

Scalloped Potatoes

serves four

6 medium-size potatoes, peeled and
    sliced thin
1 tablespoon butter
2 cups milk
1 tablespoon grated onions
½ cup grated Farm Cheese (see Index)
1 teaspoon chopped parsley

Preheat oven to 350°F.

1. Arrange potato slices in layers in a buttered baking dish, dotting each layer with butter.

2. Heat the milk, onions and cheese in a saucepan until the cheese begins to soften but not melt. Pour this over the potatoes. Bake 30 minutes until the potatoes are soft and the cheese is melted and browned.

3. Sprinkle with parsley and serve at once.

Hot Milk Hashed Potatoes

serves six

8 medium-size potatoes
1 to 2 cups milk
  dash freshly ground white pepper
  pinch freshly grated nutmeg
4 tablespoons butter
2 tablespoons chopped parsley

1. Boil the potatoes in their jackets until they are fork tender. Drain and cool.

2. Cut the potatoes into ¼-inch slices and arrange in layers in a heavy skillet. Pour milk over the slices to cover; add the pepper and nutmeg.

3. Simmer over low heat until about half the milk is absorbed. Add the butter and shake the skillet until the butter is evenly distributed. Sprinkle parsley over all. Serve hot.

Mushrooms in Milk Sauce

serves four

1 pound mushrooms, caps separated
      from stems
¾ cup Whey (see Index)
4 tablespoons butter
3 tablespoons whole wheat flour
  freshly ground pepper
1 cup milk
3 tablespoons whipping cream
2 teaspoons chopped chives
4 slices hot buttered whole wheat toast

1. Slice the caps and set aside. Chop the stems and simmer them 10 minutes in the whey.

2. Strain the whey-mushroom essence into a cup and set aside.

3. Melt the butter in the top of a double boiler over direct heat and saute the sliced mushroom caps several minutes, stirring constantly. Then blend in the flour and pepper. Stir in the whey-mushroom essence and cook, stirring, until the mixture bubbles.

4. Place the pan over, not in, hot water. Add the milk, cream and chives and cook until thick and smooth, stirring constantly. Serve hot and bubbling on the toast.

Sauces

Bechamel Sauce (Basic Cream Sauce)

yields 1½ cups

Milk-based sauces and gravies would fill an entire book by themselves. But the grandfather of them all, and the most useful sauce in any cook's repertoire, is Bechamel Sauce, more often called Basic Cream Sauce. This chameleon mixture is used in a thousand ways, as the basis for creamed vegetables, for souffles, for casseroles, for soups, and as the starting point for uncounted sauces with tongue-twisting names that gild everything from apricots to zebra steak.

This sauce first saw the light of day in Louis XIV's kitchen, where Chef Bechamel invented this gift to Western cuisine. The mainstay of millions of kitchens, from small farmholds to castles to great restaurants, it is easy to make and will hold very well in the warming oven over a wood-burning range for as much as an hour. It can be refrigerated, frozen, heated and reheated and still maintain its integrity.

2 tablespoons butter
2 tablespoons whole wheat flour
1 cup milk
1 small onion stuck with a clove
½ small bay leaf

1. In a heavy saucepan melt the butter over low heat. Blend in the flour, cooking and stirring 2 or 3 minutes. Remove from heat.

2. Scald the milk, then gradually add it to the flour mixture, stirring steadily.

3. Add the onion and bay leaf and cook over low heat, stirring, until thick and smooth. Discard the onion and bay leaf.

Sauce Fines Herbes

yields 1½ cups

This is a variation of Bechamel (one of hundreds!) that is particularly good with fish and vegetables. A few tablespoons of this sauce worked into 4 scrambled eggs turns that pedestrian dish into something splendid. Try mixing a little of this sauce into mashed potatoes—very tasty.

3 teaspoons chopped parsley
3 teaspoons chopped chervil
1 shallot, chopped
¼ cup wine vinegar
⅔ cup Bechamel Sauce (see above)
3 tablespoons heavy cream
3 teaspoons chopped tarragon

1. In a small saucepan simmer the parsley, chervil and shallot in the vinegar until most of the liquid evaporates and the herbs are soft.

2. Stir in the Bechamel Sauce and simmer gently 5 minutes.

3. Stir in the cream and tarragon and serve at once.

CHERVIL

Bread

Austrian Milk Bread

makes one round loaf

1 tablespoon baker's yeast
¼ cup warm water
1¾ cups whole wheat flour
1 tablespoon grated lemon rind
⅔ cup milk
3 tablespoons melted butter
2 tablespoons honey
2 to 3 tablespoons raisins
1 egg, beaten

1. Have all ingredients at room temperature. Dissolve the yeast in water by letting it stand 10 minutes.

2. In a bowl mix all other ingredients except the raisins and egg. Add the yeast, mixing thoroughly.

3. Knead 8 to 10 minutes or until the dough is elastic and smooth. Knead in the raisins.

4. Let the dough rise in a greased, covered bowl in a warm place until doubled in size.

5. Punch down the dough, shape into a plump round loaf and place on a greased baking sheet. Allow the dough to rise again another 30 minutes in a warm place.

6. Preheat oven to 400°F. Brush the loaf with the egg.

7. Bake in the hot oven 15 minutes, then reduce the heat to 350°F and bake 25 minutes longer.

Special Milk Dishes and Desserts

Curds and Cream

serves two or three

  1 quart raw clean milk
½ cup heavy cream
    freshly grated nutmeg
    honey (optional)

1. Let the milk stand in a crock in a warm place until sour and clabbered but not separated into curds and whey (about 12 hours to 3 days depending upon room temperature).

2. Line a colander with a double layer of damp cheesecloth and pour the clabber in very carefully. Let the clabber drain overnight. Set the whey aside and use in another recipe.

3. Chill the curd for several hours, then turn out on a shallow dish. Dust with nutmeg and serve with the cream. The cream may be sweetened.

Baked Custard

serves four

3 eggs
3 tablespoons maple syrup
2 cups milk
1 teaspoon vanilla extract
    freshly grated nutmeg

Preheat oven to 350°F.

1. Beat the eggs until foamy and light, then add the maple syrup, milk and vanilla.

2. Pour the custard mixture into individual custard cups and grate a fine dusting of nutmeg on top of each. Set the cups in a pan of hot water which comes halfway up the sides of the custard cups.

3. Bake until a knife blade inserted in the center of a custard comes out clean — about 40 minutes. Serve hot or cold.

Curd Cake

serves ten to fifteen

This custardy Swedish delicacy has the name *Smalandsk ostkaka* in its homeland. The rennet tablets called for in this recipe are the junket rennet tablets available in most grocery stores, not the much stronger animal rennet called for in many recipes in this book. The cake is traditionally served with homemade lingonberry jam.

3 rennet tablets, household strength
3 tablespoons cold water
10 quarts milk
½ cup whole wheat flour
8 eggs, beaten
3 tablespoons honey
2 cups whipping cream
½ cup chopped blanched almonds

1. Dissolve the rennet tablets in the cold water.

2. Mix a little of the milk into the flour until smooth, then add this to the remaining milk, stirring thoroughly. Heat the milk slowly in a large kettle, stirring from time to time, until its temperature is 98°F for cows' milk, 85°F for goats' milk.

3. Add the rennet to the milk and stir a few seconds. Let it set 15 to 20 minutes, or until curd starts to form. Pour into a colander lined with a double layer of damp cheesecloth and allow it to drain several hours. At the end of this time press out as much whey as you can by hand.

4. Turn the curd into a mixing bowl and add the eggs, honey, cream and almonds and stir until thoroughly blended.

5. Preheat the oven to 250°F. Butter a 3-quart low casserole, pour in the cake batter and bake 45 minutes in the slow oven or until the cake is set firm and has a light brown top. Cool to room temperature before serving.

Indian Kheer

serves two

In India this soothing dessert often follows a fiery curry and is decorated with almost transparent pure gold or silver leaf, which Indians claim adds a needed mineral to the diet. The taste of the precious metal is a subtle and fleeting tang.

2 cups milk
5 tablespoons ground brown rice
    (available at specialty food shops,
    or grind your own with a mortar
    and pestle or grain mill)
2 tablespoons chopped almonds
2 tablespoons chopped pistachio nuts
1 tablespoon honey
4 tablespoons thick coconut milk (the
    fresh-drained milk with enough
    grated coconut added to give the
    consistency of thick cream)

1. Bring the milk up to the scalding point, and, stirring constantly to prevent a boil, sprinkle in the ground rice.

2. When the milk begins to thicken, add the almonds, pistachios and honey.

3. Now add the coconut milk, stirring well. The *kheer* should have the consistency of custard.

4. Pour into individual dishes and chill. Serve cold.

    Often, in India, a few drops of rose water or orange blossom water are added for flavor. Using delicate flower honeys will achieve a similar effect.

Rice Pudding Like Grandma Used to Make

serves six

  3 eggs
1½ cups milk
  4 tablespoons maple sugar
1½ tablespoons butter
  1 teaspoon vanilla extract
    rind of ½ lemon, grated
  1 teaspoon lemon juice
  ½ cup raisins
  ½ cup chopped, dried or fresh apple
  2 tablespoons chopped butternuts
  2 cups short grain brown rice cooked
    in milk
    Devonshire Cream (see Index)

Preheat oven to 350°F.

1. In a mixing bowl, beat the eggs until light, then add the milk, maple sugar, 1 tablespoon butter and vanilla. Blend thoroughly.

2. Beat in the lemon rind, lemon juice, raisins, apple and nuts. Fold in the rice lightly.

3. Grease a baking dish with remaining butter. Pour in the batter and bake 1 hour. Serve hot or cold with Devonshire Cream.

Milk Tart

makes one 9-inch pie

2 cups milk
1 stick cinnamon
6 pieces orange rind, 1 × ½ inch, with
    pith removed
1 vanilla bean, split open
½ cup heavy cream
2 tablespoons maple syrup
¼ cup cornstarch
2 tablespoons butter
2 tablespoons applesauce or pureed
    fruit
1 baked 9-inch pie shell
2 eggs, lightly beaten
  freshly grated nutmeg

1. In a saucepan combine the milk, cinnamon stick, orange rind and vanilla bean, and, over moderate heat bring the mixture up to the scalding point. Then remove from heat, cover and let stand 20 minutes.

2. In a mixing bowl, mix together the cream, maple syrup and cornstarch. Stirring constantly, mix the cream mixture into the milk, then cook over low heat 2 or 3 minutes or until very thick.

3. Add the butter, stirring until it melts. Remove from heat and cool to lukewarm, stirring occasionally to prevent a skin forming on the top. Preheat oven to 350°F.

4. Spread the applesauce evenly over the bottom of the pie shell. Remove the orange rind, vanilla bean and cinnamon stick from the cooled custard mixture. Beat in the eggs.

5. Pour all into the pie shell and dust the top with nutmeg. Bake 35 to 40 minutes, or until the custard is set and has a golden brown surface. Cool to room temperature before serving.

Sour Milk Pie

makes one 9-inch pie

2 eggs, slightly beaten
1 cup Sour Milk (see Index)
¼ cup honey
1 tablespoon vinegar
1 teaspoon cinnamon
¼ teaspoon cloves
½ teaspoon allspice
1 cup seedless raisins
1 unbaked 9-inch pie shell

1. Combine all of the ingredients, stirring until thoroughly mixed. Let all stand 45 minutes to allow the raisins to plump up and the milk to acidify. Heat oven to 450°F.

2. Pour mixture into the pie shell.

3. Bake 10 minutes, then reduce heat to 350°F and bake 30 minutes longer or until pie is set. Cool and serve.

Sour Milk in a Hurry

One of us remembers a particularly good sour milk gingerbread from childhood days and the kitchen trick which made instant sour milk out of fresh sweet milk. To 1 cup of sweet milk add 1 teaspoon of lemon juice or cider vinegar. Let it stand 15 minutes or until it clabbers.

Old-Fashioned Vanilla Custard

serves four

2 cups milk
¼ cup honey
1 vanilla bean, split open
4 egg yolks

1. Put the milk, honey and vanilla bean in a heavy saucepan, then heat to the scalding point, stirring often. Remove from the heat.

2. Beat the egg yolks until thick, then remove the vanilla bean from the milk and very gradually add the hot milk to the yolks, beating vigorously all the while.

3. When all the milk is beaten in, return it to the saucepan and cook over very low heat until the custard thickens.

4. Pour into custard cups and chill several hours.

"To Make a Dyschefull of Snowe"

An old Apple Cream Custard recipe from *A Proper Newe Booke of Cokerye* (before 1575). In those days it was difficult to beat cream and egg whites, for there were no wire whisks or egg beaters; in this recipe the cook is instructed to make a homemade beater out of a clean stick.

Take a pottell of swete thycke creame and the whytes of eyghte egges, and beate them altogether wyth a spone, then putte them in youre creame and a saucerfull of Rosewater, and a dyshe full of Sugar wyth all, then take a stycke and make it cleane, and than cutte it in the end foure square, and therewith beate all the aforesayde thynges together and ever as it ryseth take it of and put it in a Collaunder, this done take one apple and set it in the myddes of the platter, then cast your Snowe upon the Rosemarye and fyll your platter therewith. And yf you have wafers caste some in wyth all and thus serve them forth.

4

SWEET CREAM

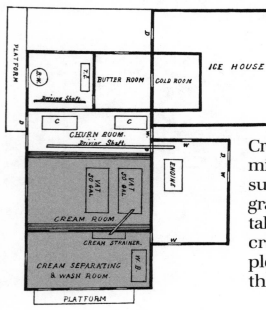

Plan of Dairy for Fifty Cows.

Cream is the butterfat portion of the milk, and it rises naturally to the surface through the principles of gravity as the milk stands. It may take as much as 36 hours for the cream in cows' milk to rise completely. The longer the milk stands, the richer the cream.

Cream has several interesting properties—it will culture into a number of regional delicacies, it whips into fluffy masses, it can be cooked to a thick, semi-solid state, and it freezes well. It is a tremendously important ingredient in Western cooking, from simple farmhouse fare to haute cuisine. Homogenization makes the milk protein in cream more sensitive to heat, and often it will flocculate, or separate, in hot, acid liquids, even though the cream is not sour.

The butterfat globules in goats' milk are much smaller than those in cows' milk, and it takes considerably longer for them to rise to the surface as cream, as much as 3 days. Most home dairy goat owners use a separator to liberate the cream from the milk quickly. On the average, a gallon of goats' milk will yield more cream than will a gallon of cows' milk. However, goats' cream is slower to whip and slower to make butter than is cows' cream.

Cereal or Coffee Cream—cream that is liberated from cows' milk after standing for 12 hours; it contains between 18 percent and 20 percent butterfat.

This is called *cereal* or *coffee cream* commercially. *Half-and-half*, is, as its name implies, a mixture of cream and milk, and contains only 12 percent butterfat.

Light Cream—contains at least 32 percent butterfat and is found on the surface of cows' milk that has stood 24 hours.

In its natural state this cream is quite free flowing, but when pasteurized under high pressure, as commercial light cream is, it becomes more viscous, and more appealing to the dairy case shopper who associates all creams with thickness. Don't be worried if your light cream is more

liquid than the stuff in the supermarkets—it's really supposed to be that way.

Goat milkers with a separator who want light cream should run the milk through the separator while it is still warm from the goat, with the screw set to an extraction rate of 1 to 1⅛ pints of cream per gallon of milk.

Separating Goats' Milk

If you only keep one or two goats, it is not worthwhile to run the daily milk take through the separator. You may save up the milk from several milkings and run it through all at once later, by pasteurizing and holding each milking.

1. Pasteurize the fresh milk at once by holding it at 180°F for 30 seconds, then cool it rapidly and store in a cool place until you have accumulated enough for the separator.

2. Before putting the milk through the separator, it must be reheated to 180°F and then cooled at once to 100°F. At least part of the milk that goes into the separator should be fresh and warm from the goat.

3. Set the separator screw at the desired setting and run the milk through.

Whipping Cream—also known as *heavy cream*, contains at least 40 percent butterfat.

With the gravity creaming method cream of this weight results after more than 24 hours' standing. A prerequisite for good whipping quality is a high fat content. Cream with 40 percent butterfat is easy to whip, while that with 30 percent and lower is difficult to whip. Commercially, cream with a butterfat level of only 25 percent is made into whipping cream by adding powdered sweet buttermilk with a high lecithin content.

Whipping cream from goats' milk is

produced by setting the separator cream screw to make ¾ pint of cream per gallon of milk.

USES FOR CREAM

Different weights of cream can be whipped, soured, cultured, worked, ripened, heated, frozen, chilled, flavored and sweetened, and are used in thousands of recipes. In many regions, such as Devonshire, Normandy and Scandinavia, and in traditional French cooking, cream is integral to the cuisine. In the following pages there are directions for making several creams, from Devonshire Cream to the Kaymak of the Near East to the Scandinavian Graddfil. (Sour cream is so versatile it has a section of its own, as does butter.) Recipes calling for quantities of cream are here, from sauces to desserts (including luscious cream soups and ice creams), from old, old favorites to inventive novelties for the delight of your palate.

It is important to note that although cream freezes well, both in liquid and whipped states, it must be securely wrapped to exclude any freezer odors.

ABOUT WHIPPING CREAM

The ideal whipping cream is easy to whip and makes a fine cream foam with a good increase in volume; the cream foam is firm and durable and does not backslide into liquid if kept for several hours.

When cream is whipped, air is beaten in and collects as a cream foam full of tiny air bubbles. The fat globules in the cream cluster on the walls of the air bubbles. The agitation of the beater forces some liquid butterfat out of each fat globule, and this liberated fat becomes the cement that holds the globules together, making a stiff whipped cream. Goats' cream will whip up to a greater volume than cows' cream, and it is always snow white, whereas cows' cream often takes on a delicate yellow patina.

To get the desirable fine cream foam, the cream *must be cold*. Warm cream contains melted liquid butterfat, and cannot be whipped. If cream has been pasteurized, don't try to whip it until it has chilled or ripened for 24 hours at 40°F.

The firmness of the butterfat in cream varies with the animal's diet and the time of year. Summer pasture makes softer butterfat, and it is usually more difficult to whip this cream unless it ripens thoroughly. Winter cream has firmer butterfat and whips easily.

Ripening Cream

Ripening cream refers to the method of storing the cream for 24 hours at low temperatures to let it develop the right proportion of liquid and crystallized butterfat globules. Ripening is essential for good whipping cream.

21146 Cream, $3.85.

21143 Cream, $2.00.

How to Whip Cream

We've all done it more times than we care to remember—poured some cream from a container that has been standing on the counter for at least an hour into a bowl hastily snatched from the kitchen cupboard, and then whipped it and whipped it with a beater straight from the kitchen drawer, only to end with a disappointing, yellowish, grainy mass and some thin separated liquid in the bottom of the bowl. This culinary disaster is common and avoidable. Here's how to make never-fail, superior whipped cream that holds its firmness and delicately enhances a thousand dishes:

1. Wait until the last minute—just before serving—to whip cream. Use a manual egg beater. Electric blenders are not good cream whips—no substitutes for the human hand and eye have been found.

2. Have the cream, the bowl and the beater *cold*, below 45°F. The bowl and beater can be rinsed in cold water and dried just before whipping. If the bowl and beater are warm, you run the risk of making butter rather than whipped cream.

3. Don't use an enormous bowl. The bowl and beater size should be balanced, otherwise the whipping process will be prolonged, will generate heat and produce a poor cream foam.

4. The bowl should be filled less than half full of cream, or it will be difficult to whip in the necessary amount of air quickly. If you have a lot of cream to whip, it is better to do it in two smaller amounts than to court failure.

5. The whipping should be rapid and vigorous and should stop in time. Care must be taken not to overwhip the delicate mass, but to stop when the cream's volume is increased two times and it holds together in large, soft globs with a shining, glossy surface. If the whipping continues after this stage it will soon become granular and liquid and will separate out in the early stages of becoming butter.

6. If you are adding sweetening or flavoring, do it toward the end of the whipping process. Adding it before the cream is whipped decreases the whippability and raises the temperature of the cream.

When Whipping Starts to Go Wrong

You are whipping merrily away and relating an adventure or bit of news, or simply daydreaming, when you notice with a start that you have whipped the cream too much and it is starting to become grainy and turn to butter! All is not lost. Add 2 tablespoons of heavy cream to the teetering mass to restore equilibrium, and proceed with the beating until the cream is whipped to your satisfaction.

Decorative Whipped Cream

If you want this very stiff cream, continue to whip the cream with caution past the point of perfection *almost* to the grainy early butter stage. Cows' cream will become thick nearly to the point of spreadability and will take on yellow shadows in the folds of cream. Now the cream can be forced through a pastry tube for the desired ribbon or fluted effects.

Decorative cream rosettes, ribbons, puffs and other pastry tube extravaganzas can be frozen for later use. Force the whipped cream through the pastry tube directly onto a sheet of aluminum foil, then quickly freeze the decorations uncovered. As soon as they are frozen, wrap them securely, put them in a shallow, crush-proof box, and return to the freezer.

FLAVORED WHIPPED CREAMS

Use these for fruit and dessert toppings, for filling cones, crepes and cream puffs. Pile them on pancakes and waffles or use them to garnish drinks and soups, hot or cold.

Fleurette—This is the charming name the French give to freshly whipped unsweetened cream, and it is used not only on fruits and desserts, but with soups, from borscht to corn chowder.

Creme Chantilly—Whip 1 cup of heavy cream, and in the final minute of beating add 1 teaspoon of honey and a little pulp scraped from the heart of a vanilla bean. If you use liquid vanilla extract, ½ teaspoon is plenty.

Maple Cream—Vermonters who have both a cow and a sugar bush use this liberally on Sunday morning waffles. Whip 1 cup of heavy cream and add 1 table-spoon or more of Grade C maple syrup, more robust in flavor than Fancy or Grade A.

Ginger Cream—Whip 1 cup of heavy cream, and in the final moments beat in ½ cup of ginger jam. A dusting of nutmeg completes the rich taste.

Lemon Cream—Whip 1 cup of heavy cream, and in the last minutes beat in 1 tablespoon honey, 1 tablespoon lemon juice and the finely grated rind of half a lemon.

Fresh Fruit Cream—Almost any ripe, fresh fruit can be pureed in a blender and whipped into the cream, with or without sweetening. A particularly happy combi-nation is raspberry cream ladled and heaped on dead-ripe peaches.

Creme Amandine—Whip 1 cup of heavy cream, and in the last minute add 1 teaspoon almond extract and a few drops of lemon juice. Fold in 2 tablespoons of toasted, shredded almonds. Another way is to replace these ingredients with ¼ cup of almond paste, whipping it into the cream in the final moments.

Vermont Snow Cream

This old-fashioned concoction was a children's favorite after or during a fresh country snowfall. It is both grainy in texture and evanescent, melting rapidly, but all children enjoy it because it is made of snow. It takes only a little imagination to fancy that the billowing snow-drifts as far as the eye can see are crystalline mounds of snow cream. . . .

  ½ cup heavy cream
  ¼ cup honey
  ½ teaspoon vanilla extract
  2 quarts fresh-fallen snow

1. Mix the cream, honey and vanilla in a bowl.

2. Gather the fresh snow, then rapidly beat in the cream mixture until the snow is thick and blended. Serve at once!

The beating is best done outside or in an unheated room.

OTHER CREAMS

Devonshire Cream I

yields about 2 to 3 cups

2 gallons fresh Jersey or Guernsey milk

1. Pour the milk into a large shallow pan and let it stand for 6 hours or until the cream starts to rise.

2. Place the pan carefully on the lowest heat possible and heat the milk very, very slowly, over a period of 1 to 2 hours. The milk must not be allowed to boil. When the milk is thoroughly hot, remove from the heat.

3. Cool the milk in the pan for at least 24 hours. Skim the cream and serve.

Devonshire Cream II

1. Pour the evening's milk into a shallow pan and let it stand in a cool place overnight.

2. The next day put it over *very, very* slow heat to cook for 6 to 8 hours, or until the cream on the surface appears yellow, wrinkled and leathery.

3. Without disturbing the cream, remove the pan from the heat and cool the cream for 24 hours.

4. Skim off the cream with a slotted spoon or cream skimmer. Stir it with a fork to smooth it out and serve in a dish with a spoon.

Devonshire Cream is enjoyed in Devon with hot scones, honey and the housewife's best jams.

Creme Fraiche

yields 4 cups

This is heavy cream matured and fermented slightly, that is served cold on fruits and as a topping. It will keep 2 to 3 weeks if stored in a tightly covered jar in the refrigerator.

4 cups heavy cream
3 tablespoons cultured buttermilk or pleasant-tasting, naturally soured milk

1. Combine the cream and buttermilk in a large jar and stir thoroughly.

2. Cover the jar and put in a warm place free of drafts for 24 to 36 hours or until the cream takes on an agreeable and mild acidity that lies between sweet cream and sour cream.

3. Chill in the refrigerator until needed.

Kaymak or Near Eastern Clotted Cream

This delicacy is used liberally with Near Eastern pastries and is equally good with puddings, fruit pies and fresh fruit.

    1 quart heavy cream

1. In a very large kettle bring the cream almost to a boil over very low heat.

2. With a ladle, scoop cream out of the kettle and pour it back in from on high so that it makes many bubbles. Continue doing this 30 minutes to 1 hour until the kettle is full of fine cream bubbles.

3. Remove from the heat and set in a quiet place to cool gradually for several hours.

4. Refrigerate and chill for 24 hours.

5. The thick carpet of cream that lies on top of the liquid is the *kaymak* or clotted cream. Remove it with a spatula to a bowl. Cut it into slices with a knife and serve as a topping. If too soft to cut, remove it with a spoon.

Graddfil or Scandinavian Sour Cream

yields about 4 cups

This cream has a texture more like yogurt than sour cream, and is used as the basis of many dishes in Sweden, Finland and Denmark. It can be substituted for yogurt in any recipe, but has its own delicious and distinctive taste.

    1 quart light cream
    4 tablespoons fresh buttermilk culture
        (see discussion, p. 47)

1. Warm the cream to 70°F and pour into a jar, leaving an inch or two headspace.

2. Inoculate the cream with the buttermilk, cover the jar and shake for several minutes to mix thoroughly.

3. Let the covered jar stand undisturbed in a warm place (70°F), 18 hours.

4. Ripen the Graddfil another 24 hours in the refrigerator before using.

Pasteurizing Cream

Equipment
    stainless steel pail
    dairy thermometer
    large kettle

1. Pour the cream into the stainless steel pail. Put in the dairy thermometer.

2. Set the pail in a large kettle of boiling water and heat until the temperature of the cream reaches 145°F. Hold the cream at this temperature 30 minutes, stirring frequently.

3. Cool rapidly to 40°F by setting the pail in cold running water. Store at this temperature. It is important that pasteurized cream stand 24 hours before it is used for making any dairy products from whipped cream to butter.

Another way of pasteurizing cream is given in the section on milk. See Pasteurizing Milk I in the Index.

SWEET CREAM RECIPES

Soups

Brussels Sprouts and Grapes in Cream

serves six

4 cups brussels sprouts
1 cup seedless green grapes, halved
4 tablespoons butter
½ cup heavy cream
   freshly ground pepper

1. Steam the sprouts over boiling water until tender-crunchy—about 5 minutes.

2. Put the sprouts, grapes and butter in a heavy skillet. Heat until the butter sizzles, agitating the pan to thoroughly coat the grapes and sprouts.

3. Add the cream, turn the heat low and cook until the cream is almost evaporated, about 10 minutes. Sprinkle with pepper.

Cold Cucumber Cream

serves four

3 large firm cucumbers
3 tablespoons butter
3 tablespoons whole wheat flour
3 cups Whey (see Index)
1 cup milk
½ onion, thinly sliced
½ cup light cream

1. Peel, seed and slice the cucumbers.

2. Melt the butter in a saucepan, then cook the cucumbers over low heat 10 minutes.

3. Blend in the flour, then gradually add the whey, stirring constantly.

4. In a separate saucepan scald the milk with the onion slices, then strain the milk into the cucumber mixture, stirring constantly. Simmer 10 minutes.

5. Puree the soup in a blender, cup by cup, and stir in the cream. Chill several hours in the refrigerator before serving.

A Classic Vichyssoise

serves six to eight

The test of a good restaurant used to be a request for their vichyssoise; it was surprising how many vaunted names failed to serve a fine, rich, cold and creamy soup with the distinctive flavor of potatoes, leeks, good stock and cream. No substitutions or inferior ingredients are possible in this, one of the world's great soups.

2 tablespoons butter
4 big leeks, sliced
1 medium-size onion, sliced
5 medium-size potatoes, peeled and
    sliced thin
4 cups rich chicken stock
2 cups milk
  a few twists of freshly ground white
    pepper
2 cups medium cream
1 cup heavy cream
  chopped chives

1. Melt the butter in a heavy saucepan, add the leeks and onion and cook until they are limp and translucent.

2. Add the potatoes to the leek-onion mixture and stir in the chicken stock.

3. Simmer 30 minutes or until the potatoes are soft to the point of disintegration.

4. Puree the potatoes in a blender, a cup at a time, then return to the saucepan. Add the milk, the pepper and medium cream and bring the soup almost to a boil.

5. Cool the mixture, and when room temperature, stir in the heavy cream. Chill 6 to 8 hours.

6. Serve in cold cups topped with the chives.

Creamed Spinach Soup

serves four to six

1 pound spinach, washed and
    picked over
1½ cups milk
  3 tablespoons butter
  2 tablespoons grated onions
  3 tablespoons whole wheat flour
  pinch each freshly ground
      pepper, freshly grated nutmeg
      and cayenne
  2 egg yolks
  1 cup heavy cream
  1 tablespoon chopped chives
  Creme Amandine (see p. 74)

1. Put the drained spinach in a heavy saucepan without water, cover tightly and cook over low heat 4 or 5 minutes. Turn the leaves over with a fork and cook, covered, a few minutes longer until the spinach is wilted and soft.

2. Puree the spinach and its liquid in a blender and set aside.

3. Scald the milk. Melt the butter in a saucepan, then add the onions and cook until translucent. Blend in the flour, then gradually add the milk, stirring constantly. Cook until the mixture is smooth and slightly thickened.

4. Puree this sauce in the blender a cup at a time, and add it to the spinach. Add the pepper, nutmeg and cayenne and cook over low heat for several minutes, stirring.

5. Beat the egg yolks into the cream, then slowly combine this with the spinach mixture, stirring all the while.

6. Stir in the chopped chives and serve, garnishing each bowl with Creme Amandine.

Gardener's Cream of Carrot Soup

serves four

   5 medium-size carrots
   4 tablespoons butter
   4 tablespoons water
   1 teaspoon honey
   2 tablespoons whole wheat flour
2½ cups milk
   1 cup heavy cream

1. Wash the carrots thoroughly and slice into very thin rounds.

2. Put the carrots into a large heavy saucepan with 2 tablespoons butter, water and honey. Cook, covered, over low heat until the carrots are tender.

3. Put aside 8 to 10 carrot slices and dice them into tiny squares.

4. Melt the remaining butter in a saucepan over low heat. Blend in the flour, then gradually add the milk, blending thoroughly to prevent lumps. Cook gently until slightly thickened to the consistency of light cream.

5. In the top of a double boiler put the milk mixture, the carrot slices and any liquid left from the carrot cooking. Cook over, not in, hot water for 30 minutes.

6. Blend well in an electric blender, cup by cup. Return to the saucepan, add the cream and diced carrots. Heat through and serve at once.

Onion Cream Soup

serves six

   2 tablespoons butter
   2 large onions, thinly sliced
   6 cups milk
   2 tablespoons whole wheat flour
     freshly ground pepper
   4 egg yolks
1½ cups light cream
   4 to 6 slices French bread sauteed
     in butter until brown

1. Melt the butter in a large saucepan and saute the onions until they are translucent and limp. Meanwhile, heat the milk in a separate pan.

2. Stir the flour into the onions thoroughly. Slowly add the hot milk and pepper. Cook over low heat 30 minutes, stirring frequently to prevent lumps. Remove from heat.

3. In a bowl, beat the egg yolks and cream. Beating constantly, very slowly drip 1 cup of the soup into the egg mixture. Gradually beat this into the remaining soup.

4. Cook over moderate heat until slightly thickened. Do not boil. Pour the soup into a warm tureen whose bottom has been covered with the sauteed bread slices.

Traditional Vegetable Soup of Lorraine

serves eight

This hearty, rich soup belongs in every vegetarian recipe file. Gardeners will want to plant chervil for this recipe alone.

½ cup dried beans
6 medium carrots
4 leeks
6 potatoes
1 small cabbage
3 medium turnips
1 large onion
1 clove garlic, minced
1 stalk celery
1 sprig thyme
1 bay leaf
6 tablespoons butter
  French bread, sliced thin
1 cup heavy cream
2 tablespoons chopped chervil or
        parsley
  large lump sweet butter

1. Soak beans overnight in cold water to cover.

2. Wash the vegetables carefully. Leave the cabbage whole, but cut all other vegetables in half.

3. Fill a large, deep soup kettle ¾ full of water. Bring to a boil and add the beans and all the vegetables. Add the thyme, bay leaf and butter. Simmer 3 hours or until the beans are tender.

4. Warm a large casserole or soup tureen and cover the bottom with the slices of French bread. Pour the heavy cream over the bread and sprinkle with chervil.

5. Put a colander over the casserole and strain the soup liquid onto the cream-soaked bread.

6. Arrange the vegetables on a warm, shallow platter with the cabbage in the center. Split the cabbage in half and put the large lump of butter in the center. Serve the vegetables at once with the soup.

Experimenter's Choice

serves four

To this basic cream soup the adventur-
ous cook can add a cup of pureed asparagus, artichoke hearts, avocado, green
beans, tomatoes, chopped watercress,
or whatever looks good in the garden
or pantry.

2 tablespoons butter
1 tablespoon grated onions
2 tablespoons whole wheat flour
1 cup Whey (see Index) or chicken or
     beef stock
1 cup milk
  freshly ground pepper
1 cup light cream

1. Melt the butter in a heavy saucepan;
cook the onions in the butter until limp.

2. Blend in the flour, then gradually add
the whey, stirring to keep the mixture
smooth. Simmer 2 or 3 minutes.

3. Scald the milk, then add to the whey
mixture, stirring to keep it smooth. Add
the pepper and cook over low heat until
slightly thickened.

4. Scald the cream and stir in slowly.

To this basic cream, add a cup of
pureed vegetables, heat thoroughly and
serve at once, or chill thoroughly and
serve in cold cups. This cream stock
freezes quite well, and a quantity can be
made up in advance. Allow frozen cream
soup to defrost gradually before heating.

Waverly Cream Ladle.

Main Dishes

Breaded Calves' Liver

serves four

    4 to 8 slices calves' liver (about
        1½ pounds)
    ½ cup olive oil
    ½ teaspoon dried rosemary, powdered
    1 cup fine dry whole grain bread
        crumbs
    ½ cup heavy cream
      juice of 1 lemon

1. Soak the liver slices in olive oil 30 minutes, turning frequently.

2. Sprinkle each piece with rosemary and dip in bread crumbs until coated.

3. Place slices on baking sheet and broil 4 minutes each side.

4. Warm the cream and the lemon juice separately.

5. Transfer the liver slices to a heated platter, then sprinkle with the lemon juice, reserving about a teaspoonful. Mix the remaining lemon juice with the warm cream and serve in a sauceboat accompanying the liver.

Trout in Cream

serves four

    4 freshly caught trout
      freshly ground pepper
    ½ cup fine whole grain bread crumbs
    6 tablespoons Clarified Butter (see
        Index)
    ½ cup sweet cider
    ½ cup heavy cream

1. Clean and rinse trout, but leave the heads on. Gash them slightly along both sides, sprinkle with pepper and then dredge in bread crumbs.

2. Heat the butter in a heavy, large skillet. When it is very hot, saute the trout on both sides, about 4 minutes for each side.

3. Pour in the cider and cook over low heat several minutes, then add the cream and a little more pepper, and simmer until the sauce blends and is slightly thickened.

Creamed Turkey and Mushrooms

serves four

Another answer to the post-Thanksgiving Dinner problem.

1 cup sliced mushrooms
2 tablespoons chopped onions
2 tablespoons butter
1 tablespoon whole wheat flour
1 cup light cream
2 eggs, beaten
2 cups cooked, diced turkey
2 tablespoons chopped parsley
   pinch freshly grated nutmeg
4 slices hot buttered whole wheat toast
4 tablespoons slivered almonds, toasted

1. Saute the mushrooms and onions in butter in a large, heavy skillet 3 minutes. Add the flour and blend until color darkens, about 1 to 2 minutes.

2. Gradually add the cream, stirring well until smooth and thick.

3. Blend half the cream mixture with the eggs, then add eggs to pan. Cook, stirring constantly, 2 minutes or until thick and creamy.

4. Add the turkey, parsley and nutmeg and heat through.

5. Serve over the hot buttered toast, topping each portion with 1 tablespoon of almonds.

Sunday Dinner Chicken Casserole with Onions and Cream Sauce

serves six

Casserole

4 tablespoons butter
1½ tablespoons olive oil
16 small white onions, peeled
¼ cup cider vinegar
¾ cup Whey (see Index)
2 mild or Spanish onions, chopped
1 frying chicken, about 5 pounds,
    cut up
½ cup chicken stock
1 sprig thyme
½ bay leaf

Cream Sauce

2 tablespoons butter
2 tablespoons whole wheat flour
¾ cooking liquid from the chicken
    with the fat skimmed off
2 egg yolks
¾ cup medium cream

Preheat oven to 375°F.

1. Heat half the butter and all the olive oil in a large skillet, add the whole small onions and cook 5 minutes, shaking so that they are browned on all sides.

2. Add the vinegar and whey and simmer 5 more minutes.

3. Heat the rest of the butter in another large, heavy skillet, then add the chopped onions and cook until limp. Add the chicken pieces and brown lightly on all sides.

4. Add the whole onions and their sauce to the chicken. Then add the stock, thyme and bay leaf. Cover and cook in the oven 30 minutes.

5. Transfer the chicken to a warm platter and surround with the whole onions. Keep warm while making the sauce.

6. Melt the butter in a saucepan, blend in the flour and cook 1 minute over low heat. Remove from heat.

7. Stir in the cooking liquid with a whisk, return to heat and simmer, beating constantly, until smooth and thick. Remove from heat.

8. Beat the egg yolks in a bowl with the cream, then blend into the sauce. Return to low heat and stir until the sauce thickens and coats the spoon.

9. Pour the sauce over the chicken and place the platter under the broiler 1 minute to lightly color the surface.

Vegetables

Creamy Potato Salad, Utah Style

serves four to six

This dish is an invention of the Mormon pioneers, and is one of the best potato salads we've ever tasted.

4 large potatoes, boiled in their jackets,
    then peeled and cut into
    1-inch cubes
4 hard-boiled eggs, peeled and diced
⅓ cup grated mild onions
freshly ground pepper
Dressing
1 teaspoon dry mustard
2 tablespoons honey
2 eggs, beaten
3 tablespoons melted butter
½ cup hot cider vinegar
1 cup heavy cream, whipped

1. Toss potatoes, eggs, onions and pepper well in a large bowl. Chill while making the dressing.

2. Blend the mustard and honey in the top of a double boiler, then stir in the beaten eggs. Stir in the melted butter and vinegar. The mixture should be smooth.

3. Cook over, not in, simmering water until thick enough to coat a spoon. Cool to room temperature.

4. Fold in the whipped cream.

5. Mix the dressing into the salad and chill thoroughly before serving.

Tomatoes Stuffed with Creme Fraiche

serves six to eight

6 ounces cream cheese, at room
    temperature
3 tablespoons chopped chives
2 tablespoons chopped chervil
  freshly ground pepper
1 cup Creme Fraiche (see p. 75)
6 to 8 small, firm tomatoes
  small head lettuce, separated, washed
    and chilled
¾ cup Lemon Vinaigrette (see below)

1. Put the cream cheese in a small mixing bowl and blend in the chives, chervil and pepper.

2. Blend in the Creme Fraiche and let the mixture stand covered in the refrigerator for an hour to develop flavor.

3. Cut off the tops of the tomatoes and set aside. Gently scoop out the interiors and set aside to use in another recipe. Drain the tomatoes upside down for an hour.

4. Just before serving, fill the tomatoes with the cream mixture, put on the covers and arrange on a bed of lettuce with the Lemon Vinaigrette on the side.

Lemon Vinaigrette

yields ¾ cup

  juice of 1 lemon
1 teaspoon prepared hot mustard
½ teaspoon honey
6 tablespoons olive oil
2 tablespoons minced chives
  freshly ground white pepper

1. In a small bowl combine the lemon juice, mustard and honey, then beat in the olive oil with a whisk until the mixture is smooth and light.

2. Beat in the chives and season with pepper. Chill until ready to use.

Dressings and Sauces

Cream sauces are one of the pillars of Western cooking. Though most of them are made with milk and are given in the Milk Recipes section, here is a palette of creamy dressings and sauces for fish, salads and meats.

Basic Cream Dressing for Salads

yields ½ cup

4 teaspoons wine vinegar
4 tablespoons heavy cream
  freshly ground pepper

1. Put the vinegar in a small bowl.

2. Beat in the cream with a fork until well blended and creamy. Add the pepper.

Experimenter's Choice

The basic cream dressing above can be varied by beating in the yolk of an egg, or ½ teaspoon good prepared mustard or by substituting lemon juice for the vinegar.

To make Herb Dressing, double the basic recipe and add 2½ tablespoons of chopped fresh herbs: anise leaves, chives, mint, marjoram, parsley, basil or thyme. Toasted sesame seeds, caraway seeds, chopped walnuts or almonds all change the character and savor of the sauce.

Horseradish Cream

yields ½ cup

This is a lively, tasty sauce that is very good with rabbit and pork roasts.

4 teaspoons prepared hot mustard
4 teaspoons wine vinegar
2 tablespoons grated horseradish
1 tablespoon honey
6 tablespoons heavy cream
¼ cup soft whole grain bread crumbs

In a small bowl mix the mustard and vinegar, then blend in the other ingredients. Let this stand at room temperature 1 hour to let the flavors mingle, then serve.

Tarragon Sauce Normandy

yields 2 cups

This simple but unforgettable sauce comes from Normandy where a distinctive cuisine built on cream, seafood, and regional ciders brings gourmets flocking. Use Tarragon Sauce with vegetables, chicken and fish. It is superb with grilled trout and as a dip sauce for steamed artichokes.

2 cups heavy cream
2 tablespoons whole tarragon sprigs
2 dashes freshly ground pepper

Put all the ingredients in a heavy saucepan. Bring to a boil, then reduce the heat and simmer 6 to 8 minutes until the sauce has absorbed the tarragon flavor. Remove the tarragon and serve the sauce immediately.

The True Tarragon

For centuries tarragon has been used to augment the flavor of foods in place of salt. The herb adds depth and savor without the deleterious effects of sodium. It is also used in diets for people who must abstain from pepper, vinegar and garlic.

Alas, in North America the true French tarragon, *Artemisia dracunculus* is hard to find. It is nearly impossible to grow French tarragon from seeds, and the plant is usually grown from root sections or propagated plants. The "tarragon" seeds some seed houses offer in their herb lists are really *Artemisia dracunculoides*, better known as False Tarragon or Russian Tarragon, and this herb is almost tasteless.

Although the flavor of most herbs is concentrated through drying, tarragon is an exception, for drying releases its essential oils that hold the flavor. Even the true French tarragon, when dried, is disappointing in flavor. For a good, steady supply of this major herb, ranked among the top six by many gourmets, grow your own in a windowsill pot or a garden border. Buy started plants from a nursery or ask a friend to divide a clump for you.

Desserts

Cream desserts from around the world could fill several cookbooks by themselves; puddings, cream cones and puffs, fruit with cream, ice cream and exotic molded creams in the shapes of hearts and turbans studded with nuts, fruit and rose petals are the culinary treasures of Western civilization. Here are only a few to get you started on your own collection.

Almond Cream Waffles

serves four to six

3 eggs, separated
1½ cups heavy cream
1 tablespoon honey
1 tablespoon melted butter
½ cup ground almond meal (process almonds in a blender at high speed)
1 teaspoon vanilla extract
1 cup freshly ground whole grain flour (half buckwheat and half rye is good)
2 teaspoons Rumford baking powder
Honey Butter (see Index)

1. Beat the egg yolks until light, then beat in the cream and honey. Blend in the butter, almond meal and vanilla.

2. Mix the flour and baking powder thoroughly, then blend into the liquid.

3. Beat the egg whites until stiff but not dry and fold into the batter.

4. Pour onto a hot waffle iron and bake until done—6 to 8 minutes. Serve with Honey Butter.

Bavarian Cream

serves six to eight

Another classic dessert, rich and utterly delicious. Bavarian Cream is often made with the addition of pureed cooked fruit, such as apricots, berries, peaches, plums or prunes.

1 tablespoon gelatin
2 tablespoons cold water
4 egg yolks
3 tablespoons honey
1 cup milk
1 teaspoon vanilla extract
1 cup pureed cooked fruit (optional)
1 cup heavy cream, whipped

1. Soak the gelatin in the cold water while preparing the mixture.

2. In the top of a double boiler beat the egg yolks and honey with a wooden spoon until thick and smooth. Heat the milk separately and gradually beat it into the egg mixture.

3. Cook the custard over, not in, boiling water, stirring constantly until it is smooth and thickened. Set aside to cool 10 minutes.

4. Add the softened gelatin and vanilla, mixing thoroughly.

5. Cool the custard, stirring now and then gently to prevent the formation of a skin. When the custard is lukewarm, fold in pureed cooked fruit, if used, then fold in the whipped cream, turn into a 1-quart mold that has been dipped in cold water, and chill for several hours before unmolding on a serving platter.

Peaches and Cream

serves four

Ripe August peaches served with peach-colored Jersey cream are about as close to perfection as you can get. Ineffable, indescribable and irresistible!

  8 peaches
1½ cups heavy cream
  1 tablespoon honey

1. Impale a peach on a fork and dip it briefly into boiling water to loosen the fuzzy coat, then peel, pit and slice into individual serving dishes.

2. Whip the cream and sweeten with the honey, then heap the cream over the peaches.

Strawberry Shortcake Supreme

serves six

Biscuit Shortcakes
2 cups sifted whole wheat flour
2 teaspoons Rumford baking powder
4 tablespoons butter
¾ cup heavy cream

Strawberry Cream
1 cup heavy cream
½ cup honey
2 tablespoons strawberry juice from
    the sliced berries

1 quart ripe strawberries, hulled and
    sliced

Preheat oven to 400°F.

1. Sift the flour and the baking powder into a mixing bowl and cut in the butter until the mixture is the size of peas.

2. Mix in the cream until the dough is soft but not sticky.

3. On a floured board, roll the dough out thinly to ¼ inch and cut into rounds.

4. Butter each round, then place 2 biscuits together, buttered sides touching, and bake on a cookie sheet 12 minutes or until golden brown.

5. Meanwhile, make Strawberry Cream. Whip the cream, and in the final stages beat in the honey and juice.

6. Split the hot biscuits and arrange on individual plates.

7. Heap with the sliced strawberries and smother in Strawberry Cream.

Wild Strawberries and Devonshire Cream

Everybody knows how delicious a dish of strawberries and cream is, but the commercially produced berries and cream most people get is a poor thing compared to wild strawberries and Devonshire Cream (see Index), one of the immortal food combinations. This is no time-saver, but for a once-a-year treat, pick a pint of wild strawberries on a sunny June day, hull the tiny sweet things carefully, and without washing them, fill two small crystal bowls and top the sun-warmed berries with chilled Devonshire Cream. Share this very special treat with the one you love best.

Pineapple Creme Fraiche

serves four

½ cup unsweetened crushed pineapple, drained
1 cup Creme Fraiche (see p. 75)
4 slices pineapple
1 tangerine, peeled, sectioned, seeded and skinned
4 mint sprigs

1. Mix the crushed pineapple into the Creme Fraiche.

2. Arrange the pineapple slices in individual serving dishes. Heap the Creme Fraiche mixture on top.

3. Top each with tangerine slices and a sprig of mint.

5

ICE CREAM

The way we make homemade ice cream today, and the equipment we use to do it, can easily be traced to Colonial days when the gentry concluded lavish dinners with desserts of frozen cream laboriously prepared behind the scenes by kitchen scullions.

Instead of pouring sweet wines and syrup over finely crushed ice or snow as the ancients did, a proper ice cream mix was beaten together and then frozen in a device called a *pot freezer*. The pot, which held the mix, was fitted into a deeper pan packed with ice and salt; then some strong-armed hearty beat the ice cream vigorously until it was frozen. The early presidents, Washington, Jefferson and Madison, boasted this frozen luxury at their tables, and Dolley Madison's zeal for ice cream is legendary.

Today ice cream making is a huge industry like cheese manufacture, and more than 300 flavors are on record. Yet the finest ice cream is still that made on the back porch with cream and milk from your own milkers, fresh, ripe fruit and willing hands. Ice cream is an ideal experimental medium; once you have the technique and a basic recipe down pat, feel free to try blending in flavors from pumpkin to persimmon to suit your taste.

It wasn't until 1846 that a woman named Nancy Johnson put the Colonial pot and pan together into a single unit by inventing the hand-cranked freezer, a machine which featured a crank-propelled can of ice cream mix spinning in the middle of a wooden bucket packed with ice and salt. The crank-type ice cream freezer is still the most popular ice-cream-making machine. There have been changes in the methods of chilling, and in the construction material, but basically today's home ice cream maker is a close relative of Nancy Johnson's invention.

THE CHURN FREEZER

This freezer has three basic parts — the *tub*, traditionally made of wooden staves and still available today in wood as well as in heavy-duty, food-grade plastic; the *freezer can*, usually of tinned steel but sometimes made of stainless steel; and the *driver*, either a hand crank and gear or an electric motor. Other essential parts are the *freezer can cover* with a hole in the middle, and the *dasher*, which consists of wooden, tinned metal or nylon agitators on a drive shaft. Touching the sides of the can are a pair of *scrapers*. Most tubs have a small hole several inches from the top for draining off the brine.

A modification of the salt and ice churn-type freezer is the *refrigerator churn*, a small unit with an electric motor, a freezing container and a dasher-scraper. The container is filled with the ice cream mix, the dasher and motor mounted, and the whole unit put into the freezer or refrigerator freezing compartment. A very thin electric cord reduces refrigeration loss. The machine runs until the ice cream is set. Although no ice or salt are needed, the churn's capacity is small, about one quart. This little machine will fit into most refrigerator freezing units.

The Improved White Mountain Ice Cream Freezer for 1895.

42740   As features of especial merit, we claim: A strong waterproof tub, bound with heavy, galvanized iron hoops; the gearing completely covered, so that nothing can get between the cogs; cans full size and made of the very best quality of tin-plate; beaters of malleable iron and tinned; all castings attached to the tub nicely galvanized to prevent rusting. It is the only freezer in the market having the **celebrated duplex dasher, with double self-adjusting wood scraping bar,** by the use of which cream can be frozen in one-half the time, yet finer and smoother than can possibly be produced in any other freezer now in use. Positively the best freezer in the world, and guaranteed if properly used to make ice cream in 3 MINUTES.

Size	2-qt.	3-qt.	4-qt.	6-qt.	8-qt.
Each	$1.50	$1.85	$2.20	$2.80	$3.75
Size	10-qt.		15-qt.	20-qt.	25-qt.
Each	$5.00		$6.80	$9.20	$11.20

42741   Extra Fly Wheel for 25 quart Freezers.
Each.. ....$3.50

STILL FREEZING

But there is more than one way to freeze milk and cream; another popular way of making ice cream at home is the still-freeze method. In still freezing no machine, no salt, no ice—only a freezer or refrigerator freezing compartment—are needed. The ice cream mix is prepared in a bowl, then poured into freezing trays and frozen. Usually the mix comes out of the freezer several times for air to be beaten in, then returned for hardening. Ordinary, multipurpose kitchen equipment will do to make ice cream this way. Mixing bowls, wooden spoons, measuring cups, a rubber scraper, a wire whisk, as well as an egg beater, an electric beater and a blender all have their uses in still-freeze ice cream making.

WHY SALTED ICE FREEZES

Until the phenomenal advances in refrigeration during this century which saw iceboxes and icehouses replaced by complex mechanical refrigerators and freezers, ice cream manufacture depended on two natural substances—rock salt and ice. When you combine salt with ice, temperatures much colder than that of the ice alone are reached. Depending on the proportion of salt to the volume of ice, it's possible to take ice at 32°F down to −5°F and lower. As the temperature is lowered, there is an increase in the rate of heat absorption.

The more salt you add to the ice, the lower the temperature drops, and the greater the amount of heat this cold mixture is able to absorb. *Heat* is anything warmer than the salt-ice mixture.

When you salt your icy sidewalk in the winter, the mixture absorbs heat from the pavement and the atmosphere and melts. In the churn freezer the salt-ice mixture will absorb heat from the warm atmosphere of the room or the summer outdoors, unless insulated by the sides of the tub—wooden staves or thick plastic walls. Since that is basic ice cream tub construction, there is only one source of heat left for the ice-salt mixture—the thin-sided, revolving tin of sweetened and flavored cream.

How to Make Ice Cream

Making the Mix

Both churn-freeze and still-freeze ice creams as well as sherbet mixtures are prepared in advance of the freezing and stored covered in a refrigerator until it's time to freeze them. If you are using a churn, chill both the freezer can and the dasher at the same time so that they will be cold when the churn is loaded. If the recipe you are following calls for scalding or cooking, it is best to prepare the mixture 12 hours ahead of time and give it plenty of hours to cool. Always use a wooden spoon for stirring partially frozen mixes and for packing ice cream—wood is a poor conductor of heat and won't melt your hard-earned treat. If the first batches of ice cream you make lack smooth texture, adding a binder to the next batch will help. Gelatin, eggs, honey and cornstarch all are good sources of smoothness. If you prefer, you can substitute milk for the cream in ice cream recipes, giving a less rich but lower caloried, lower fat treat.

Basic Vanilla Ice Cream

makes 1 gallon

1½ quarts light cream
  1 quart whole milk
1¼ cups honey
  1 tablespoon vanilla extract
  1 tablespoon gelatin, dissolved in ½
    cup water

1. Mix all the ingredients in the top of a double boiler and heat over hot water until the mixture is 150°F.

2. Cool the mixture by setting the top of the double boiler in ice water. Chill in the refrigerator until thoroughly cold.

CHURN-FREEZER ICE CREAM

Keep a tub filled with crushed ice and covered with a clean blanket handy to the churn. Hand-cranked and motorized ice crushers will pulverize ice cubes, but few people have enough trays of cubes to make sufficient ice for a crank freezer. The most common failure in making homemade ice cream is running out of ice before the mixture is frozen—you need about 20 pounds of ice. You can make large quantities of ice in your deep freeze by filling plastic gallon containers cut off at the shoulders so that they'll make block ice. To get the ice out of the containers, dip them in warm water for a few seconds. To break up the ice, put the blocks inside a double layer of clean burlap or feed bags and pulverize the ice as fine as possible with a mallet. Fine-crushed ice will touch more of the freezer can's surface than will big chunks, providing a uniform coldness and faster chilling. Fine

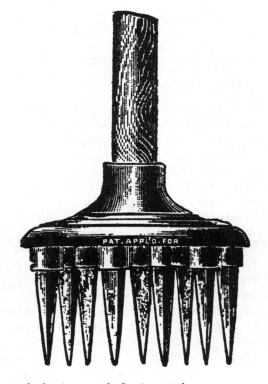

The business end of an ice crusher.

ice also reduces the possibility of an ice jam that could halt the can's revolutions.

Although common table salt will chill the ice, it costs more and doesn't work as well as coarse rock salt. The big crystals are available in 5- and 10-pound bags, sometimes sold (at a higher price) as "ice cream salt." Using the correct proportion of salt to ice is important. Too much salt makes the ice melt too rapidly, producing extremely low temperatures which lead to prematurely frozen ice cream. A mixture which freezes too fast suffers from an unpleasant, heavy coarseness, a texture linked to trapped ice crystals and emulsifiers and incomplete aeration.

Ideally, as the ice cream temperature drops during the rythmic process of churning, tiny crystals of ice form and are dispersed evenly throughout the mixture, smoothed out by such emulsifiers as cream, milk, eggs, honey and gelatin. But if the churning is stalled by too swift a drop in temperature, the emulsifiers freeze up and the crystals are not smoothed out in the mix. Instead, being of the same molecular composition, they clump together in large crystals to make a grainy ice cream.

Such a quick freeze also limits aeration. Incorporating air into ice cream is important. Without air, ice cream would be about as palatable as a milk-flavored ice cube. The amount of aeration, or *over-run* as it's called commercially, is always less in homemade ice cream than in the factory stuff. Homemade churned ice creams have about 25 percent aeration, and that's why the weights and volumes of the ingredients in the mix total one-third to one-quarter less than the finished product. If you added exact amounts totaling the yield you expected, the ice cream would bulge out of the top of the freezer can. With commercial ice creams it's common to find aeration is as much as 50 percent by volume. Heft a quart of your own and one of store-bought and you'll notice the difference.

Too little salt can lead to slow freezing and prolonged churning. If you churn the mix too long you won't make ice cream at all, you'll make a spongy, cold butter.

The ratio of salt to ice, tried and proven true over the years by ice cream makers, is: 4 parts of ice to 1 part of salt by volume. Always measure salt in a glass measuring cup, for it will corrode metal.

Churning time may be affected by the temperature of the air outside the churn, the temperature of the mix and the speed of churning, but the average time from the first twirl of the crank to the frozen confection is about 20 minutes.

LOADING THE FREEZER AND CHURNING

Before you start, remember that salt is corrosive, so put down some newspaper if you're working inside, or if it's a nice summer day, set up the freezer away from the Kentucky bluegrass and the prize petunias.

1. Crush the ice until it is fine.

2. Insert the dasher into the chilled freezer can and place it in the tub. Fill the can two-thirds full with the ice cream mixture, screw on the freezer can cover and affix the driver, either crank or motor.

3. Pack in the crushed ice halfway up the freezer can; this will make the tub about a third full of ice. Now alternate layers of ice and salt until the tub is full. With the common 4-quart freezer models it takes about 4 cups of rock salt to 16 pounds of crushed ice. The ice layers are optimally 2 inches deep and separated by the narrower salt layers.

4. Start agitating the mix. Turn the crank slowly in the beginning when the mixture is still liquid and easy to turn. As the churning gets harder, speed it up to aerate and smooth out the cream. When you have to use real effort to turn the crank and you're worrying about breaking the churn, stop. If your churn is equipped with a motor instead of a hand crank, listen for the point when the steady purr deteriorates to a skipping, straining grind, then turn it off. The ice cream is done.

5. Remove the driver and open the freezer can, then pull out the dasher. The surface ice cream will appear as soft wisps; these should be smoothed down with the back of a spoon. Cover the top of the can with a piece of foil and replace the cover. Foil is better for conducting the heat away from the ice cream during the final ripening stage than is the plastic cover. Plug the hole in the cover with a small cork. This keeps salt water from entering the can when you repack the churn for ripening.

6. Drain the salt water from the churn and repack as before with an ice base followed by alternating layers of ice and salt. This time, cover the top of the freezer can with the ice-salt mix. Wrap the blanket that has covered the tub of ice nearby around the freezer churn. In an hour the ice cream will be hard and ready to eat. If you prefer, you can ripen the ice cream in the freezer compartment of your refrigerator. Either serve it at once or keep it frozen for later use.

STILL-FREEZE ICE CREAM

Before you freeze ice cream or sherbet mixes in a refrigerator's freezing compartment or in a deep freeze, you must first determine how cold the unit really gets. Use an ordinary outdoor thermometer propped up where you plan to do the ice cream freezing. Colder freezers such as the deep freeze which keeps foods at a constant 0°F will process ice cream mix in less time than a refrigerator freezing compartment which struggles to make ice cubes. Some refrigerator freezers are capable of making only soft ice cream at best.

Once you know your freezer can make ice cream, prepare your favorite mix recipe and assemble the basic tools—ice trays, cake or bread pans (all of which can serve as the freezing can), an electric beater, a rubber scraper, foil wrap. The foil fitted tightly over the freezing can will prevent the mix from picking up refrigerator odors and will conduct heat away from the large, exposed surface of mix. It also prevents moisture in the freezer from settling and crystallizing on the cooling mix.

Because there is no dasher to smooth out the crystals and emulsifiers during the freezing process in the still-freeze system, ice crystallization is a real problem. Here the ice cream maker, armed with an electric beater, becomes the dasher, whipping air into the mixture and smoothing out the texture at crucial points in the operation.

1. Prepare the ice cream mix according to the recipe and pour it into the freezing can containers. Cover them tightly with foil and place them in the freezer. Keep the freezer door closed for one hour. (The results will be better if the mixture is thoroughly chilled beforehand.)

2. After an hour, remove the freezer can and foil and examine the mix. The top, sides, and bottom of the mix adjoining the metal container should be hardening, while the center will still be slightly soft. If the mixture is still soft on the sides, cover it again with the foil and return it to the freezer until the sides harden.

3. When the mix is frozen on the sides, scrape it into a chilled bowl and beat it with an electric mixer or egg beater. The beaters should be chilled first. This will aerate the mix, and reblend any ingredients that might have settled out while setting on the freezer shelf. As you beat, this is the time to distribute any fruit or nut additions

through the mix. Heap the mix back in the freezer can containers and cover it again with foil.

4. Freeze the mix for another hour.

5. Again take the mix from the freezer and examine it. If ice crystals are forming on the surface, beat the mix again to blend them into the hardening ice cream and to aerate. After a thorough beating, scrape the ice cream into a chilled, festive serving bowl or return it to the freezer in the freezer container. Freeze it another hour and a half, or until hard. Serve.

This ice cream can keep a week or more if tightly sealed in a plastic ice cream container and kept frozen at low temperatures. Most still-freeze ice creams are made for immediate consumption in small batches of a quart or two.

FLAVORING ICE CREAMS

Using the Basic Vanilla Ice Cream mix (see p. 98), you can make many delicious flavors by adding flavoring ingredients at the right moment in the ice-cream-making process. *The following proportions are calculated for 1 gallon of ice cream produced in a churn freezer.* There are three points when flavorings can be added to the basic mix: when the mixture is in the bowl before it is poured into the freezer can; after the mixture has been partly frozen; just before ripening when the ice cream is thick and wispy on top.

Lemon

¾ cup orange blossom honey
    juice of 4 lemons
 3 teaspoons orange juice
    rinds of 2 lemons, grated

1. Over low heat, stir the honey into the combined juices. Heat only enough to thin the honey. Add to the ice cream mix before freezing.

2. Freeze the ice cream until partially frozen, then add in the grated lemon rind. Freeze and ripen.

Maple Butter Nut

1½ cups Grade B or C maple syrup
  8 tablespoons butter
  1 cup chopped pecans or walnuts

1. Heat the syrup over low heat and add the butter, mixing until butter melts and both are blended.

2. Add the syrup and butter to the ice cream mix and start freezing.

3. When the mixture is partially frozen, add the chopped nuts and freeze until firm.

Pineapple Orange

 1 cup concentrated orange juice
¼ teaspoon vanilla extract
 1 cup unsweetened crushed pineapple

1. Add the juice and vanilla to the basic ice cream mix and begin freezing.

2. When partially frozen stir in the crushed pineapple. Continue freezing until firm.

Peach

1 pound medium-size peaches, peeled and sliced

1. When the ice cream mix has partially frozen, work in the peaches.

2. Freeze until firm.

Orange

½ cup orange blossom honey
  juice of 4 oranges
  juice of 1 lemon
  rinds of 2 oranges, grated

1. Over low heat stir the honey into the juices. Add the ice cream mix.

2. Freeze partially, then add the grated rind. Freeze until firm.

Raspberry

1 cup red or black raspberries, crushed

1. When the ice cream mixture is partially frozen, stir in the raspberries.

2. Freeze until firm.

Experimenter's Choice

You can invent your own ice creams by incorporating fruits and other ingredients. Here are a few suggestions to get you started.

wild strawberries, blueberries or
          blackberries
grated fresh coconut
toasted chopped nuts, sunflower or
          sesame seeds
ginger root, chopped and simmered in
          a honey-water mixture until
          tender
ground almond meal
fresh mint or thyme, chopped fine
dried fruits, chopped
pumpkin or other winter squash,
          pureed and flavored with pie
          spices

ICE CREAM RECIPES

You don't have to use only milk or cream to make ice cream. You can get sprightly new taste effects by using buttermilk or sour cream or yogurt. Here are some old favorites and a few recipes off the beaten path. Unless otherwise noted, these ice cream recipes are suitable for either churn freezing or still freezing.

Banana-Peachy Sour-Cream Freeze

makes 1 quart

4 ripe bananas
4 to 5 ripe medium-size peaches,
    peeled and stoned
2 cups sour cream
¾ cup honey
¼ cup lime juice

1. Puree the fruits in a blender.

2. Mix the fruits with all the other ingredients and chill thoroughly.

3. Freeze in a churn-type freezer.

Berry-Sour Ice Cream

makes 2 quarts

3 cups raspberries, crushed
½ cup water
¾ cup orange blossom honey
3 cups sour cream
  rind of 1 lemon, grated

1. Combine the raspberries, water and honey in a saucepan and cook several minutes over moderate heat, stirring constantly. Cool, then strain the mixture into a bowl.

2. Stir in the sour cream and lemon rind and chill thoroughly.

3. Freeze until smooth and hard.

Buttermilk Ice Cream

makes 1 quart

½ cup hot water
¾ cup honey
  rind of 1 orange, grated
½ cup unsweetened pineapple juice
2½ cups buttermilk

1. Boil the hot water and honey 4 or 5 minutes to make a light syrup.

2. Cool slightly, then add all the other ingredients except buttermilk. Chill thoroughly.

3. Freeze to the ice-mush point, then blend in the buttermilk thoroughly.

4. Freeze until firm.

French Vanilla Ice Cream

makes 1 gallon

This recipe for everybody's favorite makes a meltingly delicious, creamy, custardy vanilla ice cream. If you go in for lily-gilding, top it with wild grape syrup.

  1 quart plus 3 cups whole milk
12 egg yolks
  2 cups honey
  1 quart heavy cream
  4 teaspoons vanilla extract

1. Scald the milk in a large saucepan.

2. In a large bowl beat the egg yolks until light, then slowly pour in 3 cups of the hot milk, stirring constantly.

3. Pour this mixture into the pan with the remaining milk. Add the honey and cook over moderate heat until slightly thickened. Cool it.

4. Fold the cream into the cooled custard and add the vanilla. Chill until cold.

5. Freeze until hard and smooth.

Fried Ice Cream Balls

The next time someone answers, "Fried — over light," to the question, "We're having ice cream for dessert; how do you want it?" you can oblige. This slightly mad recipe makes enough to fill 5 ice cream cones.

   5 tablespoons finely crushed granola or
           dry cereal
   1 tablespoon date sugar
   dusting of cinnamon
   1 quart vanilla ice cream, frozen very hard
   oil for deep frying
   5 ice cream cones

1. Mix the granola, sugar and cinnamon on a plate for the coating.

2. Scoop out 5 round balls of ice cream frozen as hard as you can get it and still work with it. Roll the balls in the coating and return them to the freezer while you get ready to fry.

3. In a deep fryer heat cooking oil over medium heat 15 minutes.

4. Pick up each ball separately with a slotted spoon and fry it quickly all over. Drain on a paper towel and return to the freezer as soon as possible. The frying time is fast — just a few seconds to brown the coating. Do one ice cream ball at a time.

5. When the balls are frozen hard again, serve them in the ice cream cones.

Greengage Plum Ice Cream

makes 3 quarts

This is a favorite still-freeze cream.

  4 cups pitted greengage plums
  ⅓ cup water
1½ teaspoons gelatin
  2 cups whole milk
  ½ cup honey
  1 tablespoon lemon juice
  2 cups heavy cream

1. Gently cook the plums in the water over low heat until soft. Save the liquid and chill it.

2. Puree the plums in a blender until smooth, then add the gelatin to the still-hot puree.

3. Bring the milk to the boiling point and stir in the honey. Blend in the plum puree. Cool.

4. Add the lemon juice, then chill the mixture thoroughly.

5. Pour into large enough freezer containers, allowing for the cream and over-run (increase in volume from aeration). Cover and freeze until partially frozen.

6. Whip the cream. Beat the mix well, then fold in the cream. Return to the freezer covered with foil and freeze until firm.

Honey Ice Cream

makes 1½ quarts

  2 cups rich whole milk
  2 eggs, lightly beaten
  1 tablespoon gelatin
  2 tablespoons arrowroot flour
  ½ cup honey
  1 cup chopped pecans (optional)
  2 cups heavy cream
  1 tablespoon vanilla extract or rose
      water
  ½ cup non-fat dry milk solids

1. In the top of a double boiler put the milk, eggs, gelatin, arrowroot and honey. Cook over hot water, stirring, until the mixture thickens. Cool.

2. A cup of chopped pecans added to the cooled custard before mixing in the cream is a delicious variation.

3. Stir in the cream, vanilla and milk solids, mixing thoroughly. Chill well.

4. Freeze in churn freezer or by still-freeze method.

Honey-Yogurt Freeze

makes 1 quart

This is another freezer winner. The result will be best if you use half Yogurt Curd (see Index) instead of ordinary yogurt only.

2 eggs, beaten
¾ cup milk
¼ cup honey
1 cup yogurt
1 cup soft Yogurt Curd (yogurt drained 2 to 4 hours)

1. Put the eggs, milk and honey in the top of a double boiler and cook over hot water, stirring constantly. When slightly thickened, cool the mixture.

2. Stir in the yogurt and yogurt curd and chill well.

3. Pour into freezing containers, cover with foil and still freeze 1 hour.

4. Remove the foil, aerate the mix, cover again and return to the freezer another hour.

5. Check the mix. If it has settled or if ice crystals are on the surface, beat it again and return to the freezer until it is firm enough to eat.

Lemon Sherbet

makes 1½ quarts

Sherbets made with skim milk are satisfying and refreshing without the calories and cholesterol that richer ice creams possess. Here is a recipe with endless variations — substitute any fruit juice — blueberry, raspberry, peach, grape, orange, pineapple, for the lemon juice and adjust the honey to your taste. Freeze as you would ice cream.

3½ cups skim milk
¾ cup honey
½ cup lemon juice

1. Warm the milk and stir in the honey. Cool.

2. Add the lemon juice and chill thoroughly. If the juice causes the milk to curdle, don't worry, you'll never know it after churning and freezing.

3. Freeze by the churn or still method as for ice cream.

You may substitute fruit purees for the juice if you prefer. If the texture seems coarse, add 1 tablespoon of gelatin to the initial mix as an emulsifier.

New England Apple Ice Cream

makes 1 quart

Choose Russets or Greenings or other tart, richly flavored apples. An excellent new apple gaining rapidly in popularity is Empire, a cross between McIntosh and Delicious that is superior to either of its parents.

1½ cups heavy cream
1½ cups grated raw apple, including
     the skins
 ½ cup honey
 ⅓ cup lemon juice

1. Combine all ingredients thoroughly and chill.

2. Freeze in a hand-cranked or electric freezer until hard.

Mango Ice Cream

makes 2 quarts

 1 quart heavy cream
 ½ cup honey
   juice of 1 lemon
2½ cups ripe mango, peeled and
     chopped fine

1. In a saucepan warm the cream over moderate heat and stir in the honey. Cool.

2. Mix in the lemon juice and mango and chill several hours.

3. Churn-freeze until smooth and hard.

Sundaes and Banana Splits

Once you've got ice cream on hand, a modest ladle of your favorite natural fruit syrup will turn a single scoop into a simple sundae. You can embellish this treat by capping the fruit-flavored frozen mound with whipped cream and chopped nut meats. To many ice cream lovers, the ultimate ecstasy is several scoops of variously flavored ice cream heaped on longitudinally sliced bananas, enveloped in fruit syrups and covered with a lavish blanket of whipped cream dotted with chopped nuts. Several fresh strawberries or pitted black cherries perched atop each mound in this extravaganza give us the classic banana split.

Peaches and Sour Cream, Still-Freeze Style

makes 2 quarts

¾ cup date sugar
3½ cups peeled peaches, thinly sliced
¼ teaspoon lemon juice
4 cups sour cream
½ cup heavy cream

1. Stir the date sugar into the bowl of peaches. Sprinkle with lemon juice and chill in the refrigerator 1 hour.

2. Blend the sour cream and heavy cream, then fold in the fruit, mixing thoroughly.

3. Pour the fruit-cream mix into bread pans, deep trays or other freezer cans. Cover with foil and freeze in the freezer 1 hour.

4. Remove the foil and beat with an electric beater to aerate, break up the ice crystals and redistribute the fruit. Repack in the freezer cans.

5. Freeze another 2 hours or until firm. Serve at once.

Rose Water Ice Cream

makes 1½ quarts

This old Shaker recipe features rose water from the antique variety *Rosa gallica*—one of the esteemed apothecary roses noted for its rich fragrance. Imported rose water is available from some druggists or in specialty food shops. Use the most neutral-flavored honey or maple syrup for sweetening to let the elusive and delicate rose flavor shine forth.

2 cups light cream
4 egg yolks
½ cup mild honey or Grade A maple syrup
1 tablespoon rose water
2 cups heavy cream

1. Heat the light cream in a heavy saucepan over moderate heat to the scalding point. As the cream is heating, beat the egg yolks with the honey until well blended.

2. Mix a few spoonsful of the hot cream into the egg mixture to equalize the temperature, then slowly stir the egg mixture into the hot cream. Cook over low heat, stirring constantly, 3 to 5 minutes, or until slightly thickened. Cool, then stir in the rose water.

3. Mix in the heavy cream, then chill thoroughly.

4. Freeze until hard and smooth.

Spumoni

makes 1 quart mold

1 quart Basic Vanilla Ice Cream mix
   (see p. 98), churned or still
   frozen until firm but not hard
1 teaspoon each of the following,
   candied in honey and finely
   chopped: angelica, lemon rind,
   orange rind, apricot
1 tablespoon chopped almonds or
   pistachio nuts

1. Rinse a 1-quart beehive or melon mold
in ice water. Shake out the excess water.
Line the mold with 3 cups of the firm ice
cream, leaving a hollow in the center.
Cover with foil and set the mold in the
freezer for an hour.

2. Mix the candied fruit and nuts with
the remaining cup of ice cream, then
pack this into the center of the mold.

3. Cover the mold with foil and freeze in
the refrigerator freezer 1 to 2 hours or
until hard and frozen. Unmold on a
serving platter. To unmold, dip the mold
in lukewarm water a few seconds, then
invert on the serving dish.

Bombes

Today bombes are molded in all manner of
shapes and sizes, but historically they take
their name from a special ice cream mold for
still freezing which closely resembled an antique
French explosive casing. The ingredients are
layers of ice cream, usually several complementary flavors and colors, with veins or
centers of richly flavored fruits and nuts. The
shapes can be melons, cubes, hearts, ovals
and pyramids with rosettes and whipped cream
flourishes on the surface. Spumoni, formed in
a beehive mold of ice cream, chopped nuts
and candied fruits, is a famous Italian bombe.

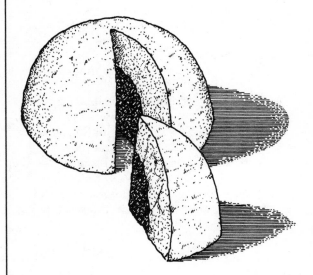

Sweet Cherry Ice Cream Made with Goats' Milk

makes 2 quarts

This ice "cream" uses whole goats' milk but no cream, and is an excellent way to enjoy the luscious dessert if you have no cream separator.

½ cup maple syrup or honey
3 tablespoons whole wheat flour
3 eggs
6 cups goats' milk
½ teaspoon rose water or almond extract
2 cups sweet cherries, crushed

1. In a large mixing bowl put the syrup, flour, eggs and 2 cups of the milk. Beat with an electric mixer until smooth.

2. Over low heat cook the mixture, stirring constantly, until it thickens. Set aside and let it cool.

3. Add remaining ingredients and chill thoroughly.

4. Freeze in a churn-type freezer.

Vermont Maple Ice Cream

makes 2 quarts

1¾ cups Grade B maple syrup
2 eggs, beaten
3 cups heavy cream, slightly whipped
2 cups milk

1. In a saucepan mix the maple syrup and eggs and bring up to a boil while beating continuously.

2. Remove at once from heat and beat in the cream and milk.

3. Chill thoroughly.

4. Freeze until hard and smooth.

Goats' Milk Ice Cream

Betty Jenks and her family live on a 50-acre farm just outside Concord, New Hampshire, where 10 years ago they started out with a Toggenburg doe and modest plans for keeping only a few goats. Today, 40 Toggenburgs and Saanens later, they have a raw milk license and supply goats' milk to stores in nearby cities.

"There's a good market for goats' milk," Betty says, adding that the demand has grown over the past two years and that their biggest problem is trying to keep up with the demand. "It would be nice to make ice cream for sale commercially; however, the milk would have to be pasteurized and that would require a lot of extra expensive equipment." So the Jenks make ice cream for themselves and for friends. "We made it about five years ago for a goat association meeting and have served it at meetings annually. We also needed something to do with all the extra milk in the summer."

Asked if she agreed with the conviction of many goats' milk fanciers that goats' milk ice cream is superior to that made from cows' milk, Betty remarked, "I must truthfully say that it tastes the same as cows' milk ice cream. The difference might be in the texture. Goats' milk ice cream is smoother."

Keeping the quality of the milk up assures a sound ice cream product untainted by "goaty" off-flavors. "Our main concern with the animals is producing a good-flavored, clean milk," she said. "We find the main reasons for off-flavor are overfeeding on grain, or a health problem. Goats are very intelligent and are easy to work with. We have converted a De Laval cow-milking machine, which makes chores a lot easier. It also cuts down on the bacteria count.

"Goat milk is naturally homogenized; therefore, you'll need a cream separator to get the cream. We were fortunate to locate a small electric table model which works beautifully. We have also purchased a home ice cream maker. The new models use four trays of ice cubes and a box of table salt. We prepare the recipe and put it in the machine before dinner. It is ready when we have finished our meal. We simply follow instructions in the recipe book we received with the ice cream maker. You can use any recipe."

The Jenks's Procedure

1. "We first separate the milk in the cream separator immediately after milking the goats. Warm milk separates better. We then chill the cream overnight. The ice cream mixture can be made ahead of time and put in the refrigerator. The colder the mixture the less time involved in making the finished product. **2.** We start with the basic vanilla ice cream mixture and add fruits that are in season. Our favorite is fresh raspberries added to the vanilla mixture. There are also a lot of ice milk recipes, and we use the whole milk which makes a richer ice milk. . . . My son is always experimenting with different flavors."

A Speed-up Hint

"We have not encountered any difficulty in making ice cream with goats' milk. With the small fat globules it does take a little longer for the mixture to thicken, but by chilling the mixture ahead of time you can speed up the process."

6

SOUR CREAM

It is possible to make good sour cream by allowing sweet unpasteurized cream to stand until it develops the right amount of the particular bacteria that give this versatile dairy product its unique flavor—possible but not probable. The odds are on the development of unwanted bacteria that will give the cream disagreeable off-flavors. It is safer and more dependable to inoculate sweet cream with a culture than to leave the souring in the hands of fate.

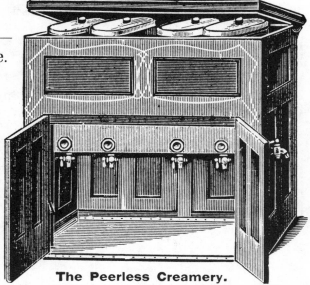

The Peerless Creamery.

For our purposes, sour cream is a cultured dairy product. Any fresh, sweet cream with a butterfat content of 20 percent or more can be made into sour cream, though the whipping weight of 40 percent butterfat will make the best. The cream is pasteurized, cooled and inoculated with a starter, the special sour cream culture containing *Streptococcus lactis* available in freeze-dried packets from dairy culture supply houses listed in the Sources section of this book. In a pinch, a few tablespoons of homemade fresh cultured buttermilk may be used.

The cream is allowed to ripen in a warm place for 15 to 24 hours, then chilled and set to mature another 24 hours. The "non-cultured" sour cream found in many supermarket dairy cases has been forced to gel through the addition of various food acids, and often contains stabilizers, emulsifiers and flavoring. You can make better sour cream than this at home with both hands tied behind your back.

Creamy smooth, rich and with an agreeable tartness, this versatile delicacy has hundreds of distinguished culinary uses. The Viennese and the Russians have done exalted things with sour cream, and it's a pity that in this country sour cream has been typecast as a topping for baked potatoes. You can use the delicious stuff in dressings and sauces, for garnishes, in general baking and cooking, to give body and interest to gravies, and to inject an unusual richness and melting smoothness into old favorite recipes.

USES

Sour cream is interchangeable with buttermilk or yogurt in most recipes calling for these ingredients, but will transform the final dishes by giving heavier consistencies and a fuller sensation of richness in the mouth. Because a cup of sour cream has about 40 percent butterfat, it will replace all or part of the fat called for in recipes for pancakes, muffins, biscuits, cookies and cakes. Sour cream has been used for centuries to make butter with a little tang to it.

WHIPPING

Sour cream can be whipped to double in volume. Whipping makes it stiffer and smoother, but care must be taken not to overwhip it, lest the cream convert to butter. Keep the cream very cold to curtail its buttering tendency. Whipping sour cream takes longer than whipping sweet cream; when you commence whipping, the sour cream becomes thin and runny, then gradually thickens and billows into creamy clouds.

It is important to note that sour cream does not freeze well unless it is incorporated into a dish that contains flour, arrowroot or cornstarch as a binder.

How to Make Sour Cream

makes 1 quart

Equipment
    double boiler
    dairy thermometer
    quart canning jar and sterile cover

Ingredients
    1 quart heavy sweet cream
    3½ tablespoons cultured starter

It is important that the cream, whether from cow or goat, be sweet, fresh and of the very best quality. The starter culture should be sound and fresh, with an acid level of at least 1 percent, and a clean, crisp taste. To prevent the development of undesirable bacteria which would taint the sour cream with objectionable off-flavors, the cream should be pasteurized first.

Pasteurizing

A large double boiler makes this job simple, but a stainless steel pot that fits inside a larger pot will do very well.

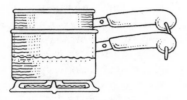

1. Pour enough cold water in the bottom pot of the double boiler so that the upper pot will touch the water. Pour the cream in the upper pot and put the dairy thermometer in the cream.

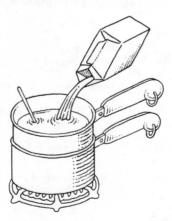

2. Over moderate heat bring the temperature of the cream up to a point between 155° and 160°F. Adjust the heat so that this temperature is maintained 30 minutes.

3. Cool the cream quickly to 85°F by setting the upper pot in ice water. Change the water if it becomes warm. It is important to lower the temperature quickly and get the culturing process underway without prolonged exposure of the cream to the open air.

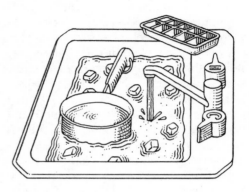

Culturing

1. Pour half the cream into the canning jar, then add the starter. Mix this thoroughly, then add the remaining cream to within ¾ inch of the top. Leave a little headroom.

2. Put the cover on tightly and shake the jar until the contents are thoroughly mixed. (Remember, too-violent agitation can start your cream on the road to Buttersville.)

3. Set the inoculated cream in a warm, draft-free place with a constant temperature between 70° and 80°F for 15 to 24 hours. You can use an insulated yogurt box (see Index) for this stage, but remember that commercial yogurt makers are set for higher temperatures — between 90° and 100°F — too much for sour cream.

If your kitchen is warm, you can get good results by standing the jar on a cork mat or a section of the Sunday paper, and covering it with a folded blanket or towel.

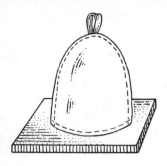

House-proud dairy makers who use sour cream frequently can stitch up a sour cream cozy in short order.

4. Test the sour cream for readiness at the end of 15 hours by scooping a little out with a clean spoon and tasting it; if more acidity is wanted, let the jar stand several hours longer.

5. Chill the sour cream in its jar for another 24 hours before using.

If your house is chilly in cold weather, don't be tempted to increase the amount of starter culture as a hurry-up trick. Better results are gained by letting the cream stand an extra 12 to 24 hours. Too much starter makes lumps.

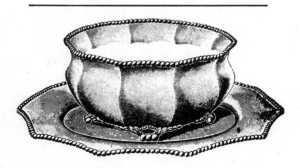

How to Make a Sour Cream Cozy

Materials

⅝ yard cotton fabric
¼ yard polyfoam, ¼ inch thick
4-inch length grosgrain ribbon
matching thread

1. Enlarge the pattern to full size on strong paper.

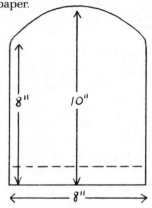

8"   10"

8"

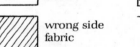 right side fabric

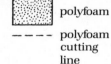 polyfoam

wrong side fabric

– – – – polyfoam cutting line

2. Cut 4 pattern pieces from fabric for outer shell and inner shell.

3. Cut 2 pattern pieces from polyfoam 1 inch shorter than fabric for inner insulation.

4. Baste 1 polyfoam piece to the wrong side of each outer shell section, aligning the tops.

5. Right sides together, stitch outer shells with a ⅝-inch seam. Leave bottom open. Turn right side out.

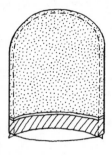 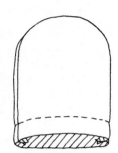

6. Right sides together, stitch inner shell.

7. Wrong side out, slide inner shell into outer shell.

8. When in place, tack the inner shell to the outer shell at the top.

9. Fold up 1-inch hems on both outer shell and inner shell. Pin or baste in place. Stitch all around the bottom ¼ inch from the edge through all layers.

 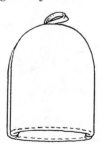

10. Pull out any basting threads. Sew a ribbon loop to the top.

SOUR CREAM RECIPES

Soups

Bavarian Sour Cream Soup

serves six

½ teaspoon caraway seeds
1½ quarts chicken stock
1½ cups sour cream
⅓ cup whole wheat flour
    stale whole grain bread cubed for
      croutons
    Clarified Butter (see Index)

1. Simmer the caraway seeds in the soup stock 20 minutes.

2. Blend the sour cream and flour until smooth, add a little soup stock, then slowly add the mixture to the simmering stock, stirring until smooth and well blended.

3. Simmer, stirring occasionally, until the soup thickens to the consistency of medium cream.

4. Fry the bread cubes in clarified butter until they are crisp and nut-brown. Garnish each plate of hot soup with a few crispy croutons.

Cold Mediterranean Avocado-Tomato Soup

serves four

6 tomatoes, chopped and pureed
      through a food mill to eliminate
      seeds
⅔ cup sour cream
½ cup milk
3 tablespoons lemon juice
2 tablespoons tomato paste
1 tablespoon olive oil
3 tablespoons chopped parsley
1 small firm cucumber
1 avocado

1. In a mixing bowl thoroughly blend the pureed tomatoes, sour cream, milk, lemon juice, tomato paste and olive oil. Stir in the parsley, cover and chill for several hours or overnight.

2. Peel and seed the cucumber, then dice it fine and set aside.

3. Just before serving, puree the avocado and beat it into the chilled soup. Garnish with the diced cucumber.

Blueberry Soup from Scandinavia

serves four

Fruit soups using lingonberries, rose hips, plums, cherries and other fruits are held in esteem in the Scandinavian countries and should be better known. Traditionally these fruit soups are served at the end of the meal, a refreshing and wholesome alternative to the dessert course. Here is a marvelous soup from Sweden. Wild blueberries have the best flavor and make a superior dish. Make this a day in advance.

1 tablespoon lemon rind
1 cinnamon stick
2 whole cloves
1 pint blueberries
4 tablespoons honey
4 cups orange or apple juice,
　　　or water
1 cup sour cream

1. Put the lemon rind, cinnamon and cloves in a small cheesecloth bag and place in a heavy saucepan.

2. Add all other ingredients except the sour cream and simmer over moderate heat until the blueberries burst. Remove the bag of spices.

3. Puree the mixture a cup at a time in a blender.

4. Cover and chill overnight. Serve in individual bowls with the sour cream heaped in the center of each serving.

　　Rusk bread is the traditional accompaniment.

Main Dishes

Beef Stroganoff

serves two or three

1 pound fillet of beef, cut into ½-inch
    slices
4 tablespoons butter
1 tablespoon grated onions
1 pound mushrooms, sliced
  pinch freshly grated nutmeg
½ teaspoon dried sweet basil or
       1 teaspoon chopped fresh basil
2 tablespoons wine vinegar
1 cup sour cream

1. Pound the beef slices thin with a wooden mallet, then cut them into 1-inch-wide strips.

2. In a heavy skillet melt 1 tablespoon butter, add the grated onions and saute 2 or 3 minutes. Add the beef strips and saute 5 minutes, turning them to brown evenly. Set aside in a dish and keep hot.

3. Melt the remaining butter in the skillet, add the sliced mushrooms and saute until they are lightly browned. Add the beef strips and season with the nutmeg and sweet basil.

4. Reduce the heat and add the vinegar, cooking 1 minute. Add the sour cream and heat thoroughly, taking care not to let the mixture boil. Serve at once over noodles or rice.

Fiery Chicken Indienne

serves six to ten

¾ cup wheat germ
6 whole chicken breasts, split
4 to 6 tablespoons Clarified Butter
    (see Index)
1 tablespoon peeled and finely
    chopped ginger root
1 garlic clove, pressed
2 small hot dried chili peppers,
    crushed
3 tablespoons whole wheat flour
1 cup chicken stock
½ cup milk or Whey (see Index)
1 cup sour cream

Preheat oven to 350°F.

1. Put the wheat germ in a large, strong paper or plastic bag. Drop in the chicken breasts 2 at a time and shake until they are well coated.

2. In a large, cast iron skillet, melt the butter. Add the ginger, garlic and chili peppers and cook 1 minute over moderate heat. Brown the chicken on all sides, adding more butter if necessary. As the pieces brown, remove them to a shallow baking dish.

3. Bake the chicken breasts 30 minutes or until the chicken is tender.

4. Add more butter to the skillet if necessary to bring the amount in the pan up to 3 tablespoons. Stir in the flour, then work in the chicken stock with a whisk, stirring until the sauce is smooth. Slowly add the milk or whey. Cook over moderate heat until the sauce is as thick as heavy cream.

5. Remove the pan from the heat and stir in the sour cream. Pour the sauce over the chicken breasts and bake another 10 minutes or until it is hot and bubbling.

Paprika Wiener Schnitzel

serves six

Veal has become a luxury meat, and deserves luxury treatment. Paprika is a mild, Hungarian hot pepper, and it should be added at the end of the cooking period since it is sensitive to heat and will lose both flavor and zing if overcooked.

3 pounds veal cutlets, cut into thin
      slices and pounded flat
4 tablespoons Clarified Butter (see
      Index)
3 tablespoons minced onions
1 teaspoon whole wheat flour
  chicken stock as needed
1 tablespoon tomato paste
1 cup sour cream
1 teaspoon paprika

1. Cut ½-inch incisions all around the edges of the flattened cutlets with kitchen scissors to keep them flat as they cook. Heat the butter in a heavy skillet and saute the meat quickly on both sides until brown. Put the meat aside in a dish.

2. To the butter in the skillet add the onions and saute until lightly browned, then add the flour and cook it until slightly brown. Slowly add the chicken stock and tomato paste until you have a smooth, boiling gravy with the consistency of light cream. Blend in the sour cream.

3. Return the cutlets to the sauce and simmer over low heat until tender, about 25 minutes. A few minutes before serving add the paprika, stir well and cook another 2 or 3 minutes.

Piquant Ginger Pork Chops

serves six

  Clarified Butter (see Index)
6 pork chops
¼ cup orange juice
1 large orange
1 teaspoon grated ginger root
1 cup sour cream

1. In a heavy skillet melt the butter and brown the chops on both sides.

2. Add the orange juice to the skillet, cover tightly and simmer 30 minutes over low heat.

3. Peel the orange and divide into sections. Sprinkle the chops with the grated ginger, and top with the orange slices. Cover skillet and cook 15 minutes longer.

4. Arrange the chops on an ovenproof serving dish. Top each chop with a generous dollop of sour cream and place under the broiler 1 minute until the cream is toasted light brown and glossy.

Pot Roast with Sour Cream Sauce

serves six to eight

Many cow owners like to raise a beef critter on the side, and here is an outstanding dish that might be called "the Best of the Bovine." This recipe has a European origin, and calls for parsley root, known in this country as parsnip-rooted or Hamburg parsley. Seed is available from most major seed companies. The thick white roots, when chopped, add flavor and interest to soups, stews and gravies. Flat or curled parsley leaves may be substituted.

     4 tablespoons Clarified Butter (see Index)
     1 tablespoon thinly sliced parsley root
     1 tablespoon chopped celery leaves
     1 carrot, sliced
     1 small onion, sliced
     3 pounds beef top round, brisket or rump
     ½ bay leaf
    20 peppercorns
     1 sprig thyme
       pinch freshly grated nutmeg and ginger
    2½ cups beef stock
     1 tablespoon whole wheat flour
     ¾ cup sour cream

Preheat oven to 400°F.

1. Melt 1 tablespoon of the butter in a skillet and over moderate heat saute the parsley root, celery leaves, carrot and onion 5 minutes.

2. Place the roast in a roasting pan that can be covered. Pour the remaining butter over the roast. Add the sauteed vegetables, bay leaf, peppercorns, thyme, nutmeg, ginger and 2 cups of the stock.

3. Cover the roasting pan and bake the roast in the oven 2½ hours, basting frequently. Remove the pan from oven and set the roast aside on a dish a few minutes.

4. Work together the flour and remaining ½ cup stock until smooth. Stir this into the roasting pan liquid. Return the meat to the roaster, reduce the oven heat to 300°F, and roast uncovered 1 hour more or until the meat is tender.

5. Remove the roast to a warm, deep platter. Blend the gravy from the roasting pan in an electric blender until smooth, then return to pan. Stir in the sour cream, bring the gravy up to a boil and serve it at once with the roast.

Roast Rabbit with Sour Cream

serves six

As many small farmholders know, there are few meat animals more economical to raise than plump, tasty rabbits. This recipe is an adaptation from a European treatment of wild hare, and if you have a hare or cottontail hunter in the family, this piquant manner of preparing them enhances their fine natural flavor.

2 rabbits, cut up into serving pieces
¼ teaspoon freshly ground pepper
5 juniper berries, crushed
4 tablespoons Clarified Butter (see Index
2 cups chopped, mixed soup greens (carrot, celery leaves, parsley root, scallions)
1 small onion, sliced
2 garlic cloves, pressed
1 to 2 cups chicken stock
5 tablespoons wine or cider vinegar
20 peppercorns
10 whole allspice berries
1 bay leaf
  pinch freshly grated nutmeg and ginger
2 tablespoons whole wheat flour
1 tablespoon currant jelly or apricot puree
1 cup sour cream

Preheat oven to 325°F.

1. Season the rabbit sections with pepper and rub each piece well with the juniper berries.

2. In a heavy skillet heat the butter, saute the soup greens, onion and garlic several minutes. Arrange the rabbit pieces atop the bed of vegetables and roast in a 325°F oven 45 minutes, basting frequently with some of the stock to keep the meat moist. Remove the rabbit pieces to a dish and keep warm.

3. To make the sauce, add 3 tablespoons of the vinegar to the remaining stock, and pour into the skillet. Bring to a boil and add the peppercorns, allspice, bay leaf, nutmeg and ginger. Cook over moderate heat 3 to 5 minutes.

4. Mix the flour, remaining vinegar and currant jelly together until smooth. Add to the simmering liquid in the skillet, stirring constantly to prevent lumps. Return the meat to the skillet, put back in the oven and roast another 40 minutes or until the rabbit is tender.

5. Arrange the rabbit pieces on a heated platter and keep hot. Strain the sauce, blend in the sour cream and heat until bubbling. Pour the sauce over the rabbit and serve at once.

Experimenter's Choice

You can adapt many of your favorite main dishes to sour cream specialties by blending this multifaceted dairy product into pan juices, stocks and casserole liquids. Pheasant, guinea hen, turkey breast, pork roast, leg of lamb, liver and many other meats are transformed from pleasant dishes to culinary poems with the help of sour cream.

1 tablespoon whole wheat flour
1 tablespoon drippings, fat or Clarified Butter (see Index)
2 cups pan juices
½ cup sour cream

1. Work the flour into the drippings until you have a smooth *roux*.

2. Gradually blend in the pan juices, stirring constantly to keep the mixture smooth. Cook 5 minutes over moderate heat until the gravy is rich and thickened.

3. Stir in the sour cream, heat thoroughly, correct the seasoning if necessary and serve with the meat or fowl.

56909 Milk or Cream Pails, tin, with bails.

	Each.	Per doz.
1 quart	$0.12	$1.30
2 quarts	.15	1.62
3 quarts	.20	2.16
4 quarts	.25	2.70

56911 Milk Peddling Cans. They are made of 4X tin with heavy brass hoop on top and bottom, spout tipped with brass; a very strong and serviceable article. Capacity two gallons.
Each................$1.56

56913 Milk Measure graduated, made of good quality tin and holds 1 quart-
Each....$0.08
Per dozen $0.87

56915 Milk Dippers, made of tin, with long handle.
Price, each.............. ... 1 pint, 10c.; 1 quart, 15c.

56917 Conical Milk Skimmer, well made of good stock.
Each.......... $0.08
Per dozen.... .90

Vegetables

German Stuffed Potatoes

serves eight

This recipe is for anyone who thinks the only thing you can do with a potato and some sour cream is heap the latter on the former.

8 medium-size baking potatoes
3 tablespoons butter
1 teaspoon finely chopped parsley
1 tablespoon chopped onions
1 cup sour cream
1 egg yolk, beaten
½ pound leftover pork roast, chopped
    fine (or pork chops, cooked and
    chopped)

Preheat oven to 325°F.

1. Peel the potatoes. Cut a thin slice off the bottom of each so that the potatoes can stand up without rolling over. Cut off the tops for covers. Scoop cavities out of the interiors with a melon baller. (Put the scooped-out portions aside to be used in soup or another recipe.)

2. Cook the potatoes and covers in boiling water 4 minutes. Drain.

3. Melt 1 tablespoon of the butter in a large skillet and fry the parsley and onions in it a few minutes. Set aside. Mix ¼ cup of the sour cream and the egg yolk together, then stir into the parsley-onion mixture. Mix in the pork.

4. Stuff the potatoes with this mixture and put the covers on.

5. Place the potatoes in a deep baking pan. Mix together the remaining sour cream and butter. Pour this over the potatoes and bake in the oven 30 minutes or until tender.

Russian Mushrooms in Sour Cream

serves four

The mushroom, like the cucumber, reaches ambrosial heights when blended with sour cream. If you are an experienced mycologist, try your favorite wild mushroom in this recipe.

4 tablespoons butter
1½ pounds small mushrooms
2 large onions, minced fine
1 cup rich beef stock
2 tablespoons whole wheat flour
2 cups sour cream

1. In a large skillet melt 3 tablespoons of the butter; turn in the mushrooms whole and brown them gently. Set them aside in a dish.

2. Add the remaining tablespoon of butter to the skillet, add the onions and cook gently until translucent.

3. Return the mushrooms to the skillet and add the beef stock. Simmer slowly until the mushrooms are tender.

4. Work a little pan juice into the flour until smooth, then blend it into the liquid in the skillet with a whisk until smooth and thickened. Add the sour cream and simmer another 5 minutes until hot and savory, and thick enough to spoon out.

Savory Rice

serves six

3 cups cooked brown rice
¼ cup chopped green onions
1½ cups large curd cottage cheese
1 garlic clove, pressed
1 cup sour cream
¼ cup milk
¼ teaspoon crushed hot pepper
½ cup grated cheddar cheese

Preheat oven to 350°F.

1. In a mixing bowl combine all ingredients except cheddar cheese.

2. Turn into a buttered baking dish, top with the cheese and bake 25 minutes.

Sour Cream Sauce for Vegetables

yields about 1½ cups

The next time you pick the millionth basket of green beans or zucchini from a never-ending garden row, try this superb sauce and remind yourself that gourmets dining in multi-starred restaurants would go mad for such a tantalizing delicacy with its ingredients fresh from the garden and dairy—if they could get it!

   2 tablespoons butter
   2 tablespoons minced shallots
   1 teaspoon honey
   1 teaspoon wine vinegar
     freshly ground black pepper
1½ cups sour cream
  ¼ cup chopped walnuts

1. Melt the butter in the top of a double boiler over direct heat.

2. Saute the shallots in the butter until they are limp and translucent. Stir in the honey, vinegar and pepper. Remove from heat.

3. Gradually stir in the sour cream. Add the walnuts.

4. Over, not in, boiling water, heat the sauce until it is very warm *but not hot.* Serve at once over tender-crisp steamed vegetables.

Care must be taken not to overheat this sauce, for there is no binder to keep the delicate cream from separating under the action of heat, but the flavor bonus makes the caution worthwhile.

Salads and Salad Dressings

Once you've enjoyed sour cream salad dressings, mayonnaise takes a back seat. Sour cream dressings range from an ethereal whipped cloud tinged with lemon and honey to a snapping Russian horseradish mixture. Experimenters can clank bottles, grind strange spices and puree exotic fruits to make unique dressings unlisted in any book of cookery.

Fruit Salad Antarctica

serves four

1 cup sour cream
2 tablespoons orange juice
1 tablespoon lemon juice
1 teaspoon honey
½ teaspoon prepared mustard
1 cup unsweetened, crushed
    pineapple
¾ cup seedless grapes, halved
¾ cup diced peaches
  lettuce

1. Have all ingredients cold, including a mixing bowl and beaters. Whip the sour cream 5 minutes or until doubled in volume.

2. In another bowl combine orange and lemon juice, honey and mustard. Slowly blend in the whipped sour cream.

3. Fold the fruit in gently. Pour into a mold and freeze several hours in the coldest part of the freezer.

4. To serve, arrange the lettuce leaves on a plate, dip the mold in hot water a few seconds and unmold the salad on the lettuce.

Russian Sour Cream-Horseradish Dressing

yields about ¾ cup

This zesty sauce makes a good dip for raw vegetable sticks, or a dressing for any green salad. It is enjoyed in Russia with a bowl of greentail onions and a loaf of dark pumpernickel or rye bread.

2 garlic cloves, pressed
2 tablespoons finely minced shallots
1 tablespoon chopped dill
¾ cup sour cream
2 tablespoons grated horseradish

Place all the ingredients in a blender, blend briefly and serve.

Sour Cream Dressing for Fruit Salads

yields 1 cup

1 cup sour cream
1 tablespoon honey or maple syrup
¼ teaspoon grated lemon rind
1 tablespoon toasted sesame seeds
1 teaspoon poppy seeds

1. Have all ingredients, mixing bowl and beaters cold. Put the cream, honey and lemon rind in a bowl and whip until light and fluffy.

2. Top each serving of any fruit salad with the mixture, then sprinkle with the sesame and poppy seeds.

Experimenter's Choice

You can invent hundreds of dressings for salads and vegetables by adding to a cup of sour cream various combinations of herbs, spices, juices and savory foods. Here are some suggestions to be tried singly or in combinations that please your palate.

curry powder
garlic, shallots, onions
chili powder
horseradish
wine or cider vinegar
dried apples, apricots, raisins
chopped nuts
lemon, lime, orange juice
fresh dill, marjoram, savory, thyme,
        tarragon
mashed banana
pureed mango, nectarine, persimmon,
        plum
caraway seeds
chopped cucumber
fresh crushed berries
cinnamon, nutmeg, cardamom
vanilla, cherry, almond extract
fresh mint leaves
carrot, green pepper, tomato juice

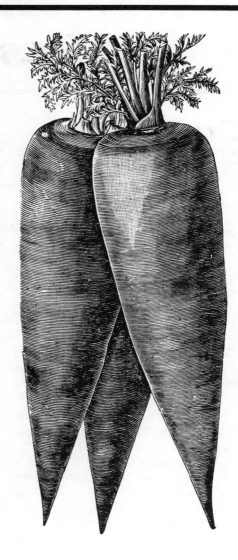

Desserts

Grapes in Sour Cream

serves one; multiply for more

This is the simplest and perhaps the most delicious recipe in this book.

1 cup seedless white grapes of the best flavor, such as Himrod or Interlaken
½ cup sour cream

1. Wash the grapes in cold water, drain, pile in sherbet or dessert glasses and chill in the refrigerator until icy cold.

2. Just before serving heap the sour cream over the grapes.

It is not necessary to add twists of lemon or chopped nuts or a little honey to this combination; the spicy sweetness of Himrod grapes balances the creamy tartness of the sour cream perfectly, and the sensations of crisp grape flesh and melting cream in the mouth are beyond description.

Prune Whip Cream

serves four

1 cup sour cream
2 cups pitted, stewed prunes
1 teaspoon lemon juice
  pinch powdered cardamom
  slivered toasted almonds

1. Put all ingredients except almonds in blender and blend until thick and fluffy.

2. Spoon into sherbet glasses and chill several hours.

3. Garnish with almonds before serving.

Sour Cream Pound Cake

serves ten to twelve

The world seems to be divided into cake lovers or pie lovers, and never the twain shall meet. Here is a top-notch candidate for the cake fancier's inventory.

- 1 cup butter
- 1 cup honey
- 6 eggs
- 1 teaspoon almond extract or rose water
- 1 cup sour cream
- 2¾ cups whole wheat flour, sifted
- ½ teaspoon baking soda
- Natural Cake Icing (see Index)

Preheat oven to 325°F.

1. Cream the butter and honey in a large mixing bowl. Beat in the eggs, one at a time.

2. Add the almond extract and sour cream and beat well.

3. Mix in the flour and baking soda.

4. Pour the batter into a well-greased, flour-dusted 9-inch springform pan. Bake 1 to 1½ hours, or until a knife inserted in the center comes out clean.

5. Let the cake cool in the pan 10 minutes before removing. Frost it, when cool, with Natural Cake Icing.

Cow Bells.

42594 The shape of these is designed to produce the loudest sound possible.

No.	0	2	3	5	7	
Size of mouth	6x4½	5½x3½	4½x3	3¼x2⅜	2⅜x1¾	in
Height	6½	5	4¾	3¼	2⅜	in.
Price, Each	$0.40	$0.25	$0.20	$0.15	$0.10	
Per dozen	4.00	2.65	2.00	1.50	1.00	

42595 Cow Bell Straps, made of leather.

Width	1½ in.	1¾ in.
Per dozen	$2.50	$2.75
Each	.25	.28

7 CHEESE

You can make many tasty and delicious cheeses in the home dairy—cottage cheese, pot cheese, ricotta, farm cheese, and cream cheese—without using salt. Most of these simple cheeses are soft or semi-soft, for nearly all the hard aged cheeses of the world call for salt, either sprinkled on the curd to help draw out the whey and firm up the solids, or rubbed into the rind to retard the growth of harmful organisms and aid in the development of the particular flavors associated with certain cheeses. Some cheeses are soaked in heavy brine solutions for days.

However, in this country so much of our food has salt added to it that as a nation of eaters we have become salt gluttons, overloading our systems with sodium, swelling our tissues with retained fluids, increasing our blood pressures and taking the risks of early heart attack, stroke and kidney failure. Just as none of the recipes in this book call for salt in their preparation, no directions are given here for salted or brined cheeses.

If you attempt to make hard cheese without salt, you must be doubly scrupulous about the cleanliness of the equipment, milk, pasteurization and cheese ripening room, and even then there will be an occasional failure. Every cheese maker now and then has an uncooperative cheese that goes wrong despite its maker's best efforts. If you want to go beyond the simple cheeses discussed here, you will find a listing of books and cheese workshops in the Sources section at the end of this book.

Most of the cheeses described below can be made either from cows' milk or goats' milk. Goats' milk cheeses can be made by using any standard cheese recipe, but better results are obtained with temperatures slightly different from those needed for cows' milk cheeses—85° to 86°F rather than the 90°F suitable to cows' milk. Goats' milk cheeses make up better if skim milk is used rather than whole milk. Goats' milk makes cheeses with a softer curd than does cows' milk. Animal rennet should be used with goats' milk, for it has superior setting qualities over vegetable rennet. Unless otherwise noted, all cheeses should be made from pasteurized milk.

Warning! Milk that contains antibiotics is no good for cheese making. If your milk animal is being treated with antibiotics, wait 2 or 3 days after you stop the medication before using any of the milk for cheeses.

Warning! Never use pasteurized milk that has gone bad under the impression that it is "sour milk"—pasteurized milk does not sour, it spoils. Trying to make cheese from this can only be a disaster.

EQUIPMENT FOR CHEESE MAKING

The section on home dairy equipment (see Index) describes the types and uses of cheese-making equipment in detail. Sources of cheese-making supplies and equipment are listed in the Appendix. Here is a brief review of the essential equipment for cheese making.

dairy thermometer

large stainless steel kettle

larger kettle that will accommodate the stainless steel kettle

stainless steel slotted spoon

long stainless steel knife

hardwood cheese drain board

plastic or stainless steel colander

butter muslin or 100 percent cotton, heavy-duty cheesecloth

cheese press, commercial, home-made or improvised

straw mats

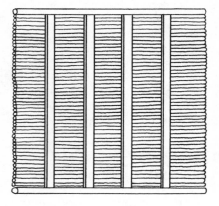

cheese molds, stainless steel, nylon or acid-resistant, food-grade plastic

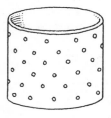

Ingredients for Cheese Making

Aside from goats' or cows' milk, there are several other ingredients needed for making cheese at home, including cheese starter cultures, annatto for coloring pale cheeses, and rennet, an enzyme which sets the curd.

Cheese Starter Culture

Many freeze-dried cheese starter cultures are available from cheese supply dealers, some of them specialized, such as those for making Camembert or bleu cheeses, Pont L'Eveque, Oka, Port Salut, and others for cheddar or Swiss. You can also buy special starter cultures for cottage cheese and other soft cheeses, and at least one specifically suited to making fresh, soft goats' milk cheeses. An hour with a cheese supply dealer's catalog will introduce you to these cultures, which you may wish to try as your skill in cheese making grows.

The starter culture directions given here are for an all-purpose culture, good for making soft and hard cheeses. Many suppliers offer it in freeze-dried packets simply as "Cheese Starter Culture."

By making up a 2-quart batch of culture, you can use some of it to make cheese whenever you like without the tedium of preparing a fresh culture from scratch every time. This culture can be frozen in convenient 1- or 2-ounce cubes in an ice cube tray, then stored in a bag in the freezer until needed.

Starter culture contains a good balance of the right bacteria for making cheeses and other dairy products: *Streptococcus lactis*, *Streptococcus thermophilus*, *Streptococcus cremoris* and *Lactobacillus bulgaricus*. Using a homemade starter culture such as this is far better than trying to inoculate milk with store-bought commercial buttermilk which is often weak and old when purchased. Unfortunately, the inadequate buttermilk route is still recommended for home cheese makers by many books and even by Extension Service personnel in dairying country! Since very fine specialized domestic and imported cultures are available at low cost, why not use them? You'll be glad you did. Always use the best, freshest materials and milk and you'll gain fame as a maker of excellent cheese.

Preparations for Making the Starter

Have enough ice cube trays at hand to hold 2 quarts of liquid. Measure the capacity of the trays beforehand to find out whether each cube compartment holds 1 or 2 ounces. Make a memorandum of that measurement since directions for making various cheeses call for the starter culture in ounces..

The milk must be fresh and clean. Do not try to make starter culture in hot, humid weather. Pick a day when temperatures are in the low 70s. The milk, jars and covers must be sterile, and all equipment clean and free from contamination.

Recipe for the Starter

Makes 2 quarts or 64 1-ounce cubes

    2 quarts raw cows' or goats' milk
    1 packet freeze-dried cheese starter
        culture

1. Boil a half-gallon canning jar and lid in water 10 minutes to sterilize, or use 2 quart jars. Drain upside down 1 minute.

2. Pour the milk into the jar and put the cover on tightly.

3. Set the jar on a rack in a deep kettle and cover with water so that the jar is submerged. Bring the water to a boil, reduce the heat to a simmering boil and hold this temperature 30 minutes. (Note: This step may be done in a pressure canner if you have one deep enough to take the jar. Put the jar on the rack and add 3 inches of water. Cover, add pressure gauge and hold 10 minutes at 15 pounds pressure.)

4. Remove the jar from the kettle and let it cool to room temperature in a sheltered corner away from drafts. (If you have used a pressure canner, set the canner in cool water to bring down the pressure, remove the jar and cool as above.)

5. When the jar cools to 72°F, inoculate the milk quickly by adding the starter culture and get the cover back on as fast as you can. Turn, swirl and twist the jar without actually shaking it into a froth until the starter culture is dissolved and dispersed through the milk.

6. Wrap a towel or folded blanket around the jar and allow the inoculated milk to ripen 16 to 30 hours at 72°F. You may ripen it in an insulated yogurt box (see Index). When the starter is ripe, the milk will have firmed up or coagulated to the consistency of firm yogurt. The starter can be used immediately to make cheese, but will remain useable for only 2 or 3 days even under refrigeration. This amount will make nearly 100 pounds of cheese.

7. To keep the starter useable for a long period, pour it into ice cube trays, cover with a sheet of plastic wrap and freeze. When solid, turn out the frozen cubes into double plastic bags, twist tightly closed and store in the freezer. These cubes will keep 4 to 6 months. Use the starter cubes for making cheese, sour cream and other cultured dairy products. Defrost at room temperature first.

Annatto

Annatto is a yellow coloring substance from the pulp surrounding the seeds of the annatto tree, a tropical plant that grows in South America.

It is used to color cheeses and butter, particularly when they are made from Holstein or goats' milk. It is unnecessary except to please the eye.

Rennet

Rennet is a natural enzyme which curdles milk or forces the solids into precipitation.

Animal rennet, widely used in cheese making, comes from the lining of the fourth or digestive stomach of calves or other young mammals. The extract is made and sold commercially.

Vegetable rennet, though less effective than animal rennet, can also be bought commercially. Lady's bedstraw or "curd flower" *(Galium verum)* was much used for curding cheeses in England. Wild thistle flowers, safflower seeds and green fig tree branches have all been used in cheese making as vegetable rennet in the past.

Rennet can be kept for several months at home in the refrigerator, but eventually it loses its strength and the cheese maker must use more of it or get a fresh stock. Animal rennet is used in all the cheese recipes given here. It should never be used full strength, but diluted to at least six times its own volume. Never make up a rennet solution in advance, but dilute the pure rennet just before adding it to the milk.

Rennet works best when the milk is slightly soured and warm. If the milk has been boiled or sterilized the rennet will not work. Pasteurized milk must be cultured with the cheese starter described above before the rennet is added to gain the right level of acidity. Together the chese starter and the rennet precipitate a firm, solid curd from the milk, the basis of hard cheeses.

How to Make Cottage Cheese

One of the world's most popular cheeses, cottage cheese is the logical item with which to start your cheese-making career. It's easy, almost fool-proof, and the results are delicious. Homemade cottage cheese is more versatile than the bland store-bought stuff. The small curd type has several names — pot cheese, Dutch cheese, *schmierkase* and farmer's cheese. The large curd type is sometimes called pop-corn cheese from the resemblance of the large curds to big white popped corn kernels. Sometimes heavy cream is mixed into cottage cheese to give it a richer, smoother texture. Pepper, chives, and herbs can be blended in to make appealing combinations.

Low-Fat Cottage Cheese

makes 1¼ pounds

1 gallon raw skim goats' or cows' milk
4 ounces Cheese Starter (see discussion, p. 138)

1. Pour the milk into a stainless steel kettle and set the kettle in a hot water bath. Put the dairy thermometer in the milk. Heat until the milk reaches 160°F and hold 3 seconds. At once remove the milk kettle from the hot water and cool it rapidly in cold water to 72°F.

2. Add the cheese starter, stirring it in thoroughly. Cover the kettle and let it stand overnight at room temperature (in the low 70s). In 12 to 16 hours the milk should have set into a soft-firm custard-like curd. If you press the side of the curd with a knife, a section should break away from the side of the kettle in a soft but clearly defined line if enough acid has developed to precipitate the milk solids. If the milk has *not* set, allow it to stand several hours longer. It may take 12 to 48 hours for the curd to set, longer if the starter was weak or the room is cold.

3. Using a long stainless steel knife, cut the curd in 3 directions, as illustrated, producing small ¼-inch to ½-inch cubes. As you cut you will notice the clear, pale yellow whey welling up as it is released from the curd by the cutting action of the knife. When all the curd is cut, allow it to rest in the kettle 10 minutes.

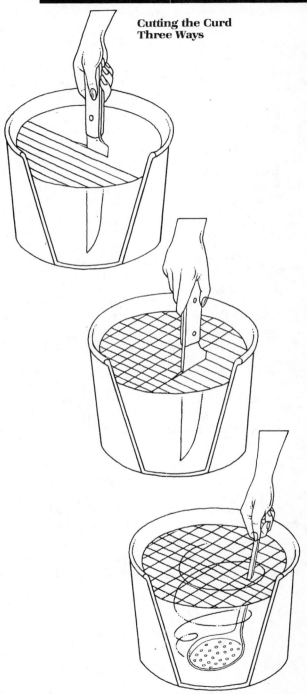

**Cutting the Curd
Three Ways**

4. Put the curd kettle back in the hot water kettle. Put the dairy thermometer in the curd, then heat *slowly* 30 to 40 minutes. Bring the temperature up to 102°F if you are using cows' milk, and to 106°F if using goats' milk. The rate of temperature increase should be about 1° per minute. During the heating, stir the curd by lifting it up gently from the bottom of the kettle with a slotted stainless steel spoon. Do not mash or crush the curd.

5. Now raise the heat slightly and stir-lift more frequently as the curds tighten up and become tougher. When the temperature reaches 115°F, reduce the heat and keep stirring until the curds feel firm and slightly rubbery to a gentle pinch.

6. Remove the kettle from the heat and dip out as much whey as you can without rupturing the curds. Save the whey for use in cooking (see Index).

7. Line a colander with a double layer of damp cheesecloth. Set it in a bowl to catch the whey. Pour in the remaining curds and whey and let them drain several minutes.

8. Gather up the ends of the cheesecloth into a bag and rinse the bag of curds 2 to 3 minutes in cool water, gently palpating the curd for a thorough rinse. Discard the water. Rinse several more times in fresh cold water to which a tray of ice cubes has been added.

9. Return the bag to the colander and allow it to drain an hour or longer.

The cottage cheese is now ready to eat. It is a low-fat, nutritious, high-protein food. You can vary the flavor and texture by stirring in several tablespoons of cream, or adding chopped chives, garlic, parsley, sage, tarragon or ground pepper. If the cheese is firm, shape it into a cylinder and roll it in chopped herbs.

Ann Koehler, Cheese Maker

Ann Koehler is President of the Granite State Capriculture Club, active in 4-H, keeps a small milk herd of Toggenburg and Saanen goats, and runs a woodworking shop where she manufactures children's toys, cribbage boards and small furniture pieces. In her spare time she raises a few pigs and a beef animal every year, as well as ducks, geese and laying hens, on 25 acres of side hill with a lot of granite ledge. She makes both a soft and a hard cheese, and many other dairy products. Here's what she says about her experiences with cheese making:

"I make two types of cheese, one a hard cheese, the other an acid-curd cheese which I use as a cottage cheese.

"I've made the acid-curd cheese for 6 or 7 years now. It's very easy. You use 1 gallon of milk. Heat it on the stove to 180°F, remove from the heat and add ¼ cup cider vinegar. You can see the curd form immediately. I drain it through a cheesecloth (fine mesh) or use gauze diapers (I bought some for cheese making). Save the whey as it is good for bread making, whey cheese, or to feed to chickens or pigs. After the curd is drained you can use it as a cottage cheese, or

1. put in a press overnight for a semi-soft cheese
2. blend with a little cream for a spreadable cheese
3. add herbs—such as snipped chives, chopped peppers [and the like]—and press.
4. For a very soft spreadable cheese use ¼ cup lemon juice in place of the vinegar. With this I usually add 1 teaspoon garlic powder, 1 teaspoon thyme, 1 teaspoon tarragon, 1 teaspoon rosemary and 3 crushed whole cloves. This is similar to Boursin cheese.

"We use this cheese as cottage cheese, in lasagne, or the spreadable varieties with crackers for snacks. I've also used the lemon-based cheese and blended it with dried fruit and nuts, then dehydrated it for a different snack food. I find apricots to be the favorite fruit.

"The hard cheese I make is very simple as well. Use 5 quarts of milk. I heat it to 86°F, and add 2 ounces of regular cheese starter, but 1 cup of yogurt or cultured buttermilk can

Large Curd Cottage Cheese

makes about 1½ pounds

> 1 gallon pasteurized goats' or cows' milk
> 4 ounces Cheese Starter (see discussion, p. 138)
> 1 teaspoon Rennet Solution (see below)

1. Pour the milk into a large stainless steel kettle. Stand the kettle in a sink of hot water. Place a dairy thermometer in the milk. Heat the milk to 72°F.

2. Add the cheese starter, mixing well. Add 1 teaspoon of the rennet solution and stir well. Cover the kettle and allow the milk to ripen at 72°F for 24 to 48 hours, or until it sets into a thick custardy consistency.

3. Line a colander with damp cheesecloth in a double layer and pour in the curd. Catch the whey and save for other uses.

4. Gather up the corners of the cheesecloth and tie up the bag of curds. Hang this over a bowl to drain for 24 hours or more. If a special shape is wanted, pack the curds instead into a perforated mold and allow it to drain.

5. Turn the cheese out and serve it at once, or chill it, or use in any cottage cheese recipe.

Rennet Solution

> 4 drops liquid animal rennet
> ⅓ cup cooled boiled water

Mix the rennet and water thoroughly just before using.

be used. I let this set for 30 minutes, then recheck the temperature, which should be 86°F. If not, I reheat it to that point. I add ½ cheese rennet tablet crushed in ¼ cup cold water. The rennet should be added slowly while stirring the milk for 2 to 3 minutes. I let it set another 30 minutes or until the curd breaks cleanly over the finger. I cut the curd into ½-inch squares, using a long stainless steel knife or spatula, first vertically, then horizontally. I use a flat skimmer and make a circular cut in a spiral from top to bottom to cut the columns.

"Now the curd is scalded. Double-boiler-style I slowly raise the temperature to 92°F and hold it there for 30 minutes. I drain the curd then, and when well drained and matted I put it on a clean board and cut it into ½-inch slices. I let it drain 5 minutes, then turn it and drain another 5 minutes, and repeat this twice more.

"Now I mix ½ ounce kosher salt into the curd, and put it into a cheesecloth-lined press. I press 30 minutes at 20 pounds pressure, turn the cheese and press 18 to 24 hours at 50 pounds pressure. Now the cheese is removed from the press and set on a mat at room temperature until a rind forms, and turned twice daily. Now the cheese can be wrapped in plastic wrap or waxed and put in the refrigerator to cure. It is useable in 1 to 14 days.

"My cheese equipment is enamel kettles (unchipped), stainless steel spoons and skimmer, a dairy thermometer, and I have a Wheeler cheese press. This is an expensive press but was a Christmas gift from my hubby. Before that I used a cut-down plastic maple syrup jug (gallon size) with holes punched from inside outward for drainage. It sat on a mat on a board with an upright dowel at each corner. I had a hardwood circle that just fit in the top of the jug and a square block above that. The lid was another board with a hole in each corner for the dowels to fit in. Bricks were piled on top of the board for weights. I got the press because the weights had a habit of sliding off onto the floor around 2 A.M. with a terrible crash."

Crowdy

yields about 1½ cups

This is the Scottish version of cottage cheese—soft and deliciously subtle.

1 quart skim or whole milk
1 ounce Cheese Starter (see discussion, p. 138)
1 teaspoon Rennet Solution (see above)
1 tablespoon heavy cream

1. Pour the milk into a stainless steel kettle and set in a hot water bath, sink or another kettle. Heat the milk to 90°F for cows' milk, 86°F for goats' milk. Remove from the hot water.

2. Add the starter and mix well. Thoroughly stir in the rennet solution called for. Cover and let stand in a warm place 2 to 3 hours or until the curd has set.

3. Cut the curd 3 ways into 1-inch cubes.

4. Return the kettle to hot water and heat until the curd reaches 90°F for cows' milk or 86°F for goats' milk. Remove at once from the hot water and let stand 10 minutes.

5. Ladle the curds with a slotted spoon into a double layer of cheesecloth, tie up into a bag and let it drain for 2 to 3 hours.

6. Turn the curds into a bowl, mix in the heavy cream, then shape the cheese into a rectangle and press lightly 1 hour between two boards weighted with a brick.

7. Wrap the cheese in foil or plastic wrap, store in the refrigerator and eat within several days.

Pennsylvania Dutch Cup Cheese

makes 3½ to 7 pounds

The Pennsylvania Dutch saved their old cups without handles for this traditional cheese. The oven baking makes a tougher curd characteristic of cup cheese. Some housewives with only one cow would pack the curd daily into a crock, salt the curd lightly and add another layer each day until they had enough to make a large amount. The cream and butter would be beaten in all at once.

3 to 6 gallons raw cows' milk, naturally soured (You may inoculate and ripen sweet milk with the cheese starter as in the recipes preceding. Allow 4 ounces starter per gallon of milk.)
½ to 1 cup heavy cream
½ to 1 cup butter
½ to 1 teaspoon baking soda
1 egg, beaten

Preheat oven to 300°F.

1. Pour the milk into a wide enamel baking pan — a scrupulously clean turkey roaster will do. Bake uncovered until the curds and whey separate.

2. Drain the curds and cool in a double-layered cheesecloth bag.

3. Soften the curds to the melting point in a stainless steel pan over steady low heat, then beat in the cream, butter, soda and egg, taking care to prevent scorching.

4. Cook gently several minutes, then pour into cups (or other ceramic containers) and cool. Cover with foil or plastic wrap.

Easy Lemon Curd

serves one

Serve this quick curd spread on warm rye bread.

2 cups cows' milk
  juice of 1 lemon

1. Heat the milk in a double boiler over hot water to 102°F. Remove milk kettle from the hot water.

2. Stir in the lemon juice, mixing thoroughly. Cover and let stand 30 minutes.

3. Line a colander with damp cheesecloth. Gently ladle in the curds with a slotted spoon.

4. Gather up the corners of the cheesecloth into a bag and hang it to drain 2 hours.

5. Turn the cheese into a bowl, scrape any cheese off the cheesecloth and use at once.

Cheese Bag How-To

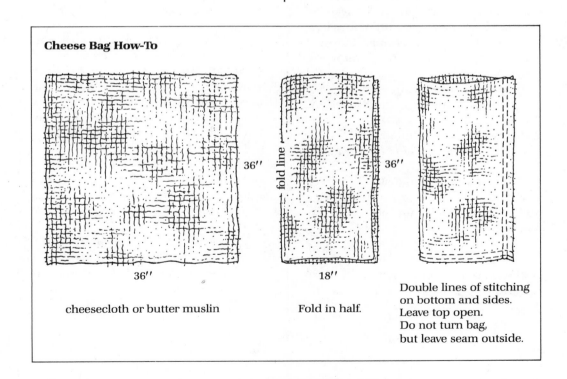

36″

36″

fold line

36″

36″

18″

cheesecloth or butter muslin

Fold in half.

Double lines of stitching on bottom and sides.
Leave top open.
Do not turn bag,
but leave seam outside.

Cream Cheese

Meltingly soft, this is one of the favorite cheeses, used for everything from Danish pastries, cheesecake, spreads, stuffings, very rich soups, dips and desserts to main dishes. Here is a version that is out of this world, similar in texture to the renowned French *Carre*.

Double Cream Cheese

Have several double layers of cheesecloth on hand for the draining stage, for the cloths may have to be changed as they become clogged with curd. Use this cheese within 2 or 3 days and always store it wrapped, in the refrigerator.

1 quart whipping cream
½ ounce Cheese Starter (see discussion, p. 138)
¼ teaspoon rennet diluted in 2 teaspoons cooled boiled water

1. Pour the cream into a stainless steel kettle, set it in hot water and heat it to 75°F. Remove the cream kettle from the hot water.

2. Add the cheese starter to the cream and mix well. Cover and let it stand in a warm place, 70° to 75°F, 2 to 3 hours to ripen.

3. Again put the cream kettle in hot water and warm the cream to 75°F. Stir in the rennet solution. Cover and let the cream stand, as above, in a warm place 12 to 16 hours, until the cream coagulates into a tender, custardy curd.

4. Line a colander with a double layer of damp cheesecloth, then carefully ladle in the curd. Gather the cheesecloth into a bag and hang it to drain in a cool place (temperatures in the 50s) 24 to 36 hours. *Do Not Place In Refrigerator*. Cream cheese is highly susceptible to picking up odors, and even a clean refrigerator can ruin the pure creamy subtlety of this delicate cheese.

5. Every 4 to 6 hours open the bag and with a spoon move the inner core of curd outward so it can drain. If the pores of the bag are clogged, transfer the curd to a new damp cheesecloth, scraping the curd from the old cloth. You may have to do this several times.

6. When the curd is thick and cohesive it has drained enough. Now shape it, wrap it in foil or plastic wrap and chill thoroughly before serving.

Though the traditional shape for cream cheese in the United States is a rectangle, in France it often comes in little round cakes.

English Colwick Dessert Cheese

makes two small cheeses

This soft, unsalted English cheese is traditionally made in small, perforated, cylindrical molds 6 inches by 6 inches. Bottomless cake pans with holes punched in the sides or clean, perforated lard cans may be used in a pinch. Some cheese supply houses carry a range of imported cheese molds. The edges of this cheese curl over toward a sunken center which is filled with whipped cream before serving.

Ingredients
  1 gallon pasteurized cows' or goats' milk
  1 ounce Cheese Starter (see discussion, p. 138)
  ½ teaspoon rennet diluted in 3 teaspoons cooled boiled water

Equipment
  stainless steel kettle
  cheese board
  straw mat
  2 molds, 6 × 6 inches
  cheesecloth
  2 saucers
  stainless steel perforated skimmer

1. Heat the milk in a stainless steel kettle set in hot water to 90°F for cows' milk or 86°F for goats' milk. Remove the milk kettle from the hot water.

2. Stir in the cheese starter. Dilute the rennet and add it to the milk. Stir well from the bottom of the kettle 1 minute.

Then top-stir 5 to 10 minutes or until the coagulation process begins. Top-stirring distributes the cream throughout the milk. Cover the kettle and let it stand 1 to 2 hours or until the curd is firm.

3. Have ready a cheese board, straw mat, cheese mold, cheesecloth and two saucers, all sterilized in boiling water 5 minutes.

4. Place the cheese board in a large shallow pan and lay the straw mat on it. Set the mold on the straw mat and line it with the damp cheesecloth which should be large enough to fold over the cheese.

5. Prepare the *tops*. Cheeses should have smooth top and bottom surfaces, and a common cheese-making step is to set aside a smooth round of curd cut to fit the mold; this is used later to top the cheese.
    To cut the tops, lower a mold into the curd ¼-inch to ½-inch in depth, then remove it by lifting straight upward. With the skimmer, scoop out the round piece of curd top very carefully and slide it onto the sterile saucer. Set aside.

6. Now remove thin slices of curd from the kettle with the skimmer and slide them in layers into the molds. When the curd reaches the top of a mold, let it stand several minutes until the level

sinks. Add more curd layers until all the curd is used up.

7. Very carefully slide the set-aside tops onto the layers in the mold. Let the cheeses drain an hour or so.

8. Pull gently but firmly upward and inward on the cheesecloth so that the curd is pulled away from the sides of the mold toward the center. Repeat several times over the next 3 to 4 hours until the cheese has the traditional curled edge and sunken center.

9. Allow the cheese to drain 24 to 36 hours longer or until it is firm.

10. Carefully remove the cheese from the mold and very gently peel off the cheesecloth. Place the cheese on a serving dish and fill the sunken center with whipped cream.

How to Make a Hard Cheese

Hard cheeses are all made essentially by the same steps and procedures — ripening the milk with cheese starter, renneting, cutting the curd, scalding the curd, draining the curd, pressing the curd and maturing the cheese. The differences in texture and taste come partly from the use of different milks, from differences in heating periods and temperature levels, from different pressing weights, durations and maturing periods, as well as from specialized microorganisms.

Almost all commercial and homemade hard cheeses need salt to retard bacterial spoilage and develop full flavor.

Moon Rocks and Cheese

Scientists Edward Schreiber and Orson Anderson reported, after study of the lunar rocks brought back from the Apollo 11 and 12 missions, that the rock samples had a compressional velocity very close to that of Muenster, Swiss and Vermont cheddar cheese. The authors commented in *Science* magazine (June 26, 1970), that the cheeses "exhibit compressional velocities that are in consonance with those measured for the lunar rocks — which leads us to suspect that perhaps old hypotheses are best, after all, and should not be lightly discarded."

A very good piece of advice from experienced cheese makers is always to make the biggest cheese you can; the labor involved in making a small cheese is the same as in making a big one.

The first time you make a hard cheese, allow the whole day for it. After you are familiar with the procedure you can work it into your regular routine.

Farm Cheese

makes 3 to 5 pounds

This good, hard cheese has been made on farms for hundreds of years. Traditionally a tablespoon of salt is rubbed into the cheese's rind before it is set away to mature. In this version no salt is used, so extra care must be taken to have all materials, equipment and ingredients ultra clean or sterile. Do not try to make the cheese in hot weather; a day in the low 70s is ideal. You will need a cool, slightly humid place to mature this cheese. A cool, well-ventilated cellar that is very clean, or a stone springhouse will do; both were favorite cheese ripening places in the past.

The Shaker Method of Making Cheese

"We set our cheese at 5 o'clock in the morning, our milk being about as warm as it comes from the cows, adding about the proportion of about one quart of water to five pails of milk. Now we let it stand one and one half hours, then cut it up and let it stand 21 minutes longer, then dip off the whey and stir it up and let it stand again three-fourths of an hour. Now we whey it down in the tub and put it into the basket, and break and tie it up three or four times according as need requires, leaving it half an hour, space between each breaking up, then tying it up the strainer we press it as clean as we can from the whey without the hoop, then cut it in pieces about half an inch square and put into water a little more than milk warm if common curd, if tender, let the water be warmer, after we take it out of the warm water we pour on cold. We believe it is essential that the milk be sweet to avoid strong cheese, as soon as the curd is out of the tub we wash it. N.B. We scald our curd in another tub."

Harvard, Massachusetts.
Fruitlands and Wayside Museum
Shaker Manuscript

This cheese is usually made in a stainless steel milk pail. Old directions tell the cheese maker to stir and test the curd's tension with the bare hand. This is not recommended here. Use a sterile stainless steel spoon or skimmer, and avoid all possibilities of bacterial contamination.

Ingredients

    2 to 4 gallons pasteurized milk
    2 to 4 ounces Cheese Starter (see
        discussion, p. 138)
    1 to 2 teaspoons rennet diluted in 3
        to 6 teaspoons cooled boiled water
    annatto coloring (optional)
    lard or Clarified Butter (see Index)

Equipment

    dairy thermometer
    cheesecloth
    stainless steel curd knife
    hardwood cheese board
    cheese press, mold and follower

1. Pour the milk into a stainless steel pail and insert a dairy thermometer. Set the pail in a sink of hot water and stir gently until the temperature reaches 90°F for cows' milk or 86°F for goats' milk. Remove the pail from the hot water.

2. *Ripening:* Add the cheese starter and stir in thoroughly. Cover the pail with a double layer of cheesecloth and let it stand 45 minutes.

3. *Renneting:* Return the pail to the sink of hot water and again bring the temperature up: 90°F for cows' milk, 86°F for goats' milk. Remove the pail from the hot water. Dilute the rennet and add it to the milk. Stir at once from the bottom of the pail up 1 minute. Top-stir to keep the cream in solution until the milk starts to coagulate. Just before it coagulates the milk will feel heavy and dense. If acidity is developing at the ideal rate, it should take 10 to 15 minutes for the milk to coagulate from the time the rennet was added. If the coagulation point is reached too rapidly or too slowly, the quality of the cheese may be impaired. Both problems can be corrected later during the *Scalding* stage in step 5.

Patty Owen, Cheese Maker

Patty Owen is a New Hampshire farm woman who makes her own cheeses as well as other dairy products. She uses Jersey milk and specializes in hard cheeses, particularly Farmhouse Cheese. She writes:

"For equipment I use mostly what I have in my kitchen — big, enameled pans for warming the milk, wooden spoons, and cheese cloth and the wood stove. It is important to sterilize everything very well and make sure you keep things clean. My cheese press is adapted from an old lard press. It is not stainless steel, but doesn't have any direct contact with the cheese so I figure I can use it until I can do something different. It's basically just a screw with a drain platform and I made a mould out of a plastic gallon jug with holes punched in it — and a wooden follower.

"I just line the mould with cheese cloth — put a cloth liner on the bottom of the press and set in the follower and apply slight pressure. This press is capable of quite a lot of pressure. I don't salt the curd. I press the cheese for a couple of hours, and then take it out and unwrap it and turn it over, rewrap it and return it to the press for a couple more hours. Sometimes, I do that again if it needs evening up — then it is removed and placed in a brine solution for several hours (or overnight if I don't finish pressing until late). After the brine soak I set the cheese in a screened cupboard down cellar. We have an old bricked-up room half-way down into the cellar — which I assume used to be the 'cool room'. It maintains a pretty even temperature so it is a good place for ripening cheese. The cheeses are set on woven mats and I wipe them every day with a brine solution, and turn them over until they form a hard rind. . . .

"Usually I have several cheeses, each at a different stage, so I check them every day and it's simple to just wipe them all and turn them over. This winter I still had a few cheeses left over from early fall production. They were becoming very dry, so I grated them and put them into plastic bags and into the freezer. We use it in cheese casseroles and it's very satisfying to think we have our own supply of hard cheese — at least for some uses. When they're not so dry they're good for sandwiches or just eating with crackers."

Patty Owen's Recipe for Farmhouse Cheese

"I use approximately 4 gallons of milk, half night milk and half morning milk. I heat the milk to 90°F, then remove from heat and add ¼+ tab of rennett which has been dissolved in water (boiled and cooled water.) I stir in well, then let it set until the curd forms, about 1 hour. I cut up the curd into cubes, then break it up into pea-sized chunks with a wire whisk. I heat it very slowly, stirring frequently, almost constantly, to 100°F, then set it aside for 10 minutes. When the curd has settled I pour off the whey and remove the curds to the cheese-cloth lined press. I press for 1 hour, take the cheese out of the mould and turn it over, then press again. I do this 2 or 3 times, and then put the cheese into the brine for 4 or 5 hours, and then it goes to the cool room."

When the milk starts to coagulate, cover it again with the cheesecloth and allow it to stand undisturbed another 30 to 45 minutes, or until the curd splits cleanly when lifted with a spoon. Do not let the curd stand so long that whey begins to separate out as a distinct liquid layer on the surface.

4. *Cutting the curd:* Cut the curd as illustrated (see p. 141). Deliberate thorough-

ness counts for much in this process. After the curd is cut, gently stir-lift 3 or 4 minutes with the skimmer.

5. *Scalding the curd:* Scalding is an important step that can't be rushed. Stand the pail in a sink partially full of warm water, put the dairy thermometer in the curd. Stir the curd gently while adding hot water to the sink until the curd reaches 100°F for cows' milk or 95°F for goats' milk over a period of about 30 minutes.

If the milk coagulated too rapidly in step 3 above, correct the problem now by heating cows' milk to 105°F, or goats' milk to 100°F in 20 minutes. If the milk coagulated too slowly in step 3 above, correct now by scalding cows' milk at 98°F or goats' milk at 93°F over a period of 40 minutes.

The curd is scalded enough if a piece is pinched between the fingers and it feels bouncy and firm and squeaky.

Remove the pail from the hot water and let the curd stand 5 minutes. While it is standing, rinse out another stainless steel pail with boiling water. Tie a double layer of sterile, damp chesecloth over the top of this pail like a porous cover.

6. *Draining the curd:* Pour the curds and whey from the first pail onto the cheesecloth of the second pail very carefully so that the curd rests on the cheesecloth and the whey flows through into the second pail. Save the whey for making ricotta cheese or for cooking.

Tie the cheesecloth full of curd into a bag and place it in the empty pail to drain 1 hour. Twist it 5 or 6 times during this period to force out the whey and to mass the curd together. At the end of the hour the curd should have a firm, rubbery texture.

Now turn the curd onto the cheese board and break it into chunks the size of walnuts. Let them drain several minutes, then break the curd apart into chunks once more, turn them over and let them drain another 4 or 5 minutes.

7. *Pressing the curd:* Line the cheese mold with damp cheesecloth large enough to fold over the top of the curd. Pack in the curd, putting the smallest pieces on the bottom and top for smoother surfaces. Fold the cheesecloth over the curd and place the wooden follower over the curd.

Press the curd at 10 pounds pressure 10 minutes; increase to 20 pounds pressure 10 minutes; increase again to 30 pounds pressure 10 minutes. Hold this pressure 4 hours.

Release the pressure, then rewrap the cheese in dry cheesecloth. Turn the cheese over and return it to the mold with the follower on top. Apply pressure to 40 pounds and let the cheese stand 14 to 16 hours under that pressure.

The next day release the pressure, rewrap the cheese in dry fresh cheesecloth, turn again, return to the mold and apply pressure of 50 pounds. Hold this pressure 24 hours.

8. *Maturing the cheese:* Remove the cheese from the press, unwrap it and rub the surface with a thin layer of clarified butter or lard. Bandage the cheese with cheesecloth, as described here:

•Cut 2 circles of cheesecloth 1 inch in diameter greater than the cheese. Slash the edges ½ inch deep at intervals all around the edge.

•Place a circle over the top of the cheese and fold down the edges. Repeat for the bottom.

•Cut a cheesecloth strip to go around the cheese and bandage it.

Store the cheese in a cool, dimly lit, slightly humid place where the temperature is steady between 50° and 58°F for 6 weeks. Air should circulate around the cheese. During the first 10 days turn the cheese daily. During the next 2 weeks turn the cheese 2 to 3 times a week. Turn the cheese once a week for the remaining time. If cracks develop, rub in more butter or lard. If mold appears, rub it off with a sterile cloth.

The cheese will be ready to enjoy after 6 to 8 weeks of maturing.

Ricotta Cheese

makes about 1 pound

This excellent, tart, grainy cheese is fast and easy to make from the whey left over from making cheese and other dairy products. It has a taste superior to anything masquerading as ricotta in the supermarket.

Always use fresh whey when making ricotta. One of our early cheese mistakes was trying to make ricotta from whey that had stood overnight—it wouldn't make! Whey that has been standing just a few hours will not precipitate properly. Whey from a Jersey cow's milk will make twice as much ricotta as will whey from a Holstein's milk. Goats' milk whey makes a fine-grained ricotta. Be sure to use double layers of cheesecloth when draining goats' milk ricotta or the small particles will slip right through.

2 gallons cows' or goats' milk Whey
    (see Index)
2 quarts milk
¼ cup cider vinegar or lemon juice

1. Mix the whey and milk, then heat in a stainless steel kettle over direct heat until the temperature reaches 185°F. Do not allow the whey to boil.

2. Add the vinegar and stir well. The solids will precipitate almost at once.

3. Strain through a double layer of damp cheesecloth. Pack the curd into a perforated mold, set in a bowl, cover and let drain overnight. Use the ricotta within a few days. Save the liquid to use in soups, whey drinks and baking.

A bag of ricotta cheese drains drop by drop.

CHEESE RECIPES

The recipes that follow suggest many ways to use these cheeses other than serving them straight.

Appetizers

Cheese Nut Balls

makes about fifteen to twenty 1-inch balls

½ pound cream cheese
½ cup yogurt
¼ cup grated farm cheese
 1 small onion, grated
¼ cup shelled pecans

1. In a medium-size bowl, combine cream cheese, yogurt, farm cheese and onion. Beat with an electric mixer until smooth.

2. Scoop the mixture out of the blender and shape into 1-inch balls with a spoon. Place them on a foil-covered plate and refrigerate until firm.

3. In a blender, reduce the pecans to fine crumbs and transfer them to a deep saucer.

4. Roll the firm cheese balls in the crushed nut particles and serve.

Sage Cheese Pots

makes 4 pots

 1 pound farm cheese, grated
½ cup sour cream
 2 tablespoons butter
 1 tablespoon finely chopped sage
      leaves
 freshly ground pepper
  Clarified Butter (see Index)

1. In a bowl work all the ingredients except butter into a stiff, thick paste.

2. Pack the mixture into opaque custard cups or small crocks, cover with a layer of clarified butter, then cap with foil. Store in the refrigerator until needed. Hold at room temperature several hours before serving as a spread on crackers or thin slices of rye bread.

Pear Chunks and Cheese

serves six to eight

 2 tablespoons lemon juice
 2 tablespoons orange juice
 4 dessert pears
½ pound farm cheese

1. In a bowl combine the lemon and orange juices. Cut the pears into 1-inch cubes and let these stand in the juice several hours in the refrigerator.

2. Cut the cheese into 1-inch cubes. Skewer cubes of pear and cheese on toothpicks. Serve.

Main Dishes

Cheese Souffle

serves four

3 tablespoons butter
3 tablespoons whole wheat flour
1 cup milk
5 eggs, yolks and white separated
1½ cups grated farm cheese

Preheat oven to 325°F.

1. Melt the butter in a skillet, stir in the flour until smooth, then remove from heat. Slowly stir in the milk until smooth. Return to heat and cook until thickened.

2. Beat the egg yolks until thick, then add the milk sauce a little at a time, beating well after each addition. Stir in the grated cheese.

3. Beat the egg whites until stiff, then fold them into the cheese and yolk mixture, working in plenty of air.

4. Butter a 1½-quart casserole and pour the mixture in. Bake 45 minutes or until the souffle is tall and golden brown.

Many's the long night I've dreamed of cheese — toasted, mostly.

Ben Gunn, in R. L. Stevenson's
Treasure Island

Cheese Toast

serves four

This is a simple but filling and good supper.

4 slices whole grain bread
1 garlic clove, pressed
4 tablespoons olive oil
½ pound farm cheese
1 mild onion, sliced very thin
1 beefsteak tomato, sliced thick
  freshly ground pepper

1. Arrange the bread slices on a baking sheet.

2. Mix the garlic with the olive oil, then spread evenly on the bread slices.

3. Slice the cheese and cover the bread slices. Arrange the onion and tomato on the baking sheet. Season with pepper.

4. Place under the broiler until the cheese is soft and just beginning to brown. With a spatula, transfer the tomato slices to the bread, and top with the onion slices. Return to the broiler until bubbling hot and slightly browned.

Cottage Cheese Cakes

makes twelve cakes

2 egg yolks
1 teaspoon chopped chives
1 teaspoon chopped parsley
1 tablespoon grated onions
1 tablespoon grated green pepper
2 cups cold mashed potatoes
2 cups cottage cheese
1 cup fine whole grain bread crumbs
1 whole egg, beaten
  Clarified Butter for frying (see Index)

1. In a bowl beat the egg yolks, chives, parsley, onions and green pepper. Beat in the potatoes and cottage cheese. Shape the mixture into cakes.

2. Roll the cakes in the bread crumbs, dip in the egg, roll again in the crumbs. Chill the cakes in the refrigerator until firm.

3. In a deep skillet heat the butter until hot, then fry the cakes until they are a deep toast brown. Drain and serve very hot.

Cottage Cheese Pancakes

makes six medium pancakes

1 cup cottage cheese
2 eggs, beaten
¼ cup wheat germ
2 tablespoons chopped nuts
2 tablespoons whole wheat flour
2 tablespoons melted butter

1. Mix all ingredients together thoroughly.

2. Cook on a hot griddle. Serve at once with applesauce, syrup or jelly.

Cottage Cheese Sandwich Filling

makes two sandwiches

½ cup cottage cheese
1 tablespoon chopped celery
1 raw carrot, grated
1 tablespoon grated onions
3 tablespoons chopped apple

1. Mix all ingredients thoroughly.

2. Use in sandwiches with lettuce or sprouts and any salad dressing.

Experimenters will like to add all sorts of delicious foods to their cottage cheese and cream cheese sandwich fillings. Here are a few suggestions: chopped walnuts, chopped green pepper, shredded radish or cucumber, chopped dried fruits, lemon or lime juice, crushed pineapple, chopped garden cress.

Cream Cheese Biscuits

makes twenty small biscuits

Use these for fruit shortcakes. They are very tender and delicate.

¾ cup cream cheese, at room temperature
8 tablespoons butter
1 cup whole wheat flour

1. Blend the cream cheese and butter, then work in the flour until the dough is stiff. Chill 1 hour.

2. Preheat oven to 400°F. Roll out the biscuit dough very thin, ¼ inch. Cut out circles with a biscuit cutter and arrange on a baking sheet.

3. Bake 10 or 12 minutes or until light brown on the surface.

Dairy Spinach Shortcake

serves eight

3 tablespoons butter
2 tablespoons chopped onions
3 cups chopped spinach, tightly
    packed
 freshly ground pepper, several turns
1 teaspoon chopped thyme
1 pound ricotta cheese
½ cup cream cheese
3 tablespoons whole wheat flour
1 egg, beaten lightly
 pinch freshly grated nutmeg
 New England Buttermilk Biscuit
    Dough (see Index)
 sour cream

Preheat oven to 375°F.

1. Melt the butter in a skillet and saute the onions until soft. Add the spinach, pepper, thyme and cook until soft. Remove from heat and place in a mixing bowl.

2. Mix the ricotta, cream cheese and flour thoroughly, then stir into the spinach mixture. Stir in the eggs and nutmeg.

3. Roll out the biscuit dough ¼-inch thick and cut 16 circles. Arrange them on the bottom of a greased baking pan. Spread each biscuit generously with the spinach cheese filling.

4. Top with the sour cream, dust with additional pepper and the nutmeg. Bake 20 minutes or until bubbling and hot.

Hot Cottage Cheese and Vegetable Dish

serves four

4 tablespoons butter
½ pound mushrooms, sliced
1 medium-size onion, chopped
1 medium-size green pepper,
    chopped
2 cups cottage cheese
4 eggs
 freshly ground pepper

1. In a heavy skillet heat the butter and saute the mushrooms, onion and green pepper until soft. Mix in the cottage cheese.

2. Beat the eggs slightly, then blend them into the cheese and vegetable mixture. Sprinkle with the pepper, fold over lightly in the pan until the mixture is firm, then serve at once.

    This recipe makes a good filling for stuffed baked tomatoes and peppers, and is good in whole wheat rolls with alfalfa sprouts on the bottom and hot sauce on the top.

Little Ricotta Omelets

serves four with eight small omelets

2 tablespoons whole wheat flour
1 tablespoon water
4 eggs
1 tablespoon butter
½ pound ricotta cheese
2 tablespoons warm water
1 tablespoon grated Parmesan
    cheese
1 cup hot homemade tomato sauce

1. Blend the flour and 1 tablespoon water until smooth. Beat the eggs with a fork and mix thoroughly into the flour mixture.

2. Melt a bit of the butter in an omelet pan and spoon in 3 tablespoons of the egg mixture. Cook on both sides. Repeat until the omelet mixture is gone. Keep the small omelets warm in a low oven.

3. Mix the ricotta, warm water, and Parmesan. Spread on each omelet, then roll the omelets up. Arrange in a wheel spoke pattern on a serving dish. Pour the tomato sauce over the omelets in a ribbon.

Pasta with Ricotta

serves four

1 pound whole wheat macaroni
4 tablespoons butter
1 pound ricotta cheese
½ cup milk
  oregano

1. Cook the macaroni until tender. Drain, return to pot and add the butter.

2. Mix the ricotta with the milk in a bowl until smooth. Pour over the hot macaroni, then simmer over low heat until the mixture is hot and bubbling.

3. Serve in warmed bowls sprinkled with the oregano.

Vegetables

Cottage Cole Slaw

serves six

6 carrots, grated
2 tart apples, peeled, cored and
    grated
1 cup cottage cheese
2 cups finely shredded cabbage
1 tablespoon honey
½ cup yogurt or sour cream
1 tablespoon lemon juice
1 tablespoon grated onions
  pinch celery seed

Combine all ingredients thoroughly. Chill and serve.

Cup Cheese Salad

serves six

1 small head lettuce, broken up, or
    3 cups fresh alfalfa sprouts
6 radishes, sliced thin
¼ cup parsley, tightly packed
3 scallions, chopped
1 stalk celery, chopped
4 tablespoons toasted sesame seeds
3 cups Pennsylvania Dutch Cup
    Cheese (see p. 144)
2 large tomatoes, sliced
1 medium-size cucumber, peeled and
    sliced

1. Combine all ingredients except the cup cheese, tomato and cucumber. Mix and toss well. Arrange in the center of a platter.

2. Turn out the cup cheeses and slice thinly.

3. Arrange the sliced cheese, tomatoes and cucumber slices alternately around the mixed vegetables. Serve with any dressing (see Index).

Eggplant Ricotta Casserole

serves four to six

 2 medium eggplants
½ cup olive oil
½ cup wheat germ
 1 teaspoon chopped oregano
 1 teaspoon chopped basil
 2 tablespoons butter
 1 cup chopped onions
 2 cloves garlic, pressed
 2 pounds ricotta cheese
 1 cup grated farm cheese
 1 quart stewed tomatoes

Preheat oven to 350°F.

1. Cut the eggplants into shoestrings, place in a bowl and pour the olive oil over them. Toss until oil coats the eggplant.

2. Bake the eggplant on an oiled baking sheet until tender, about 10 minutes.

3. Put the eggplant in a mixing bowl, sprinkle with the wheat germ, oregano and basil and toss lightly.

4. Melt the butter in a skillet and saute the onions and garlic until soft. Remove from the heat and mix in the cheeses.

5. Grease a 2½-quart casserole and arrange in it alternating layers of eggplant, tomatoes and cheese mixture, repeating until all the ingredients are used up. Cover and bake, 30 minutes; uncover last 5 minutes. Serve at once.

Garden Pie

serves six

1 unbaked 9-inch pie crust
1 cup mushrooms
5 tablespoons butter
1 garlic clove, pressed
1 cup chopped onions
1 cup finely shredded cabbage
1 cup sliced broccoli or cauliflower
    florets and stems
1 cup chopped turnip or parsnip
  pinch crushed caraway seeds
2 sprigs basil, chopped
1 teaspoon chopped dill
2 tablespoons whole wheat flour
2 tablespoons wine vinegar
2 eggs
½ cup cottage cheese
½ cup cream cheese

Preheat oven to 350°F.

1. Set pie crust aside. Separate the stems and caps of the mushrooms. Slice the caps and set aside. Chop the stems.

2. Melt 3 tablespoons of the butter in a skillet and saute the mushroom stems, garlic, onions, cabbage, broccoli and turnip until tender-crisp. Stir in the caraway seeds, basil and dill. Remove from heat.

3. Sprinkle the vegetables with the flour, mix well, then add the vinegar and toss again.

4. Beat the eggs, then work in the cottage cheese and cream cheese. Stir in the vegetables.

5. Melt the remaining butter in a skillet and saute the mushroom caps.

6. Spread the vegetable-cheese mixture in the pie shell. Top with the mushroom caps, then bake 35 to 40 minutes or until set. Serve hot or warm.

Ricotta Rice

serves four

3 cups cooked brown rice
4 tablespoons chopped green
    onions
1½ cups ricotta cheese
2 garlic cloves, pressed
1 cup sour cream
2 tablespoons milk
½ teaspoon chopped hot pepper
⅓ cup grated farm cheese

Preheat oven to 350°F.

1. Mix the rice and onions.

2. Mix the ricotta, garlic, sour cream, milk and hot pepper, then blend into the rice and onions.

3. Butter a quart casserole, pour in the mixture and top with the grated farm cheese. Bake 25 minutes until the cheese bubbles and the mixture is hot.

Green Pepper Casserole

serves six

This is a summer buffet dish par excellence.

1½ cups boiling Whey (see Index),
    chicken stock or vegetable stock
1½ cups bulgur
  3 tablespoons butter
  1 cup chopped onions
  4 garlic cloves, chopped
  4 cups chopped green peppers
  2 cups sliced mushrooms
  1 teaspoon chopped marjoram
  2 tablespoons wine vinegar
  ½ teaspoon dry mustard
  1 teaspoon grated horseradish
1½ cups cottage cheese
  1 cup grated farm cheese
  4 eggs, lightly beaten

Preheat oven to 350°F.

1. Pour the boiling whey over the bulgur in a bowl and let stand 15 minutes.

2. Melt the butter in a large skillet. Saute the onions and garlic until onions are soft and translucent. Add the peppers and mushrooms and cook until just tender. Remove from the heat.

3. To the cooked vegetables, add the marjoram, vinegar, mustard and horseradish and set aside.

4. Mix the cottage cheese and farm cheese together.

5. Butter a 2½ to 3-quart casserole, then spread the bulgur on the bottom. Add the vegetables as the next layer. Top with the cheese, spreading evenly.

6. Pour the eggs over the mixture. Bake 45 minutes and serve hot.

Stuffed Tomatoes

serves four

4 large tomatoes
1 cup cottage cheese or cream
    cheese
2 tablespoons chopped celery
1 tablespoon chopped chives
1 tart apple, peeled, cored and
    chopped
1 tablespoon raisins

1. Cut the tops off the tomatoes, scoop out the pulp and put in a bowl.

2. Add the remaining ingredients to the pulp, mix thoroughly and stuff into the tomatoes. Chill and serve.

Dressings for Vegetables

Cheese Sauce for Vegetables

yields 3 cups

This tangy sauce is an outstanding complement for all the members of the bean tribe, green, shelled or lima, and adds a memorable note to any cooked vegetable.

1 tablespoon butter
1 garlic clove, pressed
½ cup chopped onions
3 *Beurre Manie* Balls (see Index),
    crumbled into bits
2 cups milk
1 cup grated farm cheese
1 tablespoon tarragon vinegar
½ teaspoon grated horseradish
1 small chili pepper, chopped

1. Melt the butter in a saucepan and saute the garlic and onions until soft.

2. Add the *Beurre Manie*, cook gently 3 minutes while separately warming the milk. Stir the milk into the saucepan mixture, lower heat and cook, stirring often, until thick and smooth.

3. Add the cheese, vinegar, horseradish and chili pepper and heat through thoroughly. Serve at once.

Dairy Salad Dressing

yields 2 cups

1 cup yogurt
1 cup cottage cheese
1 garlic clove, pressed
2 teaspoons lemon juice
1 tablespoon chopped dill
1 teaspoon chopped oregano

Blend ingredients in a blender until smooth. Chill and serve on salads.

Creamy Salad Dressing Francais

yields 1 cup

3 garlic cloves
¼ cup chopped basil, tightly packed
¼ cup olive oil
1 tablespoon tomato paste
   freshly ground pepper
¾ cup cream cheese
2 tablespoons heavy cream

1. Crush the garlic in a wooden bowl. Add the basil. Bruise and work these vigorously until well blended.

2. Constantly beating with a fork, work in the olive oil drop by drop.

3. Work in the tomato paste and pepper.

4. Beat in the cream cheese, moistening with the cream. Serve with any green salad.

Standing Press tor Cheese.

The above illustration shows the method of making a good standing press for cheese factory or private dairy. The construction is so simple that any person familiar with the use of saw and hammer can make it. It consists ot a frame, which is supported on legs and the loose boards on which the hoops stand, and which are grooved to allow the whey to run off. For making a four-hoop press, as shown, it takes five sets of rods and saddles, four heavy press screws and four hoops and followers. The rods pass up one side and over the iron saddles shown on the top of the press and down on the other. Holes are bored through the top timber to allow the screws to project up through when raised to allow the removal of the hoops. The divisions between the hoops are made of two-inch plank and support the upper timber when the screws are raised. The presses can be made any length desired.

56823   Rods, Saddles and Washers, per set.......$1.50
56824   Screws, 1¾ by 20 inches long, per set..... 2.75
   Prices quoted on all sizes of hoops and followers.

Cheese Box Machine.

57016 For the manufacture of material into cheese boxes, machinery of some nature is required. The variety at present are as a rule too intricate and expensive, We have endeavored to present a machine that will meet the requirements of the small as well as the large maker. It has a large capacity, and is moderate in price.
Price, complete.... ......$14.50

Desserts

Banana Cream

serves four

This is outrageously, madly delicious spread on date-nut bread or carrot cake. It is also a dessert in its own right. Experimenters might like to substitute peaches for the bananas.

4 ripe, brown-spotted bananas
½ cup cream cheese
2 tablespoons heavy cream
3 tablespoons maple syrup
5 tablespoons currant jam
3 tablespoons chopped almonds

1. Mash the bananas in a bowl with a fork until smooth. Work in the cream cheese and the cream until the mixture is thick and fluffy.

2. Mix in the maple syrup.

3. Heap the mixture on a dish. Smooth the surface and cover with jam. Sprinkle all over with the chopped almonds. Chill several hours and serve cold.

Cheese Pudding

serves four

1½ cups cottage cheese
¾ cup heavy cream
1 tablespoon honey
  juice of 1 lemon
  rind of 1 lemon, grated
  cinnamon

1. Blend the cheese in a blender until smooth, then blend the cream, honey, lemon juice and ¾ of the grated rind 30 seconds.

2. Pour into sherbet glasses, sprinkle the remaining rind and the cinnamon on top and chill until firm.

Curds and Whey

This simple dish clears up a mystery for many children, for this is the curds and whey that Miss Muffet was eating when the uninvited spider sidled up beside her. The dish is simply cottage cheese, or "curds," served in a shallow dish of whey with heavy cream poured over the top and a lacing of honey traced across the surface. It is still enjoyed in England.

French Pot Cream

This fine, sprightly cheese dish has several uses. It can be unmolded on a serving dish and surrounded like a *Coeur a la Creme* with fresh cherries, strawberries or other fruit in season. It is also excellent in sandwiches with lettuce and tomatoes or other sandwich timber. Cut into cubes, it adds interest and texture to fruit and vegetable salads. Diced very small it is marvelous with a dish of garden fresh green peas.

2 cups cottage cheese
2 cups sour cream
2 cups heavy cream
  freshly ground pepper (optional)

1. Put the cottage cheese in a blender and blend until smooth.

2. Put the sour cream in a bowl, add the cottage cheese and mix. Vigorously beat in the cream. (Add the pepper at this point if the pot cream is to be used for sandwiches and salads.)

3. Line a colander with damp cheesecloth and pour in the cheese-sour cream mixture. Cover and let drain overnight in the refrigerator in a deep bowl.

4. Unmold on a serving dish.

Homestead Cheesecake

serves ten

¼ cup wheat germ
1 teaspoon powdered cinnamon
8 eggs
4 cups cottage cheese
3 tablespoons lemon juice
1 cup yogurt
1 cup honey
¼ cup whole wheat flour

Preheat oven to 350°F.

1. Mix together the wheat germ and cinnamon, then sprinkle this over a very heavily buttered 9-inch springform pan. Roll and shake the pan until the inside is evenly coated. Chill in the refrigerator.

2. Beat the eggs until foamy and thick. Gradually beat in the cottage cheese. Stir in the lemon juice, yogurt, honey and flour.

3. Pour the batter into the springform pan and bake 1 hour. Turn the oven heat off but leave cake in the oven another 2 hours without opening the door.

4. Chill overnight in the refrigerator.

Low-Fat Cheesecake

makes one 9-inch cake

4 eggs
4 cups ricotta cheese
1 cup skim buttermilk
½ cup honey
1 teaspoon vanilla extract
2 tablespoons lemon juice
1 teaspoon grated lemon rind
  pinch powdered cardamom

Preheat oven to 375°F with a shallow pan of water on the bottom of the oven.

1. Beat the eggs until light, then blend in the remaining ingredients, beating until the batter is light.

2. Grease a 9-inch springform pan, pour in the batter and bake 45 minutes.

3. Cool the cake, then chill several hours before serving.

Raspberry Parfait

serves two

1 cup raspberries
½ cup cream cheese
½ cup yogurt
1 tablespoon maple syrup

1. Crush the berries in a bowl and set aside.

2. Blend the remaining ingredients, beating hard until they are light.

3. Into parfait glasses spoon first a layer of berries, then the cream mixture, then the berries until all is used in multiple layers.

Natural Cake Icing

makes 2 cups

1 cup honey
1 cup cream cheese
1 teaspoon vanilla or almond extract

Beat all ingredients with an electric beater until thick and creamy and of a good spreading consistency. Use at once, topped with chopped nuts, shredded coconut, chopped dried fruits or all of these combined.

Strawberry-Rose Petal Sauce

yields about 4 cups

This delicate and unusual sauce comes from Linda Applegate of Perrysville, Ohio. She uses it over vanilla ice cream, pound cake or cheesecake. We have discovered that is ambrosial in a Rose Petal Sundae, over Rose Water Ice Cream (see Index).

 2 cups strawberries
 1 cup honey
 1 cup rose petals (these must be
        the old-fashioned fragrant
        "shrub" roses)
¾ cup cream cheese, at room
        temperature
½ cup heavy cream, whipped

1. Put the strawberries, honey and rose petals in a blender and blend until smooth.

2. Blend in the cream cheese.

3. By hand fold in the whipped cream. Serve at once.

Traditional Coeur a la Creme, or "Cream Heart"

This beautiful dessert, molded in a heart-shaped cheese basket or metal mold, has a special meaning on Valentine's Day.

1 pound cottage cheese
1 pound cream cheese
2 cups heavy cream
2 cups strawberries, raspberries or
        other berries in season,
        crushed

1. Cream together the cottage cheese and cream cheese, then gradually beat in the heavy cream.

2. Line a colander with damp cheesecloth and pack the mixture in; cover and let it drain in the refrigerator 6 hours.

3. Line a metal heart-shaped mold with damp cheesecloth, then pack the firm cheese mixture in. Chill several more hours, or until firm.

4. To serve, unmold on a serving plate and gently peel away the cheesecloth. Pass the bowl of berries for each guest to spoon on his/her portion. This is accompanied, traditionally, by warm French bread straight from the oven.

What to Do with the Whey?

Composition of Cheese Whey	%
total solids	6.35
fat	0.5
protein	0.8
lactose	4.85
ash	0.5
lactic acid	0.05
water	93.7

Whey is a pleasant-tasting, nutritious substance which contains about 50 percent of the nutrients that appear in whole milk—lactose, vitamins, minerals and soluble protein. It is an excellent food.

Since very early times people have been drinking whey and using it in the kitchen. From Hippocrates' days to modern times whey has been prescribed and used as a preventive and curative for a number of human ailments including dyspepsia, uremia, arthritis and gout. In the nineteenth century there were more than 400 whey spas in Europe catering to believers in whey cures. Today whey continues to be popular in Europe as a major ingredient in a number of commercially produced beverages. In Switzerland, Rivella, a crystal clear whey drink flavored with alpine herbs sells more than 30 million litres a year. In Poland, one among several whey beverages is a non-alcoholic, bubbly whey "champagne." Dozens of other whey beverages, both sparkling and still, are consumed throughout Europe, from Russia to England.

In this country, although researchers at several universities have come up with nutritious whey beverages which ranked high with taste-testing panels, commercial ventures into the whey-drink market are rare, for it is more profitable to produce and sell sugared, artificially flavored, carbonated "soft drinks."

Commercial whey beverages in Europe are usually pasteurized and clarified, then mixed with various fruit, herb or vegetable juices and perhaps carbonated. In this country, at the University of Michigan, a whey drink called "O-way" was developed as a breakfast beverage, a vitamin-packed, nutritious mixture of orange juice and whey. At the University of Arizona, whey mixed with peach and grapefruit juice delighted the palates of tasters; another excellent mixture included vinifera grape juice, whey and passion fruit juice. Other tested whey drinks have included tomato juice, prune juice and carrot juice. Whey has a particular affinity for citrus juices, and when other fruit or vegetable juices are used in combination, a dash of lemon or grapefruit juice adds interest and zest.

USES FOR WHEY FROM THE HOME DAIRY

- Drink it unadorned, chilled or hot—a satisfying, nutritious, snack drink.
- Mix it with apple cider, orange or grapefruit juice, with pineapple, peach, apricot, prune, grape, berry and other juices enlivened with a touch of lemon. Mix it with carrot, celery or tomato juice. Experiment with mint, sweet woodruff and other herbs and spices.
- Use whey in soup or gravy stock for rich, fuller-flavored results. Replace water or milk in recipes with whey. Use whey as the liquid ingredient in cakes, pies, pancakes, waffles, muffins, breads, steamed puddings, gelatin salads, casseroles, scalloped vegetables and soups.
- Use fresh whey to make whey cheeses, including ricotta and *mysost* (see box). Mysost is a mild and sweet Scandinavian delicacy made from whey by long, slow cooking until the water content has evaporated, leaving behind a golden, buttery spread composed of caramelized lactose, fat, minerals and protein. When the same cheese is made from goats' milk, it is called *gjetost*.
- Whey can be fed to livestock. Not only piglets and calves but most young animals including kittens and puppies, thrive and grow on whey.

Mysost

makes ½ pound

Mysost is a Scandinavian whey cheese which has dozens of local variations on the major theme, including making it with whole milk, as well as adding honey, cloves or cumin seed. Additions are made at the time the albumin is returned to the kettle.

2 quarts cows' milk whey

1. Strain the whey into a stainless steel kettle and cook *very slowly* over direct but low heat. Stir frequently and skim off the foamy albumin that rises to the surface. Set this skimmed material aside.

2. Cook until the whey is reduced to one-quarter its original volume. It should have the consistency of heavy cream. This may take 5 hours or longer. Bigger batches take longer than do small ones.

3. Return the skimmed material to the kettle and stir it in vigorously. Continue to cook until the whey is light brown and very thick.

4. Put the kettle in a sink of cold water and beat the whey vigorously until it has the consistency of butter.

5. Pour it into a greased mold and cool it. When it is firm, unmold the cheese and wrap it in foil.

8 *BUTTER*

Making butter in the small home dairy is usually a seasonal project— it is done during spring and summer when there is a surplus of milk—but the butter can be stored in a freezer and supply the family all year long. Making butter is a traditional and good way to utilize a perishable product.

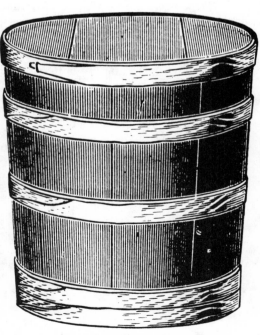

How much butter you'll get per pound of milk depends on the butterfat content of the whole milk, the fineness of separation of butterfat from skim milk, bacteria, the effectiveness of the churn, and critical temperatures throughout the process — they all play a part in the conversion of milk into butter. It takes one quart of 40 percent cream to make a pound of butter, so the ideal is to have dairy animals yielding good amounts of butterfat per gallon of milk. The more butterfat, the more butter; Jersey and Guernsey cows, whose milk contains high ratios of butterfat, are known as the best butter cows of all.

Home butter making is an easily learned skill and can be made nearly foolproof by following several logical steps with care: separating and holding the cream; churning the cream; washing, working and molding the butter. All of these steps have certain sanitary procedures linked with them.

FIRST YOU SEPARATE THE CREAM

Butter *can* be churned from whole milk, but it takes time, a lot of work, and you don't get very much for your efforts. A much more efficient method is first to concentrate that which becomes butter — butterfat — into cream before starting the churning process. Called *cream separation*, it is done commercially in giant centrifuges, but at the home level there are simpler ways. Easiest on the equipment pocketbook, but not the most efficient way, is *gravity* creaming. More efficient are the home versions of the creamery giants — centrifugal hand or "farm" cream separators which once were commonplace in rural North America but are now almost impossible to find except at country auctions.

GRAVITY CREAMING

The ideal place for gravity creaming is a springhouse or old dairy room where the temperature is no higher than 55°F and the atmosphere is free from flies and odors. A clean, cool cellar will do, although most modern cellars are musty or smell of fuel oil; root cellars are scented with onions, cabbage or apples. Milk and cream are extremely sensitive to aromas and will quickly absorb undesirable taints. A shaded and screened back porch might seem a good place, but moving air carries dust through the screening. Moreover, air currents will cause the cream to toughen and crust over. But if you have a clean, cool place on your homestead, you can try gravity creaming. Call this place the *separating room* and use it for no other purpose.

Shallow-Pan Method of Gravity Creaming

1. As soon as the animals are milked, twice daily, pour the milk into shallow pans — stoneware, stainless steel or glass no deeper than 4 inches are best — in the separating room and let them stand undisturbed for 36 hours.

2. At the end of this period most of the cream will have risen to the surface of the pans; remove it with a skimmer used only for that purpose. Goats' milk will take much longer — up to 72 hours.

3. Cool-store the cream in a cream can until you have enough for churning. Creams separated by this method have kept sound for 6 days when cooled at 40°F, but that seems to be the luckiest absolute limit. Cream exposed to the air for such long periods faces terrible bacterial odds.

Deep-Can Method of Gravity Creaming

This method, popular in the late nineteenth century, was known as the deep-set, shotgun, Swedish or Cooley system. It gave better and faster results than the older shallow-pan method. How effective deep-can separation is depends on the available supply of cold water; 40°F is the ideal, with 55°F as the high mark. Under optimum chilling conditions it's possible to separate out all but 0.2 percent or 0.3 percent butterfat in a 24-hour period. The traditional cans (and still the best) are the tinned 4-gallon shotgun cans which feature one-piece, lipped, tightly fitting tops — important, for the cans go into the cold water right to the top. They get their name from their vague resemblance to shotgun shells.

1. Have the milk can cooler filled with water as cold as you can get it and keep it. If you have a supply of ice, add it to the water.

2. While the milk is still warm from the animal, fill the cans, cap them tightly and plunge them into the icy water so that they cool rapidly. Let them stand undisturbed for 24 hours.

3. At the end of 24 hours use a sterile section of plastic tubing to siphon the cream into a glass pitcher. Start the siphon just below the surface, moving it down slowly until you reach the lighter, blueish skimmed milk.

4. Store the cream in a can maintained at the same cold temperature. You can keep a week's separations easily this way, then churn all the cream at once.

During the late 1800s when dairy herds in New England supplied numerous creameries, there was a commercial refinement of the shotgun system. Named the Cooley Creamer after its manufacturer, the device consisted of a cold water chest fitted with crank-powered elevators used to raise and lower the cream cans. The chests were generally cooled by deep spring water, an ideal source that was cold all year round, but the cans were different than most shotguns. Just beneath the top rim the cans were fitted with narrow windows which extended down to a point below a maximum cream line. At the side of the window was a simple scale calibrated in inches. When the creamery hauler arrived for the pickup, he would first measure

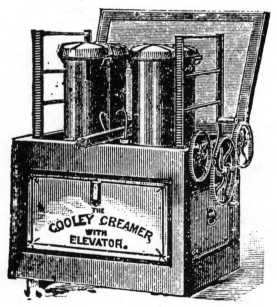

The Cooley Creamer with Elevator illustrates the famous deep-can method of gravity creaming. Four-gallon shotgun cans were filled with warm milk fresh from the cow, then submerged in cold water of 55°F. The cream rose in 24 hours and made excellent butter. A labor-saving elevator allowed the farmer to raise the cans with ease.

the inches of cream in each can before drawing it off. At the end of the month when the cream checks were sent out, the dairy farmer was paid according to the total number of inches collected. The cans were all uniform.

Hydraulic Creaming

Today this system is considered impractical and unethical, but it was used in the past on farms with cream-only markets.

Pour cold water into a can or crock of warm fresh milk. The amount of water is from one-quarter to one-half the volume of milk. Let it stand several hours, then draw the cream off the top, or, in the case of crocks with spigots, drain off the watery skim milk through the bottom, changing containers when the cream starts to pass through.

Known as the water dilution system for obvious reasons, this was the fastest of the gravity creaming systems, for when cold water is mixed with milk, the cream rises much more rapidly to the surface than it does with milk alone, usually in 3 hours. Yet there were serious drawbacks to the system: first, it intentionally adulterated a good food product, the skim milk, which had nutritional value to the farm family or livestock; then, the cream was usually on the thin side and the butter it made had little character; finally, any speed gained in the separation was lessened by the extended butter churning time and labor. Furthermore, if impure water was used, it resulted in bacterial infection, and the whole operation was a loss.

HAND CREAM SEPARATING

Following its invention and gradually increasing popularity in Europe in the late nineteenth century, the mechanical implement which separated cream from milk by centrifugal force gained a place in milkrooms all over North America. Usually called "farm separators" to differentiate them from the larger creamery separators, there were more than a dozen makes on the market at the turn of the century. The earliest ones were hand powered, but later models were electrified. Names like Sharples, Omega, Reid and Davis don't echo around the farm auctions much any more, but there are still sturdy models from yesteryear cranking out cream in small dairy operations today.

Depending on the condition and cleanliness of the separator and the accuracy of its cream setting, an operator can get creams of up to 50 percent butterfat. As with most adjustable machines used to process raw materials, the separator grows in effectiveness along with the experience of the operator. Creams of 30 percent and 40 percent make good butter, and since separator creams are made in just a fraction of the time it takes for gravity separation, the freshness of the cream usually assures lower bacteria counts and better quality butter. Though thicker cream churns faster than thinner cream, a 50 percent cream is hard to handle in cold weather. Too thick to pour, it must be ladled or spooned out, and you never seem to get all of it out of the can.

Setting Up the Separator

1. Pick a location away from animals, manure, dust, chaff, a frequently opened and closed door or any other place where there is a danger of increasing the bacteria in the milk. A proper dairy room, clean, sanitized, odorless, and with a good water supply and floor drain is best.

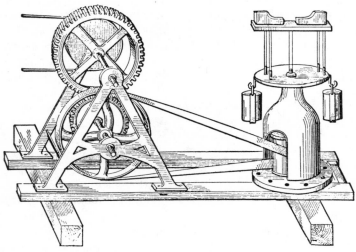

A drawing of the first centrifugal cream separator, an experimental German machine dating to the mid-nineteenth century. Two buckets of milk hung from the arms at the edge of the rotating flat plate and were whirled round and round for a while. When the machine was stopped, a good amount of the cream was on the surface and could be skimmed off. Hundreds of separator designs emerged until the efficient design of Baron Bechtelsheim of Munich was bought up by the De Laval Company and mass-produced to become the major cream separator.

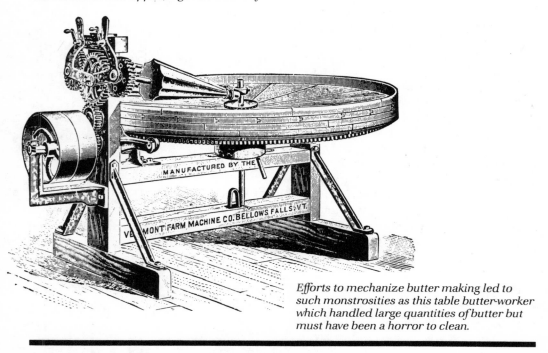

Efforts to mechanize butter making led to such monstrosities as this table butter-worker which handled large quantities of butter but must have been a horror to clean.

2. The floor, preferably concrete, must be sturdy and level, as the machine is powered by a spinning crank or pulley in one direction while building up terrific centrifugal force in another direction. If out of plumb and poorly secured, parts will wear unevenly, ending inevitably in a breakdown. Use a level and steel washers — not pieces of wood — as shims to correct the level, and then secure the separator to the floor with lag screws or bolts.

3. Assemble the separator. If the machine is new, follow the manufacturer's directions. If the machine is second-hand, you should have received the manual from the former owner. Separators are fairly complicated and the instructions, remedies for malfunctions, and especially the parts list, were once kept somewhere not too far away from the machine. When buying a separator, *always ask for the manual — it's part of the machine*. If no manual is available and the machine is an International Harvester, copies of the manual are available through the mail (see Index). If you pick up another brand at auction without a manual, you may find one which can be photocopied at the library of your state university or in extension service files.

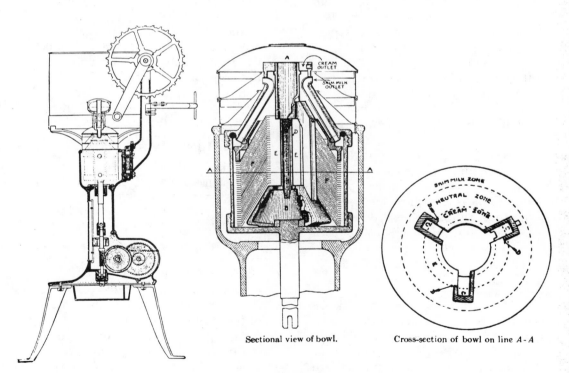

Sectional view of bowl.

Cross-section of bowl on line *A - A*

An early twentieth century International Harvester cream separator. If you bought one at an auction without the manual of diagrams and instructions, here are the essential parts.

4. Fill the oiler to the proper level. The usual indicator is a small window—either round or square—located in the frame, and the correct amount of oil is indicated when the level bisects the window on an idle machine. Keeping the reservoir filled and the oil clean is very important with all separators, as the moving parts must be thoroughly lubricated for the machine to work properly. A special separator oil was available in the days when every farm had a separator, but today we use light gear oil or transmission fluid. Depending on use, the separator should be checked for oil condition at least four times a year. Foul oil causes friction and wear, and the associated lag affects the performance in fineness of separation. If the oil is excessively dirty, flush the system after draining it by closing the drain cock and filling the reservoir very carefully with kerosene. Do this outside the dairy room and carefully wrap the rest of the separator in plastic to avoid kerosene contamination. Crank the handle or turn on the motor for a minute so the spinning worm wheel sprays the cleanser over all moving parts; after the machine comes to a stop of its own accord, drain off the kerosene and fill with fresh oil. *Be careful not to spill any kerosene on the separator as it will taint the cream.*

5. Check the set screw. The thickness of the cream is controlled by a small set screw located in the neck of the bowl shell. With De Laval models, for instance, this screw is identified by its square recess—it was designed to take a small square driver, but a small standard screwdriver fitted corner to corner

works just as well. If the machine has never been operated by you, don't touch the screw until one batch of milk has been run through. Separators of recent manufacture have the screws factory-set for optimum separation, but the same can be said for second-hand machines from someone's farm. These older machines are probably set for the higher cream ranges, but a possible exception might be a separator rebuilt by a person other than a factory-trained mechanic. If, after the first run, the cream is too thin, turn the screw counterclockwise to make it thicker. If it's too thick, and in the winter that's possible, turn the screw clockwise. Turn it just a little— $\frac{1}{16}$ of an inch is about right one way or the other—until it's correct. If you are going to separate goats' milk, you will probably have to fiddle with the screw until you get the right and optimum setting.

Separating Goats' Milk

To separate goats' milk, the cream regulating screw on the separator should be set fine enough to recover ¾ pint of cream from each gallon of milk. If such a setting were used for cows' milk, the cream would be as thick as soft paste.

---

6. Examine the bowl. Before starting the separator be sure that the bowl is at the correct height. This is done by removing the supply can and regulating cover and pressing down on the cream cover. The line around the neck of the bowl should be level with the top edge of the cream cover. If it is too high or too low, remove the lock nut and washer from the base of the worm screw housing and turn the screw up or down with a wrench until the neck and cream cover are aligned. If this is not done, the cream and skim milk will not enter the covers correctly. Then return the regulating cover to its original position.

7. Position the cream and skim milk spouts above the collecting containers, seat the float in the neck of the regulating cover and affix the supply can to the holder. The supply can faucet should be directly over the float. When the faucet is opened, the regulating can fills, causing the float to rise and control the amount of milk entering the machine.

Making the Run

Have on hand a couple of quarts of warm water, the supply of milk to be separated (at 85° to 90°F is an optimum temperature) and enough containers to handle the cream and skim milk you will process, then turn on the radio if you like and pull up a chair. Cranking a separator is a sit-down job. (Some people may prefer to stand.)

1. Start the machine by turning the crank slowly, gradually bringing it up to the correct operating speed over several minutes. Most separators are equipped with a bell or cricket which sounds a warning until the correct speed is reached, or if the pace slackens off during operation. The speed of turning should be steady and rhythmic, somewhere between 40 and 60 rpms, or whatever it takes to stay just ahead of the ringing bell.

2. When the separator is up to speed, warm it by pouring some of the warm

water directly into the regulating cover. This will pass out through the skim milk spout. Now check to see that the supply can faucet is closed, then fill the can with the milk to be separated.

3. When half of the warm water has been discharged, turn on the supply faucet and continue cranking—and refilling the supply can with milk—until all the milk is separated.

4. Keep up the same cranking pace and pour 2 more quarts of warm water into the supply can. This will wash out any butterfat stranded on the machine parts when the milk ran through the creaming and skimming disks.

5. Release the crank and let the machine slow down and stop of its own accord. A running separator should never be stopped manually by jamming the crank, nor should it be started with uneven, jackrabbit starts and jerks. This kind of abuse leads to bent shafts and broken gears.

Cleaning Up

It's desirable to have in the same room as the separator a large, double-tub laundry-type sink, a good supply of hot and cold water, and a stove for heating scalding water nearby. Cleansing agents can be sodium carbonate (washing soda) or one of the commercial dairy equipment sanitizers (see Index). *Household soaps and detergents are not recommended.* They will leave a film on tinned surfaces, and the perfumes in these products intended to make them appealing to housewives will unpleasantly taint the milk and cream. Follow this cleanup procedure.

1. Remove the supply can, disassemble the bowl so that the discs and other components exposed to the milk can get individual attention. Always rinse them in cool water first, then scrub them thoroughly with hot water, a cleanser and a brush. Don't be tempted to take a shortcut by rinsing with hot water or scalding right off under the impression that water at that temperature will devastate all bacteria. It might, but what also will happen is that the milk albumins will be cooked onto the metal to such a degree that very strong dairy acids will be needed to get them off. Acid cleansers are best avoided as they have a cumulative corrosive effect on parts coated with tin, eventually exposing the metal core to rust. It is a standard dairy rule always to rinse any machine part or implement that has been in contact with milk in *cool water first* to rinse away milky residues. After the cool rinse, the hot scrub-down with detergent and the hot rinse, you are ready to scald.

2. Thwart rust by scalding the separator parts in extremely hot water, and then hang them up to dry. Never stack wet discs or reassemble the bowl with wet parts or you'll have a new project for the tinsmith in short order. Do not wipe the parts dry with a dishtowel—this spreads bacteria from one contaminated part to many clean ones. When they were originally sold, separators came with special brushes, disc washing holders and oddly shaped wire handles to make cleaning all the parts easier. These probably have disappeared over the years, but they are easily replaced with regular bottle brushes for cleaning faucets, spouts· and covers, and with improvised special handles from heavy-gauge wire.

HOLDING THE CREAM

Keeping the cream sound and fresh until you have accumulated enough to churn butter is often a problem for people who separate milk in small amounts daily or every other day with the plan of churning at the week's end. Depending on the number and type of dairy animals you milk, you may be dealing with a few pints of goats' cream or quarts of cows' cream. If the milk was wholesome and the cream made under rigidly sanitary conditions, small amounts can be safely stored in the refrigerator, tightly covered of course.

Speedily reduce the temperature of the separated cream by placing the can in a container of ice water before storing it in the refrigerator. Surrounding the warm can's total surface with cold water is a better way to swiftly conduct heat out of the cream than enveloping it with cold but very still refrigerator air. Be sure the cream can has a tightly fitting cover to exclude refrigerator odors.

In the old days, farms without refrigeration kept fairly large amounts of cream cool and sound in cans bathed to their tops by water chilled to 40°F with ice from the icehouse. An alternative then was to salt the cream heavily to preserve it until churning. Modern alternatives are freezing and pasteurization.

FREEZING

Cream freezes well, and the home deep freezer is a good tool for the small producer building up a cream supply for later churning. As with other cold storage practices, it's good to have tight-fitting lids to keep out freezer odors. Heavy food-grade plastic containers are recommended as they will stand up under a lot of freezing and thawing, and they're easier to clean than the more coarsely finished lightweight plastics. Try to use containers that the day's cream take will almost fill up, without vast amounts of air space but still leaving an inch or so for freezing expansion. It's better to have a dozen small containers of frozen cream, than to add to one large container all through the week. Small containers will thaw faster when butter-making day comes.

Avoid using the lightweight plastic "throwaway" commercial milk containers—they do not stand up under freezer temperatures and expanding frozen liquids. Moreover, their narrow necks mean a funnel is needed to fill them—yet another piece of equipment to clean and another source of possible bacterial infection—and they are very difficult to get thoroughly clean. They hold sour odors forever.

1. Sterilize the containers with a commercial dairy sterilizing solution (see Index), fill them with the cream from the separator or pasteurizer, cool quickly in very cold water, then place them in the freezer. Pasteurizing the cream now before freezing will save time later if you plan on making sweet cream butter or soured cream butter cultured with a commercial starter. Do not pasteurize the cream if you plan to make naturally soured cream butter.

2. When churning time arrives, take the containers out of the freezer and let them thaw at room temperature. Use a dairy thermometer to check the temperature as it warms up. You'll want to keep cream a little cooler for goats' butter, for it will have smaller globules of butterfat that are slower to come than the larger fat globules in cows' milk. Chillier temperatures help the butter form.

Shaker Butter

The Shaker Manuscript at the Fruitlands and Wayside Museum in Harvard, Massachusetts, contains the following advice:

To Make Good Butter in the Spring or Winter When the Cows Are Feeding on Hay

For a sufficient quantity of cream to make ten or twelve pounds of butter, take four or five carrots (according to size) make them perfectly clean by washing and scraping, grate them with or on a grater such as you would use for horseradish; then put carrots in a quart or three pints of the new milk, squeeze out the juice and put it into the churn with the cream. It gives the butter a fine color and a very sweet taste.

PASTEURIZATION

People without freezers or with freezers that are full to the top, find that pasteurization and refrigerator storage will allow the cream to be held for later churning for almost a week. Pasteurization is simple with the small pressure or heat-style pasteurizing units designed especially for the home dairy. The smallest one, however, takes a half gallon of milk or cream—still too capacious for someone with only a pint or two of cream. A small amount of cream can be pasteurized at home without a pasteurizer this way.

1. Place the cream in the top of a double boiler, allowing the top pot to touch the water in the bottom compartment. Bring the cream temperature up to 180°F and hold this temperature for 40 minutes, then reduce the temperature as rapidly as possible by setting the cream pot in very cold water.

A primitive pasteurizer. One of the biggest problems with these early pasteurizers was their tendency to scorch the milk.

2. Add this pasteurized cream daily to a cream can which is stored in the refrigerator tightly closed. You should be able to hold the cream for a week.

If your goal is a naturally soured butter, do not pasteurize the final batch of cream but put it aside for use as a naturally soured starter (see Index). (Or, you can pasteurize the cream and use a commercial starter culture if the natural bacteria are not important to you.)

SWEET CREAM BUTTER OR SOURED CREAM BUTTER?

Both sweet cream butter and soured, or ripened, cream butter are suited to the home dairy, depending on the butter maker's preference. Sweet cream butter is simply the massed, washed and shaped butterfat from a quantity of sweet cream. Soured cream butter is made from cream that has developed a definite acidity through the natural or deliberately introduced action of benign bacteria. Most unpasteurized cream will sour naturally if left in a warm place 24 hours, and this cream will make a natural soured cream butter. Pasteurized or fresh raw cream can be purposely soured by adding either a commercial bacterial culture and allowing it to grow, or by adding a home-grown bacterial culture and letting it develop. The bacterial cultures are called *starters*.

Although the range of butter flavors will never come close to the taste spectrum of cheeses, there are different flavors, gradually acquired and deeply rooted in individual ideas of what ideal flavors should be. Unfortunately, salt has formed the basis of much butter taste; for people accustomed to salted butter, sweet cream butter may seem to be lacking in character at first, while soured cream butter without salt may taste too ripe. The prejudice passes, however, and even salt-indoctrinated butter tasters soon discover that the fresh and fragrant pleasures of sweet cream butter, and the brisk, tasty flavor of soured cream butter have their merits. Our taste for soured cream butter goes back many centuries to the days when most milk was hand-squeezed from teats into wooden buckets teeming with lactic-acid-producing bacteria, and from there went to wooden cream separation tubs where it sat exposed to the air for a day or so. Then the cream went into another wooden bucket for transport to the wooden churn where dashers of wood made the butter. Washing and working the butter was done in wooden bowls or

Firm Butter without Ice

This interesting set of instructions comes from the Shaker *Manifesto* of 1879, a rich compendium of practical knowledge:

> In families where the dairy is small, a good plan to have butter cool and firm without ice is by the process of evaporation, as practiced in India and other warm countries. A cheap plan is to get a very large-sized, porous, earthen flower-pot with a large saucer. Half fill the saucer with water, set it in a trivet or light stand — such as is used for holding hot irons will do; upon this set your butter; over the whole invert the flower-pot, letting the top rim of it rest in and be covered by the water, then close the hole in the bottom of the flower-pot with a cork, then dash water over the flower-pot, and repeat the process several times a day, or whenever it looks dry. If set in a cool place or where the wind can blow on it, it will readily evaporate the water from the pot, and the butter will be as firm and cool as if from an icehouse.

on a wooden board with bare hands or wooden butter paddles, the so-called Scotch hands. The product was finally pressed in a wooden butter mold or packed into wooden butter tubs. Such butter was fated to be a ripened product from the moment the first squirt of milk hit the bucket.

Some of the ripened butter was good, some indifferent, and some frightful — ruined by an overwhelming tide of undesirable microorganisms that conquered the benign bacteria responsible for the desirable clean, acid flavor. Butter makers, at the mercy of these invisible organisms, ascribed the butter that went wrong to the cow's diet or disposition, to witches, the weather and a hundred other sources. But by the time butter making moved off the farm and into the creameries, the commercial production of laboratory-isolated cultures was underway. These

The butter tub. This tub had to soak in brine overnight before use. The paper liner and cover circle that fit inside the tub also soaked overnight in brine. Just before the tub was used, the brine was poured off and the tub scalded with boiling water, then cooled with cold water. It was lined with the brine-soaked paper and was then ready for the butter.

Jersey Butter

The enthusiastic owner of a herd of Jersey cows whose milk he made into choice butter in Pomfret, Vermont, visited Michigan in 1874 and came home outraged by the butter he saw in his travels. The local farm paper reported his views this way:

> Mr. Tinkham said he was in Michigan some time ago, and while there, about two months, never tasted a bit of good butter. It was white, bad colored and poor in texture. This is caused largely by the feed which the cows get. Nearly all through the state they feed in low, swampy lands.

Valley Farmer
(Windsor, Vt.),
Feb. 21, 1874

A tower of butter containers for shipping the perishable stuff to market.

cultures were used in Danish creameries during the late nineteenth century and their popularity spread swiftly across Europe and to North America. By the early twentieth century 10 firms in the United States alone were manufacturing starters for the butter industry.

Today commercial cultured starters for making butter and many other dairy products can be ordered from cheese and dairy supply stores. Most of these cultures contain the acid-producing bacteria *Streptococcus diacetilactis*, or a combination of *S. diacetilactis* and *Leuconostoc citrovorum*. These starters give a clean, acid flavor to butter, especially the diacetyl, which is an important butter flavor constituent; they also increase the yield of butterfat slightly, and safeguard the butter against invading enemy bacteria by their sheer numbers.

One disadvantage of soured cream butter, one that is not a problem with sweet cream butter, is that it is prone to oxidation and off-flavors if metal ions, particularly copper and other heavy metals, are present or in contact with the butterfat.

NATURAL STARTERS

If you choose to stay away from the store and commercial products, making your own natural starter is easy to do, but there is always the risk that bacteria which give off-flavors will dominate the benign bacteria you wish to encourage.

1. Pour fresh milk into a sterile pint jar, cover it and let it stand at 70° to 75°F until pleasantly sour, about 24 to 48 hours. The milk will have thickened into a smooth, uniform clabber with mild acidity, good aroma and clean taste. You must make this starter with *raw milk* which contains no antibiotics; pasteurization will kill off all the beneficial souring bacteria as well as the harmful organisms.

2. Now mix the soured milk into half a gallon of recently pasteurized skim milk. Here the pasteurization ensures a clean medium for your homemade culture. Cover the container and allow it to stand in a warm place, 70° to 75°F until the milk forms a thick, smooth coagulum, usually 12 to 36 hours later. This is your starter.

3. Freeze the starter in several sterile ice cube trays, then store the frozen starter cubes in a plastic bag in the freezer. Each cube can culture a quart of cream.

NATURAL SOURING WITHOUT STARTER CULTURE

If you are the naturally confident type, you may not want to bother with a starter, but let each batch of cream sour on its own before churning. Of course you run the risk of losing the whole batch and the labor that went into making it, but that's the chance you take.

Place the can of sweet cream to be churned in a warm place until it sours. During a northern winter, a good place is behind the woodstove. Allow 24 hours or until the cream develops a pleasant acidity and aroma. The cream must be raw, not pasteurized, for a natural souring to take place, and any minute traces of antibiotic in the cream mean total failure. If the cream spoils instead of ripening, don't even try to make butter from it. You've lost the game.

CULTURING THE CREAM WITH A STARTER

If the behind-the-stove project failed, you are probably interested in cultured starters. Make the starter as described above, either with a homemade milk sample or with commercial freeze-dried starter.

1. Inoculate each quart of cream with one ounce of starter. If you are using frozen starter cubes (one ounce each), allow them to thaw first at room temperature. Both starter and cream should be between 70° and 75°F. Cover the cream and let it stand undisturbed at room temperature until the acidity is to your taste, about 24 hours.

2. Chill the ripened cream in an ice water bath to about 55°F for goats' cream, and 62°F for cows' cream. Now you are ready to churn.

CHURNING

The final stages of the butter-making operation are pretty much the same, whether sweet or acid cream is used, whether commercial starter or natural ripening, whether goats' cream or cows' cream, whether Toggenberg, Nubian, Holstein or Jersey. The equipment materials and models differ, and goats' cream generally comes into butter at lower temperatures than cows' cream, but basically in the

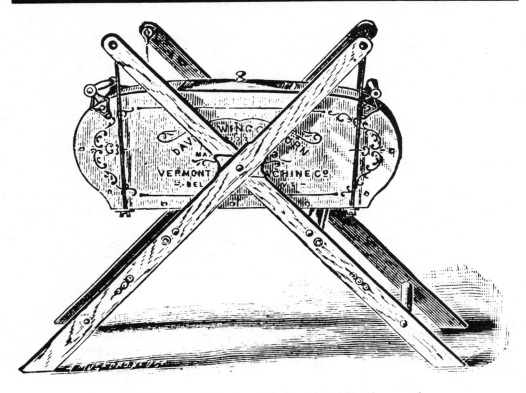

A swing churn, one of dozens of designs that fell by the wayside.

home dairy it's a dasher driven by arm or motor which makes the butter. Here are the methods of two experienced butter makers—Jill McCullough, a New Hampshire dairyist who has exhibited the results of her craft, and Howard Dickinson, a longtime dairy farmer in western Massachusetts.

SETTING UP

It is most important to plan out your butter production program in advance and set up the needed materials, because it's a nuisance trying to keep one step ahead of the game as you go along. It is,

for example, "like trying to get your wrappers laid out when your hands are all buttery," Jill notes, and Howard adds, "or you're there with a sticky mold and no pot of cold water."

1. Pick a place with access to running water, a sink, a stove and a table. If you use a table model churn, the table should be large enough to hold the churn and still allow working space.

2. Start a pot of water boiling, and while it's heating, scrub your hands thoroughly. Pay particular attention to your fingernails, as you don't want any livestock or barnyard microflora to contact the butter while you're working it.

Home Dairy Butter Making

Faced with a newly formed milk monopoly's ultimatum to join them or go out of business, Ralph and Howard Dickinson and their sister, Esther, closed down the commercial dairy operation on their western Massachusetts farm, ending a tradition of nearly 200 years of dairying since their family started homesteading in the Berkshire Mountains.

"In '60 we bought a big stainless steel bulk tank and went along," Howard says, recalling an earlier dictum that forced thousands of small New England farm families out of dairying, "but this time we thought we'd try it another way."

Now Ralph and Howard work in the farm's timber lots and Esther is the postmaster of the small village. The herd of registered Guernseys is gone, but, as Howard says, "we've never bought milk or butter and we refuse to do it now," so 2 or 3 cows remain to fill the family's needs.

Howard and Esther make the butter, with Howard at the separator, churn and butter mold, while Esther washes, works and packages the butter. Up to half their 3 cows' milk production is separated into cream which is cool-stored in 10-gallon milk cans until there is enough to charge the churn, every few days. The separator is a De Laval Model 14 "New World's Standard Series" and dates back to the 1930s. Although the machine has

Howard Dickinson and his sister, Esther, making butter in the kitchen of their Massachusetts mountain farm.

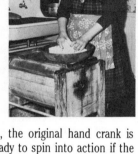

been electrified, the original hand crank is still in place ready to spin into action if the power goes off when there's a batch of milk to separate. The butter churn is a hand-cranked model of unknown manufacture with a revolving hardwood dasher that looks something like the stern-wheel paddles of an old river boat. It's been in the Dickinson family making butter for 80 years, and shows no signs of wearing out.

The North Family Farm in Canterbury, New Hampshire, is a small, diversified farm with a dairy described by the principal people involved, Tom and Jill McCullough, as being "a little larger than family scale, but not much." The McCulloughs have 3 draft horses and 9 Jersey cows, produce their own hay and oats for the livestock and have wheat, carrots, onions, maple syrup and dairy products for sale. From their dairy room come milk, cream, yogurt, cheese and about 8 pounds of butter a week, produced in a wooden crank churn of 6-quart capacity.

The McCulloughs are happy farming, and though they have backgrounds in farming, have learned mostly by doing and asking. They both are involved in the complete farm life. "We both try to learn all the skills and not divide them as in the more traditional past," Jill said.

3. Place a bowl of cold water on the table, one that's large enough to hold the butter mold, paddle and Scotch hands, if you use them. If wooden butter tools are cold and wet, the butter won't stick to them. Add another bowl large enough to hold the butter you'll make.

4. If you are like the McCulloughs and Dickinsons and use freezer paper for wrappers, cut and stack them on the table. Regular "parchment" butter wrappers are available commercially at low cost.

5. If you save the buttermilk to drink, sterilize as many bottles and lids as you think you will need and the funnel to fill them, and set them near the churn. On the opposite side of the churn place a bucket large enough to catch the wash water. "Save the first rinse water for the pigs, chickens or compost," Jill advises, "as there is still a lot of buttermilk in it."

6. Put the butter mold, paddle and Scotch hands in the pot of boiling water for a minute, then cool them under the cold water tap. When cool, place in the bowl of cold water.

7. Pour the boiling water into the churn (if it's wooden) and crank it for a minute so that the dashers and all wooden surfaces are exposed to the liquid. Churns of stoneware will usually survive scalding, but light ceramic and glass churns should be sterilized as you do canning jars—in a deep hot water bath or the dishwasher. Keep them out of drafts when they are still hot.

8. Pour off or flush out the sterilizing water.

MAKING BUTTER

A churn can be as simple as a preserve jar half filled with cream and shaken briskly over the shoulder, or a bowl with an egg beater for a dasher, but for the serious butter maker it's a good idea to invest in a machine made especially for the purpose—the butter churn. Many models and sizes of churns are available. At both the Dickinson and McCullough farms they use wooden crank churns to churn separator cream and they're happy with the results.

However, the authors have tasted both sweet and soured butters made in old wooden churns, and almost always there has been a detectable hint of rancidity in the butter. No matter how thoroughly and conscientiously the churn is cleaned after each use, at one time or another some part of the wooden surface escapes sterilization. Cleaning and sterilizing wooden implements is difficult, and we feel a glass churn, easily cleaned, is better for the home dairy maker.

1. Taking the temperature of the cream to check if it's within the right range is very important. The low to mid-50s F is the base for goats' cream, and the low 60s F for cows' cream. Review these conditions which might affect the churning.

A cold room—If the room is cold, the cream temperature might fall below the base temperature, causing the butterfat to harden. To counter this, start with warmer cream.

A hot room—When the temperature of the room is warmer than the cream, a condition which can seriously soften the butterfat, start with colder cream. It is true that it's faster and easier to beat higher temperature creams into butter but the results are disappointing. Warm butter is lumpy and greasy and contains an excess of buttermilk which makes it a prime medium for spoilage bacteria. Too cold a temperature, on the other hand, causes the cream to become too thick, almost gum-like, clinging to the dashers like wet bread dough, preventing agitation of the cream and yielding no butter.

Other butter makers argue that the season of the year, the breed of dairy animal and the nature of the feed all influence the selection of the churning temperature since they are factors which are linked to the hardness or softness of the butterfat. Spring and summer are the soft fat periods for dairy animals since they are dining on grass and forage instead of the grain and hay that produce harder butterfat. A butter maker's rule of thumb is: the higher the melting point of the butterfat, the higher the churning temperature should be; conversely, the lower the melting point, the lower the churning temperature.

Butter made with soft fat not only has a shorter storage life than hard-butterfat butter, but also causes exasperation in the kitchen. On a hot summer day a pound of soft-fat butter will melt into a puddle and run all over the table. This mess is useless as a spread and always manages to spill when you try gingerly to put it into the refrigerator to harden up again. It's a common country kitchen disaster for a cook coming out of wintertime and used to cooking with hard-fat butter, to scorch the first pans of soft spring butter.

Jill McCullough and Howard Dickinson churn their Jersey and Guernsey creams at the same temperature—62°F—with the temperature determined by a dairy thermometer, an essential piece of equipment. "A dairy thermometer is important," Howard advises, "because the cream *has* to be 62°F. If it's colder, the cream takes longer to churn; if it's warmer, much warmer, more butterfat globules will escape in the buttermilk and during washing, lessening the yield."

Since the cream has usually been cool-stored, the temperature will rise just by bringing it into a warm room. The sterilizing water in the churn can either help or hinder. If the cream is cooler than you want it, it will warm up a bit when it's poured into a churn still steaming from the boiling water. If the cream is too warm, putting it into a hot churn will make it warmer yet, so the foresighted butter maker rinses the scalded churn with cold water before beginning.

2. To avoid splashing cream and buttermilk all over the room, fill the churn only half full. A half-filled churn also assures that an abundance of oxygen will be present — and oxygen is crucial to the development of diacetyl, soured cream butter's most important aromatic.

3. Crank the churn at a slow, steady pace, or, if you're using an upright dasher, plunge it into the cream rythmically. Electric churns are usually governed not to exceed the right *break* speed. The break speed is the point at which the cream gives up its butterfat, determined for the electric churn by a factory-specified temperature. The exact churning time will depend on the temperature of the cream and the butterfat hardness and is impossible to predict precisely. For example, Howard Dickinson vows that it always takes him 30 minutes to churn his separator Guernsey cream, while Jill McCullough says it takes her about 5 to 8 minutes to churn separator cream from her Jerseys, but 15 to 40 minutes to reach break with skimmed cream.

You will recognize that you are nearing the point where the butter forms as the churning grows more stiff and difficult, and then suddenly the cream "breaks" the butterfat free and the crank turns easily again. If you look inside you'll see the butter forming around the dashers, with golden or snowy flakes of butter swirling in the cream which is now thinning into buttermilk. Continue to churn until the butter is massed in the bottom of the churn.

4. Drain off the buttermilk. Use a section of cheesecloth over a funnel to catch any elusive butter granules. When the buttermilk is drained off, pour into the churn an equal amount of water warmed to the same temperature as the buttermilk. If you use a crank churn be sure to close the drain cock before adding the water. Crank, or start the churn for the first washing, and let the butter wash 1 minute. Drain and rinse again with two washes of cool water or as many as needed until the water runs clear.

5. Transfer the butter from the churn to a bowl and start working the mass. Jill McCullough and Howard Dickinson's sister, Esther, work their butters with their hands, but for people who choose not to go up to their wrists in butterfat, Scotch hands are the answer. You can work butter in a bowl with your hands, but it's more difficult to manipulate a pair of wooden paddles in the bowl—much easier to work the Scotch hands and butter on a flat,

---

Choice Butter—The Secret Disclosed

A hundred years ago choice butter brought fabulous prices, for those days, on the luxury market. Dairymen who could get the quality of butter that brought those prices were few and far between, and dairy papers commonly ran columns describing the manufacture, price, cows, feed—everything affecting butter except scrupulous sanitation, which was the real source of choice grade butter. Here is a typical butter story from the Windsor, Vermont, *Valley Farmer* of 1874:

Three Essentials for Butter

In making fancy butter there are three essentials—color, texture and flavor. The color must be a rich golden yellow; the texture firm, tenacious, waxy, with that nutty flavor and smell which impart so high a degree of pleasure in eating it. Butter of the very highest quality will bring $1 a pound readily. A Philadelphia maker who receiveds this price gave J. B. Lyman of Boston these facts as to his management: he feeds on clover or early-mown hay; cuts fine, moistens, and mixes in corn-meal and wheaten shorts; feeds often and but little at a time; uses no roots except carrots; keeps his pastures free from weeds; keeps the temperature of the milk room at 58 degrees; skims clean; stirs the cream in the cream-pot; churns once a week; just before the butter gathers he puts a bucket of ice-cold water into the churn; in working he works out all the buttermilk without the use of the hand, absorbing the drops with a fine linen cloth wrung from cold water, and at the second working handles delicately with fingers as cold as may be; salt nearly one ounce per pound; packs in one-pound balls.

sterile surface. Work the butter as you would knead bread dough. The Scotch hands are grooved for a better grip in breaking, flopping, folding, shaking, pressing and working the butter against a hard surface. Quarter-pound and half-pound lots are the easiest to work. Try to get rid of all the buttermilk and rinse water you can in the working process. "If there's water trapped in the butter, the butter may sour more quickly," Jill warns.

6. After the excess moisture is worked out of the butter, return it to the bowl and pick up the butter mold and paddle. Both should be cold and dripping wet. The paddle works best if it's the same width as the mold. Press the butter in firmly, filling the bottom ends and corners first. Work upward, pressing the butter in hard to avoid air pockets. These holes are traps for air and they don't look as good in butter as they do in Swiss cheese. Fill the mold a little

Making Goat Butter

Bobbi Moriarty is a young but retired registered nurse who lives with her husband Bob, a pharmacist, and their four-year-old daughter Sarah on a very small farm in Farmington, New Hampshire. In the eight years they've been farming, the Moriarty goal of self-sufficiency through diversified agriculture has drawn closer through the production of all meats — beef, veal, lamb, rabbits, chickens, ducks, geese and chevon — most of their own fruits and vegetables and all livestock feed except grain.

The Moriartys have a herd of 10 milking goats, and a substantial portion of their cream goes into butter making. "My butter making is very simple except for washing the cream separator after use," Bobbi says. "If you've ever used one, you know what I mean — the parts don't fit easily into a kitchen sink."

Most of the Moriarty goats are Nubians; 2 are Saanens. The Saanens average 3.8 percent butterfat, and the Nubians 4.5 percent to 5.0 percent butterfat in their milk. "I save morning milk from all does in a 4-gallon tote pail and separate all of it immediately. Then I pour the thin cream through the separator once again, then a third time, so I end up with very thick cream. I then chill it quickly. We don't liked aged goat butter so it is made fresh.

"When the cream is very cold — refrigerator temperature — I put it into an antique glass butter churn, which is similar to a wooden egg beater in a bottle, and let it stand 10 or more minutes at room temperature depending on the time of year. During the summer it warms up quickly.

"Then I crank the butter maker until I hear a sloshing sound which means that the buttermilk has started to separate out. When the separation is complete, I pour out and save the buttermilk and add icy cold water to the churn and beat again. As the water gets cloudy I pour it out and add fresh. This is continued until the water is clear."

She then turns the butter into a bowl and works it until the excess moisture is out. Her yield is 1 pound of butter from 4 gallons of milk. "I read so many books concerning cow butter making which sounded so complicated. I have never ever had butter that wouldn't come — if it's slow coming, I just chill the cream again. It's so simple once done.

"Our lives seem to revolve around the goats, for they are our favorites. We make many more barn improvements for them than home improvements for us," says Bobbi. "We think goat butter is best except when very old, for then it may develop a 'goaty' flavor which I detest! Our milk is tasty so the end product is good. I suppose goats with off-flavored milk would produce off-flavored butter, too."

over the top, then scrape it level with the butter paddle edge.

7. Center the full mold on the butter wrapper and depress the plunger. Voila! A handsome pound of butter! Now fold the wrapper closed as you would a small parcel and refrigerate the butter for immediate use, or freeze it for the future.

Some butter is salted during the working period, roughly at the rate of ¾ tablespoon per pound. Neither Howard nor Jill salts butter. "We only salt our butter if someone asks for it," comments Jill.

"Sweet cream butter is a specialty and it seems a shame to salt it." Adds Howard, "When you're freezing butter, it's always better to freeze sweet butter than salted butter. The salting seems to intensify after being frozen."

There is more to do with butter than spreading it on bread. A major ingredient in cooking the world over, butter is used in pies, pastries, breads, sauces, soups, desserts, with vegetables, meats, poultry, fish and, of course, on crumpets, scones and toasted English muffins. Here are some suggestions for various butters and ways to use them.

CLARIFIED BUTTER AND VARIATIONS

This simple butter is the drawn butter of seafood menus. It has many uses in the kitchen, in cream sauces, in baking and for frying in place of oil. Moreover, the keeping qualities of clarified butter are superior to ordinary butter. In India the staple cooking fat is a kind of clarified butter called *ghee*, made from the butterfat of water buffalo milk—90 percent of all *ghee* is made at home in India. In this country dairy manufacturers and food processors are clarifying butter oil and storing it. Not only is this *anhydrous fat*, as it's called in commercial circles, easy and cheap to store for long periods, but the skim milk byproduct of the process can also be stored cheaply and for long periods. The dairy processor therefore can save a quart of milk for a rainy day, for by adding water and a dash of anhydrous fat to the skim milk, stirring and chilling, you have reconstituted milk.

A good source of fat-soluble vitamins and essential fatty acids, butter oil is rich in energy. If the oil is made from Jersey or Guernsey cream it will have a light golden color, but if the cream source is the goat, the oil will be clear.

In India *ghee* is made by the *Desi* method by heating whole milk to the boiling point in an earthenware container, then cooling it to lukewarm and culturing it with a traditional starter. When the milk clabbers it becomes a product called *dahi*, and this is churned with a wooden dasher until the butterfat and skim milk separate. After being worked, the butterfat is clarified by direct pan heating. There are many regional variations in the flavors of different *ghees*, and this oil is the bedrock of Indian cooking.

How to Make Clarified Butter

yields about 2 cups

1. Heat a pound of butter over low heat. Remove from the heat when completely melted and let it stand in a warm place until the milk solids precipitate out to the bottom of the pan.

2. Skim the clear butterfat from the solids with a spoon or a turkey baster.

3. Pour the clear butter oil into small sterile jars and seal. If the jars are hot when they are covered, a vacuum seal will form. Since the oil is affected by light, store it in a cool, dark place. The oil will keep up to a year if sealed and stored this way. Here are a few traditional ways to use clarified butter aside from frying chicken and dipping seafood into it.

Beurre Noisette

This has a delicious nutty flavor on asparagus, fiddlehead ferns, the first tender dandelion greens and broccoli, or with pasta, with the addition of 1 teaspoon of lemon juice to the *beurre noisette*.

In a heavy saucepan heat clarified butter steadily until it turns a light toast brown. Pour it over hot tender-crisp vegetables and season to taste. Serve at once.

Beurre Noir

This is *beurre noisette* carried one step further and enlivened with a little tartness.

In a heavy saucepan slowly heat clarified butter until it is dark brown, then stir in 1 teaspoon of vinegar and serve at once with fish, vegetables or eggs.

Lemon Butter or Beurre Meuniere

This simplest of sauces is the natural companion of brook trout, salmon or other delicate fish.

Make *beurre noisette*, above, then add 2 teaspoons chopped parsley and 1 teaspoon lemon juice and pour over the fish at once.

Herb Butters

Garden-fresh vegetables steamed until tender-crunchy are delicious and excellent foodstuffs. The home dairyist can bring dishes of garden produce to perfection by including herb butters in the kitchen repertoire. Here are some wonderful herb butters which make instant superb vegetable sauces.

Basic Herb Butter

yields about ½ cup

¼ pound butter, at room temperature
1 tablespoon each finely chopped
    parsley and chives
½ teaspoon each finely chopped thyme,
    rosemary, basil
½ teaspoon grated lemon rind
  pinch freshly ground cayenne
  freshly ground pepper

1. Cream the butter with the herbs, lemon rind and seasoning.

2. Place the mixture on a rectangle of foil and shape into a cylinder. Wrap and chill.

3. Cut off 2 or 3 tablespoons at a time as needed to sauce vegetables.

    You may make up different herb butter rolls and freeze them to be used as needed. Place the rolls in an air-tight plastic bag before freezing. Parsley butter is excellent with nearly every vegetable that grows, but try the following suggestions for something out of the ordinary,

mixing the herbs with ¼ pound of butter as in Basic Herb Butter, and serving the result with the matching vegetable.

Beets

1 tablespoon chopped fresh dill
½ teaspoon pulverized dried
    cardamom

Broccoli

1 tablespoon chopped chervil
  pinch powdered ginger
1 teaspoon chopped parsley
½ teaspoon dry mustard

Carrots

1 tablespoon chopped dill
1 teaspoon each chopped parsley,
    thyme, mint, marjoram

Cauliflower

½ teaspoon scalded, bruised caraway
    seeds
1 teaspoon chopped tarragon
1 teaspoon chopped rosemary

(continued on next page)

Celery

1 teaspoon chopped basil
1 teaspoon chopped thyme

Green Beans

½ garlic clove, pressed
1 teaspoon each chopped sage and
    sweet basil
1 teaspoon scalded, bruised dill seeds

Green Peas

1 teaspoon each chopped mint,
    thyme, fennel

Lima Beans

1 teaspoon scalded, bruised caraway
    seeds
1 teaspoon each chopped oregano
    and thyme

Other Butters

Almond Butter

yields about ¾ cup

¼ cup butter, at room temperature
½ cup almonds, ground fine

1. Cream the butter until smooth and light.

2. Blend in the almond meal. Serve.

Basil Butter

yields about ½ cup

This is a favorite Italian seasoning traditionally served with gnocchi when the first spring basil appears.

2 tablespoons chopped basil leaves
2 garlic cloves, pressed
1 tablespoon chopped parsley
6 tablespoons butter, at room
    temperature

1. In a mortar pound the basil, garlic and parsley to a paste.

2. Cream the butter in a bowl, then work in the herb paste until thoroughly blended. Chill while making the gnocchi.

Garlic Butter Extraordinaire

yields about 1 cup

This marvelous mixture is not for the fainthearted; redolent of garlic, it favors French bread and snails.

½ pound butter, at room temperature
 1 tablespoon finely chopped shallots
 4 garlic cloves, pressed
 1 tablespoon chopped parsley

     Cream the butter in a bowl, then work in the shallots and garlic, then add the parsley.

French Bread

Slice a crusty loaf of French bread and spread each slice with the garlic butter mixture. Wrap the loaf in aluminum foil and heat in a hot oven 10 to 15 minutes.

Snails

Preheat oven to 450°F. Have 2 dozen snails and their shells separated. Into each shell put some of the garlic butter mixture, then the snail, then more garlic butter. Arrange on a flat baking pan with shallow sides, and put 2 tablespoons water in the bottom. Sprinkle the opening of the snail shells with fine bread crumbs, then bake in the oven until the crumbs are brown. Serve at once.

Honey Butter

yields about 1½ cups

Here's a butter treatment for hot popovers, muffins, pancakes and such.
½ cup aromatic, best-quality honey
½ pound butter, at room temperature

1. Blend the honey and butter with an electric beater until light and pale in color.

2. Scoop into a tightly covered container and store in the refrigerator.

Mint Butter

yields about ½ cup

This nippy butter is good with lamb, spinach and broiled tomatoes.

 2 tablespoons chopped mint leaves
¼ pound butter, at room temperature

1. Blend 1 tablespoon of the mint into the butter, whipping with a fork until light. Reserve the other tablespoon of mint.

2. Shape the mint butter into a cylinder. Roll it in the remaining mint.

3. Wrap in foil and chill until needed.

Rose Butter

yields about 2 cups

This is an unusual recipe, but the fragrant butter is delicious on crackers, warm bread and morning toast. No salt gets in the butter.

2 quarts fragrant rose petals (shrub or
    damask roses are best)
1 pound butter

1. Choose a covered bowl or crock considerably larger in diameter than the length of butter. Put a layer of rose petals in the bowl and sprinkle with salt. Repeat until all the petals are used.

2. Set a small saucer on top of the rose petals in the bowl, and arrange the pound of butter on the saucer.

3. Cover the bowl tightly and store it in a cool place 48 hours or longer. The butter will absorb the scent of the roses. When the butter is ready, discard the petals and salt.

I never had a piece of toast
    Particularly long and wide
But fell upon the sanded floor
    And always on the buttered side.
        James Payne, *Poem*, 1884

Scandinavian Creamed Butter

yields about 1 cup

This fluffy butter is beautiful to look at and delicious on vegetables. Chopped dill or other herbs may be beaten in.

½ pound butter, at room temperature
    a few drops of warm water
    parsley sprigs

1. Put the butter in a large, slightly warmed bowl. Cream the butter 5 to 7 minutes with an electric beater, adding a drop or two of the warm water to speed the creaming process. The butter should be fluffy and airy.

2. Heap in a small bowl and garnish with tiny sprigs of parsley.

Sesame Butter

yields about ½ cup

This is excellent with hot vegetables.

2 tablespoons sesame seeds
6 tablespoons butter, at room
    temperature

Preheat oven to 350°F.

1. Toast the sesame seeds lightly in the oven about 20 minutes, stirring often.

2. Cream the butter in a bowl with a fork, then work in the sesame seeds.

Sweet Pepper Butter

yields about 1¼ cups

 1 medium-size green pepper, seeded
½ pound butter, at room temperature
 1 teaspoon each chopped parsley,
    thyme, rosemary, basil
 1 tablespoon grated onions

1. Steam the pepper until soft. Chop fine.

2. Cream the butter, then gradually work in the pepper.

3. Work in the herbs and onions. Allow the butter an hour to absorb the flavors and serve.

Whipped Mushroom Butter

yields about 1½ cups

This savory, flavorful butter is excellent with snow peas.

½ pound butter, at room temperature
⅓ cup Mushroom *Fumet* (see p. 201)
⅓ cup lemon juice
 1 tablespoon mixed chopped parsley
    and tarragon

1. Beat the butter until soft and yielding.

2. Gradually beat in the mushroom *fumet*, and then the lemon juice. Beat with an electric beater or balloon whip 7 to 10 minutes or until the mixture is the consistency of whipped cream.

3. Just before serving mix in the chopped herbs.

Butter Sauces

Here are more butter sauces to use as dips, on broiled liver, chops, game, and fish, with fried squid, on vegetables — especially baked potatoes — and whatever seems good to you.

Frozen Honey Butter Hard Sauce

makes 16 to 18 tablespoons

This is out of this world served frozen on hot desserts. Try it with Apple Brown Betty.

⅓ cup butter, at room temperature
¾ cup honey
   rind of ½ lemon, grated
   juice of 1 orange

1. Beat the butter with an electric beater until soft. Add the honey gradually.

2. Beat in the lemon rind and orange juice.

3. Place 1 tablespoon of the mixture on a small square of plastic wrap. Fold over and seal with tape. Repeat until all the mixture is wrapped in small packages. Place in the freezer. When ready to serve, unwrap and place on a hot dessert.

Juniper Berry Butter

yields about 1 cup

The flavor of juniper berries varies surprisingly from climate to climate. The berries that cover the low bushes in old pastures look tempting and smell aromatic, but their flavor cannot compare with the pine-scented juniper berries from the Mediterranean countries. Still, they can be used in a pinch. After picking them in the late summer, dry them outdoors in a shady place for several days; then store them in well-corked bottles. For game and liver dishes there is no more complementary and intriguing flavor.

¼ pound butter
3 tablespoons finely chopped onions
1 garlic clove, pressed
3 to 5 juniper berries, crushed
2 tablespoons lemon juice
1 tablespoon chopped parsley

1. Melt the butter in a pan over low heat and cook the onions and garlic until they are soft but not brown. Remove from the heat.

2. Add the juniper berries, lemon juice and parsley. Blend thoroughly and serve with game or liver.

Mushroom Fumet

yields ⅓ cup

¼ pound mushrooms, sliced
1½ tablespoons butter
  a few drops lemon juice

1. In a saucepan simmer the mushrooms barely covered with water.

2. Add the butter and lemon juice, bring up to a boil, then reduce the heat and simmer 10 minutes.

3. Strain, then reduce the liquid to ⅓ cup.

Sauce Bearnaise

yields about 1½ cups

Caloric madness served on broiled or grilled fish and choice cuts of meat.

 3 sprigs each tarragon and chervil
 2 shallots
⅓ cup tarragon vinegar or white
        wine vinegar
  freshly ground pepper
 3 egg yolks
 1 tablespoon water
½ pound butter, at room temperature
  pinch freshly ground cayenne

1. Chop 2 sprigs each of the tarragon and chervil with the shallots and put in the top of a double boiler with the vinegar and a few grindings of pepper. Reserve 1 sprig of the tarragon and chervil.

2. Put the double boiler top over simmering but not boiling water, then beat in the egg yolks and water gradually with a whisk until the mixture is light and foamy.

3. Beat in 1 tablespoon of the butter until the mixture is smooth. Repeat until all the butter has been worked into the sauce.

4. Season with the cayenne, add the remaining chervil and tarragon, then blend for a few seconds in a blender. Serve at once.

Beurre Manie Balls

makes six

If you make a lot of cream sauces or soups, you will bless the day the French invented *beurre manie*. These are little balls of flour and butter in the right proportion made up ahead of time. Then, when a *roux* of butter and flour is needed to thicken a sauce or soup, the cook simply reaches for a *beurre manie* ball or two, pinches off small bits and blends them into the simmering liquid. Voila! Instant cream sauce.

6 tablespoons butter, at room
        temperature
6 tablespoons flour

1. Cream the butter with a fork. Work in the flour until the mixture is smooth.

2. Roll into 6 balls of equal size, wrap in an air-tight bag and refrigerate until needed.

Beurre manie balls may be frozen in a tightly covered container and moved to the refrigerator as they are needed.

BUTTERMILK

Buttermilk, real buttermilk, is simply the liquid that remains after cream has been churned into butter. It has been recognized as a delicious and healthful drink for centuries in many cultures. As an all-purpose cooking ingredient it is unsurpassed, useful for everything from gravies to desserts.

Biscuits are just biscuits, but buttermilk biscuits are something special. Pancakes, breads, gingerbread, cold and hot cakes, cookies and pastries are lighter, richer tasting and have a more tender crumb when buttermilk is used instead of whole fresh milk. Part of the secret lies in the lactic acid content of buttermilk, for this reacts with baking soda, an alkaline, to make a gas which permeates the dough and causes it to rise. The tiny flecks of butter that remain give smoothness and depth of flavor.

But not all buttermilk is the same. There are three basic kinds of buttermilk.

Sweet Cream Buttermilk — the liquid residue after sweet cream is churned into butter. This lacks the tanginess of cultured or soured cream buttermilk, and can seem flat and characterless to people unfamiliar with it as a beverage. But this buttermilk is excellent in the kitchen, and makes delicious ice creams and milk sherbets.

Buttermilk from Soured Cream — buttermilk from cream that has been soured either naturally or with a culture. It is a popular beverage with a great culinary reputation. Depending on individual taste, there is a point at which excess acidity makes this tangy buttermilk too sharp to drink, but still very useful in soups and baked goods.

Commercial Buttermilk — called "cultured buttermilk" at the dairy counter in the supermarket, but not really buttermilk at all. It is actually skim milk (often reconstituted powder) which has been acidulated with a bacteria culture. To give the drink more credibility, flecks of butterfat are sometimes added. Commercial buttermilk always tastes the same, and is a standard product. It is usually a low-calorie food — 10 calories per ounce — because it is made with skim milk. The fact that it's cultured and convenient makes it a handy source for someone who wants to make cultured buttermilk at home, provided that duplicating the taste of the commercial brands is acceptable.

Making Buttermilk from Buttermilk

1. Into 1 quart of your own whole or skim, raw or pasteurized milk, stir 1 cup of your favorite commercial buttermilk, as fresh as possible.

2. Cap the jar, shake it vigorously to mix in the culture thoroughly, then store it 12 to 14 hours in a warm place — 80° to 85°F.

3. Check the buttermilk. If it has thickened and tastes like your favorite commercial brand, put it in the refrigerator, and when it's chilled, drink it.

If you prefer the taste of the acid buttermilk yielded by the churn after making butter with soured cream, you may culture milk in the same way by adding to it a cup of this homemade buttermilk and letting it ripen. Flavors will vary, sometimes superb, and sometimes not so memorable.

Commercial buttermilk cultures are available from dairy and cheese-making supply sources. Convenient and easy to use, the cultures are freeze dried and packed in foil envelopes. Each packet contains enough culture to inoculate one gallon of milk. When these packets are stored in a freezer, the culture remains potent for a year. (These cultures should not be confused with the new powdered buttermilk sold in food stores. This product is commercial buttermilk which has had its liquid removed, and is best used as a cooking and baking ingredient. It must be cooked and is not suitable for beverages, ice cream or sherbet.)

Making Buttermilk from a Culture

1. Assemble a kettle for heating a gallon of milk, a dairy thermometer, 4 sterile quart jars and lids, a buttermilk culture of your choosing, the milk and an incubator, which can be as simple as a cardboard box.

2. If your milk is raw, heat 1 gallon to the scalding point (180°F) and then cool it to 105°F by putting the kettle in a sink of cold water. Either whole or skim milk can be used. If you are culturing pasteurized milk, just warm it to 105°F.

3. Stir in the culture thoroughly.

4. Have the sterile quart jars warm, fill them with the cultured milk and screw on the lids.

5. Put the jars in an incubator that will hold the warmth for up to 6 hours without a loss of more than 5°F. Yogurt incubators, electric ovens or gas ovens with pilot lights all have been used to culture buttermilk. We have had good luck with two very simple methods. In the wintertime when the wood range is burning endlessly, we move the thermometer around the stove until we find a steady 105°F temperature. Then we pull up a chair to that place, set the jars of cultured milk in a cardboard box on the chair and close the top flaps. Five or six hours later the buttermilk is ripened to perfection, and it goes into the refrigerator. During the summer we drag out a battered but sound cooler chest and fill it with hot water. This warms the cooler. The water is then poured out and the 4 quarts of cultured milk go into the cooler (now a warmer). A jar of hot water which doesn't touch the jars of milk is added to keep up the warmth, and the lid is put on. Five or six hours later the buttermilk is done.

There are several ways to use buttermilk in the kitchen besides drinking it straight down. See recipes that follow.

Buttermilk and Longevity

An 1874 farm paper carried a news item on buttermilk and long life, predating the yogurt-longevity thesis of Metchnikoff decades later. M. Robin's comparison of the combustion that occurs in human bodies to that in chimneys, and his belief in the use of lactic acid to clean out the detritus of combustion, was destined to be forgotten. Here is the story.

M. Robin of Paris read a paper lately before the French Academie, in which he thus sets forth the great value of buttermilk as an article of daily food; Life exists only in combustion, but the combustion which occurs in our own bodies, like that which takes place in our chimneys, leaves a detritus which is fatal to life. To remove this, we would administer lactic acid with ordinary food. This acid is known to possess the power of removing or destroying the incrustations which form on the arteries, cartilages, and valves of the heart. As buttermilk abounds in this acid, and is . . . an agreeable kind of food, its habitual use . . . will free the system from these causes which inevitably cause death between the seventy-fifth and hundredth year.

Valley Farmer
(Windsor, Vt.),
Feb. 21, 1874

BUTTERMILK RECIPES

Soups

Buttermilk Carrot Soup

serves four to six

2 pounds carrots, sliced
2 medium-size potatoes, peeled and
    diced
4 cups Whey (see Index) or stock
4 tablespoons butter
½ cup chopped shallots
2 garlic cloves, pressed
¼ cup coarsely chopped almonds
1 cup buttermilk
1 teaspoon grated ginger root
1 teaspoon grated horseradish

1. Simmer the carrots and potatoes in the whey until tender.

2. Melt the butter in a skillet and saute the shallots, garlic and almonds 5 minutes.

3. In a blender puree the shallot-garlic mixture alternately with the carrot-potato mixture, cup by cup. Return to the saucepan in which the carrots and potatoes were simmered.

4. Blend in the buttermilk and heat thoroughly until hot. Stir in the horseradish and ginger root and serve at once.

Buttermilk Cucumber Soup

serves four to six

2 to 3 medium-size cucumbers
1 quart buttermilk
1 tablespoon chopped green onions
¼ cup chopped parsley, tightly packed
Garnish
  cucumber slices
  parsley sprigs

1. Peel and seed the cucumbers. Grate them to make 1½ cups.

2. Combine the cucumbers with the buttermilk; add the onions and parsley and chill several hours.

3. Serve in chilled cups garnished with the cucumber slices and parsley sprigs.

Cold Buttermilk Soup

serves four to six

 5 thin slices pumpernickel bread
½ cup seedless raisins
 2 tablespoons honey
 2 teaspoons grated lemon rind
   pinch freshly grated nutmeg
   pinch cinnamon
1½ quarts buttermilk

Preheat oven to 250°F.

1. Put the bread slices on a baking sheet and toast them in the oven, turning several times, until they are crisp and bone dry, about 30 minutes. Put them aside to cool.

2. Put the raisins in a mixing bowl and pour a little boiling water on them to cover. Let them stand 5 minutes, then drain on paper towels.

3. Pulverize the toast to coarse dust in a blender, then put it in a mixing bowl.

4. Add the raisins, honey, lemon rind, nutmeg and cinnamon and stir until well blended. Stirring constantly, slowly add the buttermilk.

5. Chill several hours, and before serving, dust lightly with cinnamon and nutmeg.

Tomato Buttermilk Cream

serves six

 6 large tomatoes, peeled and chopped
 1 shallot, minced
 2 garlic cloves, pressed
½ cup chopped green pepper
 1 small cucumber, peeled and
   chopped
½ cup chopped watercress, tightly
   packed
 1 cup buttermilk
 1 cup heavy cream
 1 tablespoon chopped chives
 1 teaspoon finely chopped dill
 1 small dried chili pepper, crushed
   sour cream, yogurt or whipped
     cream for garnish

1. Put half the amount given above of each of the following into a blender: tomatoes, shallot, garlic, pepper, cucumber, watercress. Blend until thick and liquid. Pour into a large bowl.

2. Add the remaining ingredients, unblended; stir thoroughly and chill for several hours. Serve in chilled cups topped with sour cream, yogurt or whipped cream as garnish.

Main Dishes

Buttermilk Pop

serves four

This is a very old Pennsylvania Dutch recipe traditionally served to the children for supper. Try it for breakfast instead.

1 quart buttermilk
3 tablespoons cornmeal
  maple syrup

1. Heat the buttermilk gently in a shallow pan on the stove, stirring constantly to keep it from separating into curds and whey.

2. Just before the buttermilk reaches the boiling point, sift in the cornmeal, stirring until it thickens. Cook several minutes or until the raw corn taste is gone.

3. Serve in bowls with maple syrup for sweetening.

Buttermilk Pork Roast

serves eight

Buttermilk can be basted or brushed onto baking or broiling meats—it makes an attractive and tasty glaze.

  2 tablespoons Clarified Butter (see Index)
  3- to 4-pound pork shoulder
  2 cups buttermilk
  1 cup Whey (see Index)
  2 tablespoons cider vinegar
  2 garlic cloves, crushed
  ¼ teaspoon dried thyme
  2 large onions, sliced
  6 carrots or parsnips
  8 small potatoes, scrubbed but not peeled
16 tiny white onions, peeled (optional)
  1 to 2 *Beurre Manie* Balls (see Index)

1. Heat the butter in a heavy Dutch oven and sear the meat on all sides. Pour off the excess fat.

2. Add to the roast the buttermilk, whey, vinegar, garlic, thyme and onions. Cover, and simmer over low heat until the pork is tender.

3. Add the carrots, potatoes and small onions, cover and cook until the vegetables are tender.

4. Set the meat and vegetables aside on a heated platter and keep them warm.

5. Thicken the gravy with 1 or 2 *beurre manie* balls or 1 to 2 tablespoons whole wheat flour.

Vegetable Dish

Mushrooms in Buttermilk Sauce

serves four

3 tablespoons butter
½ cup chopped onions
3 tablespoons whole wheat flour
1½ cups buttermilk
¾ pound mushrooms
¾ cup minced parsley, tightly packed
¼ teaspoon freshly grated nutmeg
½ teaspoon dry mustard

1. Melt the butter in a heavy saucepan and cook the onions until soft. Work in the flour and cook 3 minutes.

2. Gradually stir in the buttermilk, and cook over low heat until thickened into a sauce the consistency of cream.

3. Add the mushrooms, cover lightly and simmer until tender.

4. Add the parsley, nutmeg and dry mustard, blend well and correct the consistency of the sauce, if necessary. If it needs to be thinned, add a little buttermilk.

Breads

Buttermilk Waffles

serves four to six

2 cups whole wheat flour
1 teaspoon baking soda
3 egg yolks
1½ cups buttermilk
½ cup melted butter
3 egg whites

1. Sift the dry ingredients into a mixing bowl.

2. Beat the egg yolks until light, then stir in the buttermilk. Add this to the dry ingredients and stir until smooth.

3. Beat in the melted butter.

4. Beat the egg whites until stiff but not dry, and fold them gently into the batter.

5. Bake on a hot waffle iron until golden brown.

Country Buttermilk Cornmeal Bread

makes one loaf

2 cups cornmeal
1½ teaspoons baking soda
1¼ cups buttermilk (from soured cream)
2 tablespoons Clarified Butter (see Index)

Preheat oven to 425°F.

1. Grease an 8½ × 4½-inch loaf pan and put it in the oven to heat.

2. Sift the dry ingredients into a mixing bowl. Add the buttermilk and butter. Mix rapidly and well.

3. Pour the batter into the hot cake pan and bake 20 minutes or until well browned. Serve piping hot.

New England Buttermilk Biscuits

makes eight large biscuits or twelve small ones

2 cups whole wheat pastry flour
½ teaspoon baking soda
4 tablespoons butter
few sprigs thyme, cut fine
¾ cup buttermilk

Preheat oven to 400°F.

1. Sift the dry ingredients into a mixing bowl. Cut in the butter and thyme with a pastry cutter, until the dough is the size of small peas.

2. Stir in the buttermilk.

3. Pat out the dough on a lightly floured board until it is about ½ inch thick. Cut out circles with a round cutter, place on a greased baking sheet, brush with buttermilk and bake 15 minutes.

Desserts

Buttermilk-Pineapple Ice

serves six to eight

1 quart buttermilk
4 cups crushed unsweetened
    pineapple and juice
½ cup honey

1. Mix all ingredients thoroughly in a large bowl. Pour into a freezer tray and freeze until mushy.

2. Return to the large mixing bowl and beat very vigorously with a wooden spoon until the mixture is light.

3. Pile into sherbet dishes and freeze again until dessert time.

Buttermilk Turban

serves four

This recipe calls for a turban mold, but any decorative ice cream or gelatin mold will do.

  ½ cup cold water
  2 tablespoons powdered unflavored
    gelatin
1½ cups honey
  1 cup lemon juice
2½ cups buttermilk
  1 cup whipped Lemon Cream (see
    Index)

1. Pour the water into a saucepan. Sprinkle the gelatin on top, then let stand 5 minutes.

2. Place the saucepan over low heat and stir gently until the gelatin is completely dissolved. Set aside.

3. In a bowl combine the honey and lemon juice. Stir until the honey is completely mixed in, then add the buttermilk. Mix thoroughly.

4. Pour the buttermilk mixture into the gelatin mixture and stir until blended.

5. Pour into a lightly oiled 1-quart turban mold. Refrigerate until firm, about 2 to 3 hours.

6. Unmold the chilled dessert onto a cold serving dish and serve with the lemon cream on the side or surrounding the turban.

10 *YOGURT*

A decade ago yogurt was still a quirky health-nut food to most North Americans, until one commercial producer shrewdly capitalized on our national addiction to sweets and marketed a yogurt product loaded with heavily sugared fruit. It was so well received that most of the yogurt sold today still resembles this stickily sweet junk. However, many people have learned the pleasures of eating and cooking with "plain" yogurt and have taken to making it at home.

Yogurt is easy to make—in fact, it's difficult to fail. Devotees have their own traditional methods, often involving Granny's hallowed yogurt crock or a particular insulating blanket, but we have made yogurt with success in half a dozen different ways, from towel-wrapped jars set in the sunshine to picnic cooler overnight yogurt, to fancy electric yogurt gizmo. They all worked well.

WHICH MILK FOR YOGURT?

Either cows' milk or goats' milk makes good yogurt, though there are differences. Goats' milk yogurt will not cast off as much whey as does cows' milk yogurt, and goats' milk yogurt is softer and creamier in texture. Morning milk is reputed to make the finest yogurt.

Raw Milk—Yogurt made with raw milk can vary since the properties of the milk change with the season and the animal's feed. Unless you're sure that your milk and dairy practices approach the standards of certified milk, it is sensible to pasteurize raw milk. Not only is the milk safer, but the quality of your yogurt will be more consistent if the culture doesn't have to struggle against teeming hordes of wild bacteria.

Pasteurized Milk—A consistent type of yogurt is made from this milk, though the texture and taste may be slightly different from raw milk yogurt.

Whole Milk—This dairy staple yields a delicious, creamy yogurt, very satisfying and good.

Whole Milk with Cream Added—This blend makes the queen of yogurts, a rich, melting delicacy well suited to dessert dishes.

Skim Milk—Here is the basis for a yogurt that is the dieter's standby, but skim milk alone without filler of some sort makes a thin, runny yogurt. Ordinarily ½ to 1 cup of powdered skim milk solids is added to each quart of skim milk to give the finished yogurt body and a more pleasing texture.

Dried Milk—The powder can be reconstituted and makes an inexpensive, fairly good yogurt that is vastly improved by the addition of a little fresh milk.

Evaporated Milk—This product is not recommended for yogurt making.

YOGURT STARTER

Essential to the yogurt-making process is the starter. It can be one of the following:

1. A few tablespoons of good-quality commercial yogurt as fresh as possible

2. A little yogurt saved from your last homemade batch

3. An imported Bulgarian or domestic freeze-dried culture known as "yogurt mother" by some people

Always use plain, unflavored yogurt as a starter, never the sweet, flavored stuff. If you save a few tablespoons of each batch of yogurt to use as a starter culture for a new batch, you may notice over a period of months that its power to yogurtize milk is faltering, like a run-down battery. It's then time to get some fresh starter or to increase the dosage of the enfeebled culture.

YOGURT CULTURES

Basic Yogurt Culture—contains *Lactobacillus bulgaricus* and *Streptococcus thermophilus*. This is also what you get when you buy commercial yogurt to use as a starter.

Acidophilus Yogurt Culture—combines the Basic Yogurt Culture with *Lactobacillus acidophilus*. The yogurt made from this is very popular in Europe where it is known as *bioyurt*.

Goat Yogurt Culture—a special strain used by the French dairy goat industry (although goats' milk responds well to both yogurt cultures listed above). It is imported to this country and available through cheese supply companies listed in the Appendix.

EQUIPMENT

Containers—These can be cup-size individual serving containers or quart canning jars. Whatever size, they should be glass, crockery, earthenware, stone, enamel, stainless steel or other acid-resistant smooth-surfaced material. Covers can be anything from plastic wrap to parchment paper.

Canning jars make good yogurt containers.

Thermometer—A dairy thermometer is very useful. Temperatures above 125°F will kill the yogurt culture; below 90°F the culture will go dormant. While many yogurt makers swear by the time-honored tests of holding a little finger in the warm milk while counting ten without feeling an uncomfortable hotness, or sprinkling a little milk on the inside of the wrist, human tolerances to heat and cold vary, and a thermometer saves ruined yogurt.

Kettle—The milk is heated in a large kettle of stainless steel, unchipped enamel or glass. Never use aluminum pots or old, chipped pans, for the acid in the milk will react with the metal and adversely flavor the milk and the yogurt.

Incubator—Yogurt makers have come up with an astounding variety of incubators in which the containers of yogurt stand or lie undisturbed while the lactobacilli multiply into creamy custard. Some suggestions for effective and simple incubators follow.

1. Wrap the jars in an old towel or a sheet of bubble plastic to hold in the warmth.

The Incubator

swathed in old blanket

2. A polystyrene picnic cooler is a good incubator. Rinse the cooler with very hot water. Fill two quart mason jars with hot water and place inside the cooler, which now becomes a warmer. Put the containers full of cultured milk with their covers on into the cooler, but do not allow them to touch the hot water jars. Put the cooler cover snugly into place and let everything stand undisturbed overnight.

3. A hot-water-bottle box is fast, cheap and easy. Line a small cardboard box with several layers of crumpled newspaper. Fill a hot water bottle with hot water, wrap it in a towel and put it in the box. Add the covered containers of cultured milk. Pack newspaper in loosely between the containers, then cover the box with a section from the Sunday *New York Times* or a thick towel and leave undisturbed 3 to 5 hours.

4. Use a cardboard box lined with newspaper for the basic incubator, but wrap the cultured milk containers in a down comforter or jacket. Many old-country yogurt makers have their favorite down or thick woolen blankets especially for yogurt making. Both down and wool will hold in the warmth of the jars long enough for the culture to multiply, 3 to 5 hours.

Old Iron Pot Yogurt

5. The old iron pot is an example of making do with what's on hand. Here in Vermont there are plenty of old iron pots left from the days of farm potash production and home soap making. Today most of these pots are used for growing geraniums on the front lawn or holding kindling behind the stove, but they make excellent yogurt incubators. Put hot water in the kettle to a

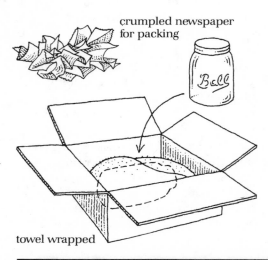

crumpled newspaper for packing

towel wrapped

level that will be an inch or so below the yogurt jars, and allow it to stabilize at 110°F *before* you put the yogurt jars in. Add the jars of cultured milk and cover the kettle with an old piece of plywood or a blanket and allow it to stand undisturbed 3 to 5 hours. In cool weather you may have to add a little hot water to keep the temperature from dipping below 90°F.

Solar Yogurt

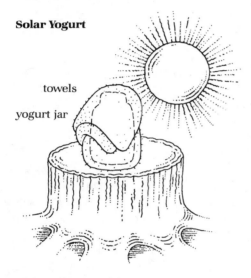

towels

yogurt jar

6. Solar yogurt is well known to yogurt-loving campers. On a morning when the yogurt is low and the sky is clear, use a few tablespoons of yogurt to culture a jar of warmed milk (reconstituted dry milk for backpackers), wrap the jar in towels and set it in the sun 3 to 4 hours. Voila! You're back in yogurt again.

7. A heating pad set on low, a Christmas tree light bulb in a metal bread box, the pilot light in a gas oven, all provide the gentle low heat you need for yogurt making. With some very-low-heat methods like the oven pilot light

the yogurt may take overnight to make. Generally the faster the yogurt makes, the milder in taste it is and the more beneficial bacteria there are in the tasty custard. When yogurt incubates over-night, it is often quite tart and has a high lactic acid content. Some people prefer their yogurt with this extra zip. You may have to make several experimental batches until you find the right balance of temperature.

8. The yogurt box is a handsome, per-manent piece of equipment that can be made in the home workshop easily. It is based on the principle of the traditional "haybox" incubator, a double box insulated with packed damp hay. Damp hay gives off small amounts of heat, and this primitive incubator worked well for earlier European gen-erations. Indeed, some gardeners bury their yogurt jars in their compost heaps where the heat urges the process to completion in a few hours.

The yogurt box illustrated in this section is an insulated box that holds and reflects radiant heat from the warm jars. Our box is lined with Styro-foam insulation, but anything that holds heat can be used—vermiculite, wood shavings, fiberglass board, ther-max or whatever insulation medium you like. The inside should be faced with reflective foil which will bounce back conducted heat to the interior of the box and keep it warmer for longer periods than if no reflective facing were used.

9. The thermos bottle yogurt maker is easy. Rinse a wide-mouthed thermos bottle with hot water, pour in the cul-tured milk, put on the cover and let it stand 3 to 5 hours.

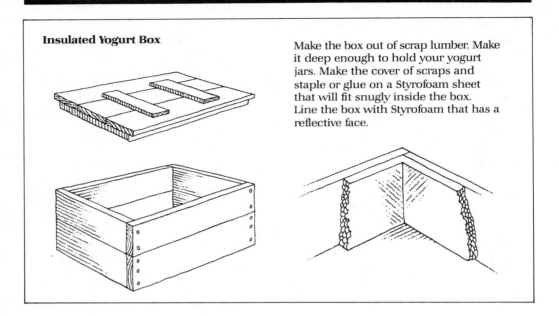

Insulated Yogurt Box

Make the box out of scrap lumber. Make it deep enough to hold your yogurt jars. Make the cover of scraps and staple or glue on a Styrofoam sheet that will fit snugly inside the box. Line the box with Styrofoam that has a reflective face.

10. Commercial yogurt machines, from electric plug-in types with individual half-pint yogurt pots to avant garde creations in acrylic and stainless steel, are on the market everywhere. Some of these are fancy modifications of the insulated box design, others little more than a simple electric heating element with a thermostat, some glorified thermos bottles. None of them functions any better than do homemade yogurt incubators, so buy one only if the design is irresistible.

MAKING YOGURT FOR THE FIRST TIME

If you are a first-time yogurt maker, or are making yogurt in a new house with untried equipment, make the first few batches in the daytime when you can keep an eye on the temperature and incubation time. Make the yogurt in half-pint jars (jelly jars are fine) so that you can test one at the end of 3 hours, 4 hours or 5 hours, and see precisely when the yogurt is done without disturbing the whole batch. It's much safer to check a small jar than to risk exploratory complications in an entire quart.

Get all your equipment and raw materials together and make sure everything is scrupulously clean. If the incubator you have decided on needs prewarming, start it now. If you are using a refrigerated starter culture, put it out where it can reach room temperature. The starter culture may be a few tablespoons of fresh, good-quality commercial yogurt, *or* a packet of freeze-dried commercial starter, *or* a few tablespoons from a good batch of homemade yogurt, the fresher the better. If you know a friend who makes superb yogurt from a special strain perhaps brought over from Lebanon or Bulgaria, ask for a little starter.

How to Make Yogurt from Raw Milk

yields 1 quart

> 1 quart whole raw milk
> 1 to 2 tablespoons yogurt starter culture

1. Heat the milk to 180°F, stirring frequently for even heating and to prevent a skin from forming. Stand the kettle in cold water and bring the temperature down rapidly to 110° to 115°F, stirring occasionally.

Heat the milk to 180°F.

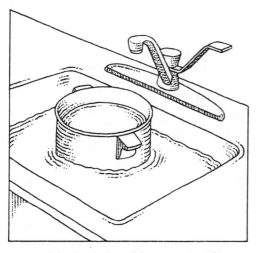

Cool the kettle in cold water to 110°F.

2. Dilute the starter with a few tablespoons of the warm milk, then stir this into the milk thoroughly so that the starter is truly well dispersed through the liquid.

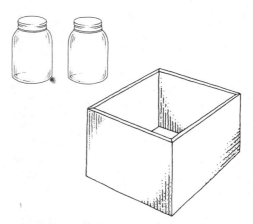

Dilute the starter with a few spoons of warm milk.

3. Pour the cultured milk into sterile jars, put on the covers and place the jars in the incubator. Put a thermometer in the incubator so that you can check its heat-holding capabilities. Let the milk stand undisturbed 3 hours.

Pour the cultured milk into sterile jars, cover and put the jars in the incubator.

4. At the end of 3 hours, check on one of the small jars. Yogurt is ripe when it has a

firm appearance and rocks slightly from side to side as the jar is gently tipped.

Yogurt made from cows' milk will have a thin layer of whey atop the opaque, firmer yogurt. Do not agitate the yogurt and do not try to stir the whey back in. If the yogurt is ready, chill it thoroughly before serving.

Yogurt is *not* ripe if it is still liquid or semi-liquid, though goats' milk yogurt will be softer and creamier in consistency than that made from cows' milk. If the test jar is not ready, put it back in the incubator and check again an hour later. When the yogurt finally "sets," note the time, incubator, culture source and other conditions so that you can duplicate, shorten or lengthen the incubation time on your next try.

How to Make Yogurt from Pasteurized Milk

yields 1 quart

1 quart pasteurized whole milk
2 tablespoons yogurt starter culture

1. Heat the milk to 110° to 115°F and add a little of the milk to the starter culture to dilute it. Stir the culture into the warm milk and mix gently but thoroughly until it is dispersed throughout the milk.

2. Pour the cultured milk into the sterile jars, cover and proceed as in steps 3 and 4 in *How to Make Yogurt from Raw Milk.*

Creamy Yogurt

To make a very rich, cream-textured yogurt, replace 1 cup of the whole milk with a cup of cream. Proceed as in making yogurt from pasteurized milk.

Skim Milk Yogurt

To each quart of skim milk add ½ cup to 1 cup of dry skim milk solids. Use 3 tablespoons of starter.

There are many other kinds of yogurt—special strains from other cultures and different lands—and there is more to yogurt than the plain custardy type described above. Once you have the technique down pat for making regular yogurt, try some of these variations.

YOGURT CURD

This is the result of a draining procedure which gives yogurt an interesting new texture. Variations in the draining time make dairy products ideal for dips, or with the appearance of cottage cheese or cream cheese. All of these can be augmented with herbs or spices, or made more delicate by rinsing the curd with cold water.

As it drains, a cup of yogurt will yield up 25 percent of its total volume in only 5 minutes. A quart of yogurt will release only 12 percent of its volume in 5 minutes. Always use spanking-clean cheesecloth for draining yogurt; never, never use old dishtowels or other discarded household linens which may impart unwanted flavors to the curd.

How to Make Yogurt Curd

1. Line a colander with a double layer of damp cheesecloth, and set the colander in a large bowl.

Line colander with cheesecloth.

2. Gently stir 1 quart of plain yogurt, pour it into the cheesecloth, then gather up the margins of the cloth to make a bag.

Pour stirred yogurt into cheesecloth.

3. Suspend the bag over the bowl (you can hang it from the faucet of the kitchen sink), and let the yogurt drain until the desired consistency is reached.

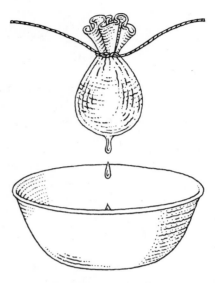

Suspend cheesecloth bag over a bowl to let yogurt drain.

Yogurt Cottage Cheese—Let the bag drain for 24 hours, then turn out the curd which will have a slightly dry consistency and a finer curd than ordinary cottage cheese. Old yogurt will have a sharper, tangier flavor because of its higher lactic acid level. New yogurt will be more delicate. If you want a bland cottage cheese, stir 1 quart of cold water into the yogurt before draining it.

Yogurt Cream Cheese—Follow the procedure for yogurt cottage cheese, but drain the curd only 6 hours. Turn out the curd into a bowl and work in 1 tablespoon of heavy cream or 1 tablespoon of sesame or safflower oil.

Yogurt Dip Base—Drain the yogurt for only 1 hour. Turn the thick, soft curd into a bowl and work in chopped parsley, onions, chives, pressed garlic, horseradish, caraway seeds, dill, grated cured cheese, chili pepper, curry powder or whatever herbs, spices or savories you like. Let this mixture stand covered in the refrigerator overnight to allow the flavors to mingle and permeate the soft curd.

Yogurt Whey—Don't toss out the pale, straw-colored whey in the bowl after draining the curd. It's good-tasting and good for you. Use it to replace water or stock in soups, breads, casseroles; drink it chilled or mixed with vegetable or fruit juices. See the Index for ways to use whey.

More Ways to Use Yogurt

Yogurt curd makes a very fine ice cream when added to a basic ice cream mixture containing eggs and milk. It is best eaten right out of the ice cream freezer.

Yogurt makes a very good meat tenderizer. The acid content partially breaks down the protein in tough cuts of meat or aged barnyard hens, and renders them tender, juicy and of excellent flavor. Set the meat or poultry in a bowl, pour the yogurt over it, cover and let it stand overnight. Cook by your favorite recipe next day.

LABAN

Laban is a very popular Lebanese fermented milk product similar to yogurt in consistency and appearance. The taste, however, is different than yogurt—mildly acid, but with a nutty, yeasty flavor. It is made in Lebanon from the milks of camels, sheep, goats and cows. The Lebanese eat it straight, as it is, or sprinkled with honey or other sweetening, as well as mixed in cakes, in soups and beverages and drained to make a thick, creamy cheese.

Home dairy makers who wish to try Laban will have to find some Lebanese friends who make it at home with imported culture. The culture, native to Lebanon, is quite special, containing 5 different organisms, including yeasts, each of which contributes an essential part to the final flavor. Here is the procedure.

1. Bring the milk to a boil and boil 1 minute.

2. Cool the milk to 120°F.

3. Inoculate the milk with Laban culture, in an amount equal to 2.5 percent of the milk volume. (This is about 2 teaspoons of culture per quart of milk.)

4. Let the milk stand, covered, for 12 to 15 hours at room temperature, then chill.

LABNEH

Labneh is another interesting dairy product, a concentrated thick yogurt cheese preserved in oil and eaten daily with bread in the Arab sections of Israel. It is an ideal food preservation technique for a hot climate with no refrigeration. The process for making it is not unlike that for making Laban. Although a commercial yogurt starter culture is often used to make Labneh, a native, homemade strain handed down from the past exists, called *robee* in Israel. So far its microorganisms have not been analyzed or identified.

The procedure for making Labneh may tempt some experimenters.

1. Cows' milk is brought to a boil and held there several minutes.

2. The milk is cooled to 102° to 106°F and inoculated with the starter culture, in an amount equal to about 2 percent of the milk volume, or a scant

Martha B. Davis, Firm Believer in Yogurt

Martha B. Davis of Henniker, New Hampshire, says, "I am a firm believer in yogurt and all dairy products. . . . I was sick last fall with a severe stomach flu. For 1½ weeks I couldn't eat or drink. I was craving milk and finally decided to try some homemade yogurt. The next day, I began to have an appetite again, and I am convinced that the bacteria in the yogurt culture did a lot for my recovery."

Martha Davis has been making yogurt for 12 years, and has exhibited her yogurt on New Hampshire Home Dairy Products Day. She began making yogurt when she was away at school with an electric yogurt maker her mother gave her. "The yogurt was a welcome change from school food when mixed with different flavorings (honey, maple syrup, fruits). As soon as I had a kitchen of my own, I began experimenting with mixing it into different foods." Now she lives near 2 dairy farms with plenty of milk available. "All the milk I use now is raw. I have never used goats' milk." Here, in her own words, is how Martha Davis makes yogurt.

"I generally make 1 or 2 quarts of yogurt at a time to feed 2 people. My yogurt dishes, which are heated on a tray, each hold 1 cup. (This is a nice size for individual servings since once any yogurt is spooned out of a dish it becomes watery when left setting.) I sometimes set a stainless steel bowl with the cultured milk under the woodstove, where it sets up very nicely.

"I buy plain yogurt to use as a starter if I don't have any homemade on hand. Homemade cultures seem to weaken with time, so when the finished yogurt is watery and really tangy, I buy commercial plain yogurt again.

"My first step in yogurt making is to wash the yogurt dishes or bowl thoroughly with hot, soapy water, then rinse. I let them drain while I'm warming 1 or 2 quarts of milk. If I'm using the warming tray, I plug it in at the same time so it will preheat. I warm the milk over medium heat until a drop on my wrist feels warm, not hot.

"I then add about ½ cup warm milk to ¼ to ½ cup starter. I mix it gently but thoroughly, and pour that into the rest of the warm milk. I stir it well, then pour this into the warming tray dishes or into a bowl to turn. . . . My 'spots' are usually 95° to 100°F. The warming tray takes 6 to 8 hours. Under the stove takes approximately 24 hours.

"I let it cool to room temperature before refrigerating. It keeps well—over a week in the refrigerator if tightly covered. I put aside ½ cup to start the next batch.

"I use yogurt in cooking, salad dressings, dips and baking. I enjoy cooking, and the variations with yogurt can be endless. The following are some of my favorites:

1. After potatoes are baked, cut them in half and scoop the potato out of the skins. Mash with some grated cheddar cheese, herbs, freshly ground pepper and yogurt to moisten. Stuff skins with this mixture, sprinkle with more cheese and paprika, then put in oven until the cheese melts.

2. Mix 1 cup yogurt with 1 or 2 mashed cloves of garlic and a little olive oil. Combine this with cubed or sliced cucumbers and chill well. Fresh, finely chopped mint may be added or substituted for garlic.

"I also use yogurt in meat dishes, such as Beef Stroganoff, added to meat and vegetable skillet dinners just before serving, blended with gravy from pot roasts or stews.

"There are 2 problems I have encountered when adding yogurt to hot foods.

Curdling: I try to avoid this by adding a small quantity of the hot food to the yogurt first, stirring thoroughly, then adding yogurt slowly over low heat.

Thinning: Sometimes the yogurt thins out when added to hot mixtures. This can be remedied by adding 1 tablespoon cornstarch to 1 tablespoon cold water, then mixing that with each cup of yogurt. I rarely find this necessary; more often I tend to leave the food on low heat and let some of the moisture evaporate. This *must* be done on low heat or the mixture will curdle."

2 teaspoons of starter culture per quart of milk. The inoculated milk is allowed to stand until it reaches room temperature.

3. Now the milk is covered and set to ferment very, very slowly in the refrigerator 10 to 12 hours. At the end of this time the curd is poured into a fine-meshed cheesecloth bag and hung in a shaded, cool place to drain for 1 week. During this draining period the curd is salted and mixed daily by hand by palpating the cheese bag. The curd is considered "done" when it reaches a fairly dry, cream cheese consistency.

4. Now the cheese is rolled into small balls, packed into glass jars and covered with olive, soy or sunflower oil. The cheese balls will keep this way up to a year without refrigeration.

USING YOGURT

Yogurt is one of the most versatile, useful foods in the kitchen. Its creamy texture makes it ideal for dips, sauces and gravies; its smoothness makes it an excellent emollient in dry casseroles, in salad dressings and as a dessert topping; its tart

---

Yogurt Hints

•Experienced yogurt lovers put aside the correct amount of yogurt as starter for their next batch as soon as the current batch comes out of the incubator. This insures that the last bit won't be used unthinkingly in a casserole or salad, and keeps the future-batch starter clean and uncontaminated from dipped-in spoons and frequently opened jar covers.

•Yogurt stays tasty and useable in refrigerator storage for up to 2 weeks, though most regular users of the creamy delicacy make up a batch weekly to get the full benefit of the digestion-aiding bacteria, and some heavy users make yogurt daily as part of the regular kitchen routine.

•Each batch of yogurt you make will be a little different since yogurt is permeated by living organisms which do not always grow and multiply predictably. Usually the consistency will range from a creamy custard to a firm custard. If you like firm yogurt, add 1 tablespoon of dry milk powder for each quart of milk. Once in a while, especially if the culture is losing strength after some months of use, yogurt will stubbornly keep the consistency of buttermilk. You can use this yogurt in baking,

to make yogurt-curd cheese, or you can freeze it and use it later for yogurt-batter pancakes.

•The longer yogurt stands in the incubator, the more solid the consistency and the more pronounced the acidity.

•Don't go overboard on using starter on the false assumption that if a little starter is good, a lot will be better and faster. Too much starter makes a coarse-grained, somewhat gritty yogurt, a foodstuff that ranks way down there with lumpy oatmeal, cold fried eggs and overcooked pasta. Starter culture needs plenty of room to expand, and too much starter leads to a crowded mass of bacterial colonies.

•Keep the milk temperature between 105° and 115°F when adding the starter culture. Temperatures over 115°F will kill the yogurt-making bacteria. Under 90°F the culturing process drags to a halt. If you inadvertently kill your starter culture by adding it to too-hot milk, you can save the day by letting it cool to the correct temperature, adding more culture and making yogurt-curd cottage cheese (see p. 221).

•Always use fresh milk for yogurt. The older the milk the longer it takes the yogurt to mature.

acidity brings out the flavors of the food with which it is blended, enhancing the natural tastes of everything from almonds to zucchini. Its easy digestibility and its nutrient content, especially its power to aid the intestinal absorption of calcium, make it an important food. Lactose-intolerant people can enjoy it, for the lactose content is converted to lactic acid in the fermenting process. People on low-fat diets can benefit from the healthful attributes of skim milk yogurt without raising their lipid levels. Yogurt can literally span the menu from appetizer to dessert. Here follow some traditional and some unusual ways to use yogurt, from other cultures and from modern North American adaptations.

Yogurt Cream I

yields 2 cups

This is a delectable dairy product similar in taste to *Creme Fraiche.*

> 2 cups whipping cream
> 2 tablespoons yogurt

1. Have both cream and yogurt at room temperature. Stir the yogurt into the cream, cover and let it stand at room temperature 1 hour.

2. Chill and serve over fresh fruit, or as a topping for carrot cake, date bread or oatmeal bars.

Yogurt Cream II

yields 2 cups

> 2 cups whipping cream
> 2 teaspoons yogurt

1. Heat the cream to 85°F.

2. Put the yogurt in a sterile glass jar, then pour in the warm cream, stirring gently but thoroughly.

3. Place in an incubator as in yogurt making, 3 to 5 hours.

4. Chill and serve.

Both yogurt creams may be whipped after they are chilled. They can be sweetened or seasoned. See the section on whipped sweet creams (see Index) for ideas on ways to vary yogurt cream.

YOGURT RECIPES

Appetizers, Dips and Sauces

Avocado Cream Dip

yields 1½ cups

1 large avocado
1 cup Yogurt Curd, dip base consistency
    (see p. 221)
1 garlic clove, pressed
  few drops lime juice

In a blender combine these ingredients. Chill several hours before serving.

This dip and other dips are excellent with sesame seed crackers, carrot or celery sticks, pineapple or cucumber chunks.

Dilled Cucumber Slices with Yogurt

yields 1½ to 2 cups

3 to 4 small cucumbers
1 tablespoon chopped dill
1 cup yogurt

1. Score the skins of the cucumbers with a fork their full length, then slice thinly. Place the slices in a bowl, cover with a saucer, weight them and let stand at room temperature several hours.

2. Drain the cucumbers, sprinkle with the dill and mix in the yogurt. Cover and chill several hours.

Greek Yogurt Cheese Balls

makes ten to twelve balls

2 cups Yogurt Curd, cottage cheese
     consistency (see p. 221)
1 tablespoon chopped thyme
2 cloves garlic, pressed
 olive oil

1. Combine the yogurt curd, thyme and garlic. Shape into 1-inch balls.

2. Dry on a clean cloth in a shady place 12 hours, covered with a piece of cheesecloth.

3. Put the balls in a jar, cover with olive oil and store in a cool place several days before serving.

   These cheese balls bear a close resemblance to the Arab Labneh (see p. 222). They are particularly good with chunks of fresh bread.

Green Fire Dip

yields 1 cup

1 cup Yogurt Curd, cream cheese
     consistency (see p. 221)
4 tablespoons chopped green chili
     peppers
1 garlic clove, pressed
 few grains powdered cardamom
 warm breadsticks

   Blend the yogurt curd, chili peppers, garlic and cardamom. Let the mixture stand 1 hour before serving it with the breadsticks.

Little Herb Yogurt Pies

makes sixteen pies

These unusual tidbits make good hot or cold appetizers. They can be made in advance and reheated.

New England Buttermilk Biscuits
      dough (see Index)
1 cup Yogurt Curd, cream cheese
      consistency (see p. 221)
1 tablespoon finely chopped mint
2 tablespoons grated onions
  freshly ground pepper

Preheat oven to 400°F.

1. Roll out the biscuit dough on a lightly floured board to the thickness of pie crust. Cut out rounds with a circle cookie cutter.

2. In a bowl mix the yogurt curd, mint, onions and pepper thoroughly. Put a spoonful in the center of half the dough circles.

3. Moisten the edges of the circles with a pastry brush dipped in milk. Top each filled circle with a second circle and press the edges together with the tines of a fork.

4. Bake the pies 10 or 12 minutes. Serve oven-hot or cold.

Yogurt-Fig Spread

yields 2 cups

If you are bored with peanut butter or on a diet, try this excellent spread on whole wheat bread.

1 cup figs
2 to 3 tablespoons apple juice
1 cup yogurt

1. Simmer the figs in a little water several minutes until they soften.

2. Remove their stems, and with enough apple juice to moisten them, blend in a blender until smooth and thick.

3. Fold in the yogurt. Use at once.

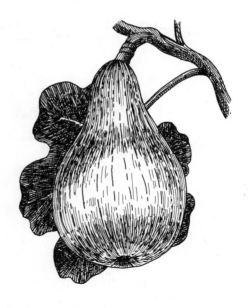

Experimenter's Choice: The All-Purpose Yogurt Sauce

yields 1 cup

This all-purpose sauce is good on cold cooked vegetables, on salads, or with chops or liver. Warm it up and mix it with rice, heap it on chick-peas, lentils and stir-fried bean sprouts. Add a tablespoon as a garnish to your favorite soup or stew. Marinate chicken in it overnight, then bake until tender.

1 cup yogurt
2 tablespoons lemon juice
2 tablespoons chopped mint
2 garlic cloves, pressed

Thoroughly blend all ingredients in a bowl, cover and let stand 1 hour before using.

Soups

Armenian Barley Soup   *serves six*

4 tablespoons butter
½ cup chopped onions
1 cup sliced mushrooms (dried Polish
        mushrooms are best)
2 garlic cloves, chopped
1 cup barley
6 cups Whey (see Index; chicken stock
        may be substituted)
¼ cup chopped parsley, tightly packed
¼ cup chopped mint, tightly packed
4 cups yogurt
1 tablespoon whole wheat flour

1. In a soup kettle melt the butter, then cook the onions, mushrooms and garlic until soft. Add the barley, stirring so that each grain is coated with butter.

2. Add the whey, parsley and mint and simmer slowly until the barley is tender, about 30 minutes. Reduce heat to a barely moving simmer.

3. Stir a little yogurt into the flour, then add this to the rest of the yogurt. Mix several tablespoons of the hot stock into the yogurt, then gently stir the yogurt into the soup. Do not let the soup boil. (High heat will make the yogurt separate, so keep the broth hot but not boiling.) Serve at once.

Cold Cucumber Yogurt Soup

serves four

2 firm, medium-size, cucumbers
4 cups yogurt
2 garlic cloves, pressed
2 tablespoons sesame seed oil
1 tablespoon wine vinegar
1 tablespoon finely chopped dill

1. Peel the cucumbers and seed them, then grate coarsely.

2. Put all ingredients in a blender and blend thoroughly.

3. Chill several hours until very cold, then serve.

Mediterranean Yogurt-Eggplant Soup

serves four

This is particularly good with goats' milk yogurt.

½ cup olive oil
 1 medium-size eggplant (about 1 pound) cut into 1-inch cubes
 1 green pepper, seeded and chopped
½ cup Whey (see Index)
 2 garlic cloves, chopped
 1 small chili pepper, crushed
 1 tablespoon chopped mint
 1 teaspoon lemon juice
 3 cups yogurt
 2 tablespoons chopped chives
 1 tablespoon chopped parsley

1. To a heavy cast iron pot add the olive oil, eggplant and green pepper. Cook for 5 minutes over moderate heat. Stir often from the beginning to coat the pieces well with oil.

2. Cover the pot and let the vegetables steam several minutes, then add the whey, garlic and chili pepper. Simmer until the vegetables are tender.

3. Puree the simmered vegetables in a blender with the mint, then add the lemon juice. Cool to room temperature.

4. Mix in 2 cups of the yogurt, reserving the last cup. Chill the soup several hours.

5. Ladle the cold soup into chilled bowls, then put 1 tablespoon of yogurt in the center of each serving. Stir it in partially to give a spiral effect, then top the soup with the chives and parsley.

Middle East Cucumber-Grape Soup

serves two

3 cups whole milk yogurt
¾ cup cold water or Whey (see Index)
1½ cups grated cucumber
½ cup white seedless grapes, halved
1 tablespoon chopped dill
½ cup chopped walnuts
2 garlic cloves, pressed
   freshly grated white pepper

1. Beat the yogurt until it is light and thick. Gradually beat in the water.

2. Stir in the cucumber, grapes and all the other ingredients and mix well. Chill several hours until ice cold.

3. Serve in chilled glass bowls with a paper-thin slice of cucumber for decoration.

Mushroom Soup with Yogurt Cream

serves six

2 tablespoons butter
1 pound mushrooms, sliced
1 tablespoon grated onions
1 tablespoon chopped parsley
1 tablespoon lemon juice
2 *Beurre Manie* Balls (see Index)
5 cups Whey (see Index; chicken stock
   may be substituted)
1½ cups yogurt
¼ teaspoon Hungarian paprika
1 cup Yogurt Cream, whipped (see
   p. 225)
   parsley sprigs

1. In a saucepan melt the butter, saute the mushrooms with the onions, then add the chopped parsley and lemon juice, simmering until the mushrooms are soft.

2. Gradually stir in the *beurre manie* balls, breaking off small pieces at a time. When smoothly blended, gradually stir in the whey. Cook over low heat until smooth and slightly thickened.

3. Stir a little of the mushroom stock into the yogurt, then carefully blend the yogurt into the stock without allowing it to boil. Add the paprika.

4. Serve at once with 1½ tablespoons whipped yogurt cream in the center of each bowl floating on the soup. Garnish with parsley sprigs.

Russian Borscht

serves six

½ cup chopped carrots
2 medium-size onions, coarsely
    chopped
2 garlic cloves, chopped
2 cups peeled, chopped beets
4 cups Whey (see Index)
1 tablespoon butter
1 cup stewed tomatoes
1 green pepper, chopped
1 large potato, peeled and chopped
1 cup coarsely grated red cabbage
2 tablespoons lemon juice
1 bay leaf
1 tablespoon chopped parsley
1 cup yogurt
2 tablespoons grated cucumber
1 tablespoon chopped dill
6 slices pumpernickel bread, thickly
    buttered

1. In a large soup kettle put the carrots, onions, garlic and beets and cover with water; cover and simmer gently 20 minutes.

2. To the vegetables in the kettle add the whey, butter, tomatoes, pepper, potato, cabbage, lemon juice, bay leaf and parsley and simmer until all the vegetables are tender, about 30 minutes.

3. While the borscht is simmering, mix together the yogurt, cucumber and dill.

4. Ladle the hot borscht into bowls and heap several tablespoons of the yogurt mixture in the center of each serving. Serve at once accompanied by the bread and butter.

This soup is equally good chilled, then pureed in a blender with the yogurt topping blended in.

Snow Pea Yogurt Soup

serves four

1 pound snow peas
1 cup chopped watercress, tightly
      packed (set aside a few whole
      sprigs for garnish)
2 cups Whey (see Index)
1 tablespoon chopped shallots
2 cups yogurt
1 tablespoon chopped chives

1. Cook the snow peas in a steamer over boiling water until just tender. Set them aside.

2. In a heavy pan put the watercress, whey and shallots and simmer 15 minutes.

3. Puree the watercress stock in a blender until smooth, then return to the pan. Add the snow peas and heat slowly. Do not let it boil.

4. Mix 2 or 3 tablespoons of the hot soup into the yogurt, then stir the yogurt into the soup. Serve at once, garnishing each bowl with the chopped chives and a sprig of watercress.

Spinach Yogurt Soup

serves six

2 cups Whey (see Index)
2 cups chicken stock
1 cup chopped celery
3 tablespoons Clarified Butter (see
      Index)
1 small onion, chopped
1 garlic clove, pressed
3 tablespoons whole wheat flour
1½ cups cooked, chopped spinach
1 tablespoon chopped parsley
1 tablespoon chopped dill
¼ cup wine vinegar
4 egg yolks
1 cup yogurt

1. In a soup kettle combine the whey and stock. Add the celery and simmer until tender.

2. In a skillet melt the butter and saute the onion and garlic until soft. Stir in the flour, then gradually add the stock, stirring constantly to keep the mixture smooth. Add the spinach, parsley, dill and vinegar and simmer 10 minutes.

3. Beat the egg yolks until light, then beat in the yogurt. Gradually add 2 or 3 tablespoons of the hot soup stock to the yogurt-egg mixture, then add this to the hot soup. Do not allow it to boil.

Tomato Sherbet Soup

serves four

4 cups homemade tomato juice cocktail
1 teaspoon lemon juice
1 garlic clove, pressed
  freshly ground pepper
1 teaspoon chopped oregano
1 cup yogurt
4 slices lemon

1. Mix all the ingredients except the yogurt and lemon slices in a blender until smooth.

2. Freeze this mixture in ice cube trays until it has the consistency of soft ice.

3. Just before serving put the frozen juice mixture in the blender again with the yogurt. Blend until the soup takes on the consistency of sherbet.

4. Serve at once in chilled sherbet cups with a slice of lemon.

Yogurt Fruit Soup

serves four to six

3 cups unsweetened pineapple juice
1 banana
1 apple, peeled and chopped
1 teaspoon chopped mint
1 nectarine, peeled and chopped
2 tablespoons grape juice
3 tablespoons honey
1 cup yogurt

1. Place all ingredients in a blender and puree until smooth and thick.

2. Chill several hours, then serve in chilled cups.

Yogurt Gazpacho

serves four

2 large tomatoes, quartered
1 sweet pepper, seeded and sliced
1 Spanish onion, peeled and sliced
    paper-thin
1 cup peeled, seeded cucumber
½ cup chopped mixed herbs:
    marjoram, parsley, tarragon,
    chervil, thyme, savory, chives,
    basil, oregano and the like
2 garlic cloves, pressed
½ cup olive oil
3 tablespoons lime juice
3 cups Whey (see Index; chicken stock
    may be substituted)
1 cup yogurt
1 cup stale whole grain bread cubes,
    ½ × ½ inch
2 tablespoons butter

1. Place all the vegetables, herbs and garlic in a large wooden bowl and chop them very fine. (A blender pulps the ingredients too severely.)

2. Slowly beat in the olive oil, lime juice, whey and yogurt.

3. Chill several hours.

4. Just before serving saute the bread cubes in the butter in a heavy skillet until they are brown and crisp and sizzling hot. Ladle the cold soup into chilled bowls and top with the hot croutons.

Main Dishes

Curried Chicken Breasts

serves four

4 tablespoons Clarified Butter (see Index)
1 large onion, chopped
1 tart apple, peeled and chopped
2 garlic cloves, pressed
2 tablespoons curry powder
1 tablespoon finely chopped ginger root
1 tablespoon tomato paste
1 tablespoon lemon juice
1 cup Yogurt Curd, cream cheese consistency (see p. 221)
½ cup raisins
4 chicken breasts

1. In a heavy skillet melt 2 tablespoons of the butter and saute the onion, apple and garlic until soft. Add the curry powder, blending thoroughly, and stir over moderate heat 1 minute. Add the ginger root, tomato paste, lemon juice and yogurt curd, stir for a moment gently, then add the raisins and set aside.

2. In another skillet heat the remaining butter and brown the chicken breasts. Add the breasts to the curry sauce and simmer, uncovered, over very low heat 30 minutes or until the chicken is tender. Turn the breasts from time to time for a thorough saturation of flavor. Add a little water occasionally if necessary.

Pike and Dill Sauce *serves four*

If there is a fisherman in the household, you can enjoy this fine dish to repletion, for the pike is a large fish.

1 tablespoon chopped dill
  freshly ground green peppercorns
1 cup yogurt
3 cups cold, steamed pike (salmon, tuna or haddock may be used instead) in chunks
  tender lettuce leaves

1. Mix the dill and pepper into the yogurt.

2. Arrange the chunks of cold fish on the lettuce leaves and serve the yogurt on the side.

Pork Chops and Yogurt

serves four

4 pork chops
3 tablespoons whole wheat flour
1 teaspoon dried crushed sage
   several twists freshly ground pepper
4 tablespoons Clarified Butter (see
      Index)
1 cup cider
1 tablespoon heavy cream
1 cup Yogurt Curd, cream cheese
      consistency (see p. 221)
1 tablespoon chopped chives

1. Dredge the pork chops in the flour, sage and pepper.

2. Heat the butter in a heavy skillet until hot, then sear pork chops on both sides until brown.

3. Add the cider, lower the heat, cover and simmer 15 or 20 minutes or until the chops are done. Put the chops on a warm platter and keep hot.

4. Reduce the pan juices over moderate heat to about half a cup. Stir in the heavy cream and yogurt curd, stir until thoroughly heated, then pour over the chops and sprinkle with the chopped chives.

Yogurt Quiche

makes one 9-inch quiche

4 eggs
1 cup yogurt
½ cup Yogurt Curd, cottage cheese
      consistency (see p. 221)
½ cup cottage cheese (see Index)
1 tablespoon chopped parsley
2 tablespoons butter
2 tablespoons finely chopped shallots
1 large onion, sliced thin
1 baked 9-inch pie shell in a quiche pan

Preheat oven to 375°F.

1. In a mixing bowl beat the eggs and yogurt.

2. In another bowl mix the yogurt curd with the cottage cheese and parsley.

3. In a heavy skillet melt the butter and saute the shallots and onion until limp and transparent, then transfer to the pie shell.

4. Spread the yogurt curd-cottage cheese mixture over the onion. Pour the egg and yogurt mixture over the top.

5. Bake until set, about 30 minutes. Serve warm or cold.

Vegetables and Salads

Vegetables and yogurt were made to go together. The creamy yogurt serves as a vehicle for the delicate vegetable juices, and the acidity gives bland vegetables a new piquancy and intensity of flavor.

Asparagus with Dilled Yogurt Sauce

serves four to six

2 pounds asparagus
2 egg yolks
1 cup yogurt
1 teaspoon lemon juice
1 tablespoon chopped dill
2 tablespoons heavy cream

1. Steam the asparagus in a steamer until tender. Set aside and keep warm.

2. To make the sauce, beat the egg yolks until thick, place in the top of a double boiler, stir in the yogurt and lemon juice and cook over simmering water until smooth and thick.

3. Stir in the dill and heavy cream, cool slightly, pour over the asparagus and serve.

Baked Zucchini in Yogurt

serves four

No cookbook is complete without another way to deal with the prolific zucchini.

2 to 3 small zucchini
2 tablespoons butter
¾ cup yogurt
¼ cup grated Farm Cheese (see Index) or other aged cheese
2 or 3 sage leaves, chopped fine

Preheat oven to 350°F.

1. Cut the zucchini into thin rounds and arrange in layers in a greased medium baking dish, dotting each layer with butter.

2. Mix the yogurt, cheese and sage. Spread this over the zucchini.

3. Bake until the zucchini are tender and the yogurt-cheese mixture browned.

Gingered Carrots

serves two

6 medium-size carrots
2 tablespoons butter
1 garlic clove, pressed
1 tablespoon chopped scallions
1 teaspoon finely chopped ginger root
½ teaspoon honey
2 tablespoons whole wheat flour
½ teaspoon dry mustard
    several twists freshly ground pepper
1 cup yogurt
1 teaspoon chopped mint
1 teaspoon chopped parsley

1. Cut the carrots into shoestrings and steam over boiling water until tender-crisp. Set carrots aside and reserve ½ cup of the steaming water.

2. In a saucepan, melt the butter and saute the garlic, scallions and ginger for 1 minute, stirring well. Blend in the honey, flour, mustard and pepper; then gradually add the reserved carrot water, stirring until smooth. Simmer until the sauce thickens.

3. Add a little of the hot sauce to the yogurt, then blend the yogurt into the remaining sauce. Do not let the mixture boil.

4. Add the carrots, heat and serve hot sprinkled with the mint and parsley.

Grilled Tomatoes under Yogurt

serves four

2 tablespoons butter
2 tablespoons olive oil
½ cup yogurt
4 tablespoons whole grain bread
    crumbs
1 garlic clove, pressed
1 teaspoon chopped oregano
¼ cup grated Farm Cheese (see Index)
1 tablespoon chopped parsley
4 large beefsteak tomatoes (allow 1 per
    person)

Preheat the broiler.

1. In a small saucepan heat the butter and olive oil, then add all the other ingredients except the tomatoes. Stir and cook until hot and the cheese is melted.

2. Slice the tomatoes in 1-inch thick slices, arrange on an oiled baking sheet and broil 1 minute. Remove from the broiler.

3. Spread the tomatoes with the yogurt-cheese mixture and return to the broiler until the topping is melted, bubbling and slightly browned.

Spring Parsnips with Yogurt

serves four

Parsnips that have wintered under the snow and are dug up in early spring are considered a treat in northern New England.

2 pounds spring parsnips, scrubbed and sliced
1 tablespoon olive oil
2 tablespoons Clarified Butter (see Index)
2 tablespoons chopped parsley
1 teaspoon grated orange rind
½ cup yogurt
½ cup medium cream

1. Steam the parsnips over hot water until tender but not mushy. Set aside and keep warm.

2. Heat the olive oil and butter in a large skillet, mix in the parsley and orange rind and cook 1 or 2 minutes over moderate heat.

3. Add the yogurt and cream, stir 1 minute over lowered heat, then add the parsnips. Do not let the mixture boil. Serve at once.

Yogurt Nectarine-Cucumber Salad

serves six

This is a Middle Eastern dish that is as beautiful as it is delicious. It is a spectacular summer salad when served in a clear glass bowl.

2 cups yogurt
2 tablespoons chopped mint
1 large garlic clove, pressed
2 pounds nectarines, sliced thin in circles
2 medium cucumbers, unpeeled, sliced thin

1. In a bowl mix the yogurt, mint and garlic.

2. In a shallow, clear glass serving dish make alternate layers of nectarine slices, cucumber slices and the yogurt mix, repeating until all ingredients are used.

3. Chill overnight or for several hours before serving.

Experimenter's Choice: Vegetarian Plate

Pick the finest, most brilliantly colored, well-flavored vegetables in your garden early in the morning. Wash, trim, and chill them for several hours. Arrange them on a white platter and serve with a bowl of Vegetable Dip. Possibilities are: greentail onions; green pepper strips; carrot sticks; broccoli (side flowerets); celery stalks; cherry tomatoes; red, white and black radishes; snap beans.

Vegetable Dip
yields 2 cups

2 cups yogurt or Yogurt Curd (see p. 220)
1 tablespoon lemon juice
  several twists freshly ground green
      peppercorns
2 tablespoons chopped herbs in the
      combination of your choice
      (watercress, parsley, celery
      leaves, garlic, summer savory,
      rosemary, sage and the like)

1. Puree these ingredients in a blender briefly.

2. Chill and serve.

Experimenter's Choice: Yogurt Fruit Salad

Make this early in the day to let the juices of the ripe fruits mingle, their fragrant aromas and sweet flavors blend.

1. In a bowl mix 4 cups of clean, ripe fruit, hulled, sliced, sectioned or whole. Here are some possibilities: apples, avocados, bananas, blackberries, blueberries, cherries, dewberries, figs, grapefruit, grapes, mangoes, melon, nectarines, oranges, peaches, pears, pineapple, plums, raspberries and strawberries. Cover and chill several hours.

2. At the same time you prepare the fruits, mix 2 cups of yogurt or yogurt cream cheese with a handful of raisins, chopped dried apricots, slivers of dried dates, apples or figs. Add pinches of any of the following herbs and spices that please your palate: tarragon, woodruff, cardamom, cinnamon, nutmeg, rose water or vanilla. Chill this mixture.

3. Just before serving, arrange Bibb or other tender lettuce leaves on a serving platter, heap with the fruit and top with the yogurt. Chopped nuts and fresh-grated coconut add piquancy and rich texture.

Desserts

Apple Omelet

serves four

4 tablespoons butter
3 good-flavored apples (Empire is
        superb), sliced, but not peeled
1 teaspoon cinnamon
  pinch powdered cardamom
2 tablespoons maple syrup
1 cup yogurt
5 eggs
2 tablespoons water

1. In a skillet melt half the butter. Saute the apple slices a few minutes on each side, then add the cinnamon, cardamom and maple syrup, and cook until the apples are tender but not mushy. Gently stir in the yogurt and set aside in a warm place.

2. Beat the eggs and water until well blended but not foaming, and cook 4 omelets (one at a time) in an omelet pan. As each omelet sets, spoon on the filling of yogurt and apples, fold over the omelet, cook another minute, then slide onto a warmed plate. Keep the omelets warm in a low oven until the last one is done.

Blueberry-Grape Cream Whip

serves two

2 cups wild blueberries
1 cup seedless green grapes, halved
1 cup Yogurt Cream (see p. 225)
1 tablespoon honey

1. Wash the fruit, drain, mix together and chill several hours.

2. Just before serving whip the yogurt cream and honey until light and fluffy, then blend in the fruit gently. Heap high in chilled glass cups.

Butternut-Carrot Cake

makes one 9 × 13-inch cake

Yogurt in cake or bread mixes makes a very tender, melting crumb. The flavor of butternuts goes extraordinarily well with carrots, honey and yogurt, but walnuts can be substituted if these rich nuts are not native to your region.

6 tablespoons butter
1 cup maple sugar
3 eggs
2 cups whole wheat flour
1 teaspoon baking soda
½ teaspoon cinnamon
1 cup yogurt
2 cups grated carrots
1 cup coarsely chopped butternut
    meats
½ cup grated coconut meat (optional)

Preheat oven to 350°F.

1. In a mixing bowl, cream the butter until soft. Beat in the maple sugar until light, then beat in the eggs one by one.

2. Sift the flour, soda and cinnamon into another bowl.

3. Add the yogurt and the flour mixture alternately to the butter mixture. Gently fold in the carrots, butternuts and coconut.

4. Pour into a greased 9 × 13-inch pan and bake 1 hour. Cool before turning out. Allow the cake to ripen 24 hours before serving with cream.

Frozen Yogurt

serves four

1 tablespoon gelatin
1 tablespoon lemon juice
2 tablespoons water
1 cup berries, nectarines, peaches,
    banana, mixed and chopped
1 cup mild yogurt
½ cup heavy cream

1. Soften the gelatin in the lemon juice and water 5 minutes, then dissolve over very low heat, stirring constantly. Remove from heat.

2. Mix the fruit and yogurt, then blend in a blender until smooth but not liquefied. Tiny chunks and pieces of fruit are desirable.

3. Pour the mixture into ice cube trays, cover and freeze. Remove from freezer 20 minutes before serving, allow to soften slightly, then break into chunks and blend in a blender until creamy, but still thick and frozen. Add cream, 2 tablespoons at a time, until mixture reaches desired consistency. Serve quickly in chilled cups.

Pear Custard Cake

makes one 9 × 13-inch cake

In September the pears on our neighbors' ancient tree ripen and hang in heavy golden teardrops until the branches bend down. Pear juice, pear butter, canned pears, stewed pears and gingered pears make kitchens fragrant all up and down our road. Here is one of our favorite ways to deal with the harvest.

Pears

6 large pears, peeled, cored and halved
1 cup water
1 tablespoon honey
1 teaspoon chopped ginger root

Cake

½ cup butter
½ cup maple syrup
2 eggs
1 teaspoon vanilla extract
2 cups whole wheat flour

Custard

1 tablespoon whole wheat flour
3 eggs, beaten
2 cups yogurt
½ cup maple syrup
¼ teaspoon freshly grated nutmeg
¼ teaspoon grated ginger root

Topping

Yogurt Cream (see p. 225)

Preheat oven to 325°F.

1. In a large skillet simmer the pear halves in the water with the honey and ginger until tender. Set aside.

2. In a mixing bowl, cream the butter, then beat in the maple syrup, eggs and vanilla.

3. Gradually mix in the flour until the batter is smooth and well blended. Bake in a greased 9 × 13-inch pan 15 minutes. Remove the cake but do not turn off the oven.

4. While the cake layer is baking, make the custard. Mix all the custard ingredients in a bowl until well blended.

5. Arrange the pear halves on the cake layer and sprinkle with any remaining stewing liquid. Pour the custard over the pears. Bake 45 minutes longer. Serve while still warm with Yogurt Cream I or II.

India Yogurt Pudding

serves four

4 cups Yogurt Curd, cream cheese
    consistency (see p. 221)
4 tablespoons honey
½ teaspoon ground cardamom
¼ teaspoon saffron, soaked in
    1 tablespoon warm milk
¼ teaspoon freshly grated nutmeg
¼ teaspoon ground cinnamon
2 tablespoons slivered pistachio nuts

1. In a mixing bowl combine all the ingredients except the pistachio nuts.

2. Chill several hours in the mixing bowl.

3. Invert on a serving dish and garnish with the pistachio slivers.

Snow Apple Simplicity

serves four

We always dry quantities of apple slices in the autumn, and this simple, satisfying mixture is good as a dessert or a snack. There are endless improvisations you can make by adding spices, other dried fruits like apricots, figs, pears, raisins, a few tablespoons of granola, a teaspoon of dulse seaweed, wheat germ or whatever you enjoy.

1 quart yogurt
2 tablespoons maple syrup
1 cup dried apples, coarsely cut

    Mix the ingredients, cover, and let mature 12 hours in the refrigerator.

Viennese Yogurt Cream

serves two

2 cups yogurt, creamy style
½ cup honey
1 cup chopped hazelnuts or almonds
2 cups currants or blackberries

1. In a glass serving bowl, stir the yogurt and honey together until thoroughly blended. Fold in the nuts.

2. Chill several hours, then serve with the fresh fruit on the side.

Yogurt Banana Split

makes two

1 peach, peeled and halved
1 large banana
2 tablespoons wheat germ
1 cup mild yogurt, creamy style
¼ cup chopped nuts and mixed dried
　　fruits (almonds, apples, apricots,
　　pineapple)

1. Put the peach in a blender and puree it smooth. Put half the puree in the bottoms of 2 sundae dishes.

2. Cut the banana in quarters and put 2 quarters in each dish. Sprinkle with 1 tablespoon of the wheat germ.

3. Add ½ cup of the yogurt to each dish and top with the rest of the pureed peach. Sprinkle with the remaining wheat germ and the chopped nuts and fruits.

Yogurt Cream Pie

makes one 7-inch pie

1 baked 7-inch pie shell
1 cup yogurt, whole milk or creamy
　　style
1 cup cream cheese
1 tablespoon honey
½ teaspoon vanilla extract

1. Beat all the ingredients to the consistency of heavy whipped cream with an electric beater.

2. Pour into pie shell and chill until set.

Yogurt-Sesame Drop Doughnuts

makes about two dozen small doughnuts

½ cup sesame seeds
½ teaspoon powdered cinnamon
2 cups yogurt
2 tablespoons grated orange rind
2 tablespoons orange juice
½ teaspoon baking soda
2+ cups whole wheat flour
    sesame oil or vegetable oil for frying

Glaze
1 tablespoon butter
1 cup honey
½ cup water

Preheat oven to 350°F.

1. On an oiled baking sheet toast the sesame seeds 15 minutes, stirring often to prevent uneven browning. Sprinkle with the cinnamon and set aside.

2. Have all ingredients at room temperature. In a mixing bowl combine the yogurt, orange rind, juice and soda.

3. Stir in the flour thoroughly. Cover the bowl with a damp towel and let the dough stand 1 hour.

4. In a heavy skillet or deep fryer heat 3 or more inches of oil to frying temperature—370°F.

5. Slide 1 tablespoon of dough at a time into the hot oil and fry until golden and puffy on each side, about 3 minutes. Do not crowd the skillet.

6. Drain the doughnuts on absorbent paper until cool, then glaze and coat with the sesame seeds.

7. To make the glaze, boil the butter, honey and water together 5 minutes. Cool this mixture until warm, then dip each doughnut into the glaze. Roll each doughnut in the sesame seeds and cinnamon.

11

DELICIOUS DAIRY DRINKS

These drinks — some thick and hearty for nutritious snacks, some ice cold and refreshing for sweltering dog days, some hot and spicy for mid-winter warmups, others soporific to help worriers relax and fall asleep easily, and some nourishing and tempting to build up invalids or the elderly — should be a spur to your imagination rather than rigid prescriptions.

Almond Cream

serves one

1 cup blanched almonds
2 tablespoons honey
½ cup medium cream
½ cup water

1. Blend the almonds in a blender until they are reduced to a fine meal. Add the remaining ingredints and blend 30 seconds.

2. Strain the mixture through a double layer of damp cheesecloth. Chill and serve.

Apple Milk

serves two

This tangy, minty drink is perfect after a hot September morning in the garden picking beans or the last of the tomatoes. Pick a few mint sprigs as you go up to the cool, shady kitchen.

½ cup yogurt
½ cup buttermilk
1 cup sweet cider
1 tablespoon mint leaves

Put all the ingredients into a blender and blend briefly.

Big Banana Shake for Two

1 cup milk
1 tablespoon honey or maple syrup
    (optional)
½ cup pitted chopped dates
1 cup mashed banana
1 cup yogurt
½ teaspoon vanilla extract

1. Put the milk, honey and dates into a blender and blend until smooth.

2. Add the banana, yogurt and vanilla and blend until thick and light.

Breakfast Drink

serves one

1 medium-size sweet carrot, grated
1 tablespoon honey
1 cup Whey (see Index)
⅓ cup yogurt

Put the carrot, honey and whey into a blender and blend until smooth; then briefly blend in the yogurt.

Classic American Strawberry Milkshake

serves two

½ cup light cream
½ cup milk
1 cup vanilla or strawberry ice cream
1 tablespoon honey
1 cup strawberries
2 tablespoons crushed ice

Put all the ingredients into a blender and blend until thick.

Eggnog

serves one

1 egg
1 cup milk
2 tablespoons heavy cream
½ teaspoon vanilla extract
  dash freshly grated nutmeg

Put all the ingredients into a blender for 30 seconds. Serve dusted with nutmeg.

Fruit Smoothie

serves four

1 cup orange juice
1 cup unsweetened crushed pineapple
1 banana, sliced
1 cup milk
1 tablespoon honey
1 teaspoon vanilla extract
3 tablespoons crushed ice
  mint sprigs (optional)

1. Put everything except the mint into a blender and blend until smooth.

2. Pour into chilled glasses and serve with mint sprigs.

Gayelord Hauser Special

serves one

The health food advocate of the thirties claimed that these three ingredients, if eaten regularly, could help people live long and healthy lives.

1 cup yogurt
1 tablespoon blackstrap molasses
¼ teaspoon wheat germ oil or
    1 teaspoon wheat germ

Blend all the ingredients in a blender and serve.

Hot Posset Cup *serves two*

Posset drinks of hot milk mixed with spices and often with fiery spirits have been favorite beverages since the Middle Ages, and old cookbooks list many. This one makes a very pleasant nightcap for two. It's also a restorative when you come in from the howling blizzard to the warmth and comfort of the fire.

2 cups milk
2 egg yolks
3 tablespoons honey
 rind of ½ lemon, grated
1 cup sweet cider
 freshly grated nutmeg

1. Combine the milk, egg yolks, honey and lemon rind and pour into the top of a double boiler.

2. Heat over hot water, stirring constantly until smooth and thickened.

3. Stir in the cider, heat through and serve in a warmed mug dusted with nutmeg.

Grape Cooler

serves one

1 cup yogurt
½ cup grape juice
1 teaspoon lemon juice

Put all the ingredients into a blender and process until frothy and light.

Indian Buttermilk Drink

serves two

1 cup buttermilk
1 cup water
 crushed ice
 pinch ground cumin (or 1 teaspoon
     honey and ½ teaspoon rose
     water)

1. Stir the buttermilk and water smooth. Pour into a glass of crushed ice.

2. Add the cumin. Stir thoroughly and serve.

Indian Saffron Milk

serves one

Milk and buttermilk drinks are very popular in India where their high nutritional value is recognized. On the eleventh day of each month devout Hindus abstain from all foods except fruit, nuts, milk and honey. Here is a delicious drink based on these ingredients.

1 cup milk
  few threads saffron
1 whole cardamom pod
1 whole clove
1 small piece cinnamon stick
2 tablespoons chopped, blanched
        almonds
  honey

1. Warm 3 tablespoons of the milk to lukewarm and soak the saffron threads in it 10 minutes.

2. Heat the rest of the milk in a saucepan until very warm. Add the spices and the saffron milk, stir, remove from the heat and let stand 5 minutes.

3. When the milk has taken on a light golden color, strain, add the nuts and honey, stir well and serve warm.

Maple Milk

serves one

1 cup cold milk
1 teaspoon maple syrup
  pinch ground coriander

Blend all the ingredients thoroughly in a blender, then serve.

Milk Pick-Me-Up I

serves one

1 cup cold milk
½ cup orange juice
2 tablespoons honey
1 egg
2 drops almond extract

Put all the ingredients in a blender and blend until rich and thick.

Milk Pick-Me-Up II

serves one

1 cup cold milk
1 tablespoon heavy cream
1 small banana

Put all the ingredients in a blender and blend until creamy.

Molasses Milk

serves one

When we were children we enjoyed this drink. The molasses went into the glass first, then the creamy Jersey milk and a long-handled spoon. No matter how long you stirred, watching the milk change from white to caramel color, there was always some stubborn molasses that refused to blend on the bottom of the glass.

1 cup cold milk
1 tablespoon molasses

Blend the ingredients in a blender, or with a spoon in a glass.

Moroccan Almond Milk

serves six

¾ cup whole blanched almonds
¼ cup honey
3 cups Whey (see Index)
1½ cups milk

1. In a blender combine the almonds, honey and whey. Blend until smooth, then strain, getting as much liquid as possible.

2. Add the milk and chill thoroughly. Stir well before serving.

Nightcap

serves one

scant 1 teaspoon honey
1 cup milk
1 cardamom seed, bruised, or pinch sweet woodruff or 1 drop vanilla extract

1. Put the honey in the bottom of a mug and set in a warm place.

2. Heat the milk and flavoring over low heat until it steams. Do not allow it to boil or scald. When hot, pour into the mug through a strainer. Stir well and sip.

Purple Cow

serves two

¾ cup frozen grape concentrate (do not add water)
1 egg
¾ cup milk
1 tablespoon honey
¼ teaspoon vanilla extract

Put all the ingredients into a blender and blend 30 seconds.

Sweet Cider Cream

serves four to six

2 cups freshly pressed sweet cider
2 cups vanilla ice cream
1 tablespoon lemon juice
1 cup cold Whey (see Index)

Put all the ingredients into a blender and blend until creamy and thick.

Tomato Shake

serves six

1 cup yogurt or buttermilk
1 cup cold milk
3 cups homemade spiced tomato juice
   parsley sprigs (optional)

Put all the ingredients except parsley in a blender and process 30 seconds. Serve in chilled glasses garnished with the parsley sprigs.

Wild Blackberry Creamer

serves one

½ cup blackberry juice
½ cup milk or yogurt
½ cup heavy cream
1 tablespoon honey

Have the juice and milk very cold or add 2 tablespoons crushed ice. Blend all the ingredients in a blender until cold and foamy. Serve in a chilled glass.

12 *CHOOSING EQUIPMENT*

Home dairy equipment can be as basic as the pot, bowl, cheese-cloth and knife found in a cottage cheese maker's kitchen or can be as sophisticated as the completely furnished room, where a small bulk milk cooler stands ready to supply a whirring separator, churn, ice cream freezer and steaming kettles which, in turn, will nourish a cheese press. The family's tastes, possibly a market for surplus and certainly the pocketbook will shape the appearance and performance of the dairy. However, big or small, a case must be made for understanding the equipment and then getting the best.

Before deciding firmly on any dairy utensil, consider foremost its chances of meeting your rigid sanitary standards. If it can't be thoroughly and easily cleaned look around a little further. Does some design fault create hard-to-get-at nooks and crannies—hiding places for harmful bacteria? Will the material itself deteriorate with time and wear to provide other microbial sanctuaries? In addition, your equipment should be durable. Milk pails are kicked by animals, culturing containers dropped, cheese kettles scalded, ice cream forms frozen—so consider strength.

Home dairy equipment is available in a range of both natural and man-made materials. Probably the hardest to work with and clean are the antique wooden implements, while the tools of streamlined, mirror-like chromium steels, especially stainless, are the easiest. In between are the modernized antiques, such as glass-lined butter churns, stoneware and other ceramicware, glassware, as well as implements of enameled metals, tinned metals, aluminum and a variety of different plastics.

Wood—As a rule the condition and complexity of a wooden implement will determine the advisability of its use. Such simple tools as butter molds and paddles are constructed of solid hardwood or a few joined pieces, then smooth-sanded, and because of their small sizes and seamless, or near-seamless, construction, scrubbing and scalding are easy. Antique upright dasher churns, box and barrel crank churns and most wooden buckets, on the other hand, are made of joined staves or squares. Depending upon the care they received when they were in use and during the ensuing years, they can range from fairly sound to downright rotten. When inspecting an old churn you are consid-

ering for modern use be sure to look inside and at the bottom—places which escape the drying and bactericidal benefits of sunlight. Mold and decay will frequently appear where butterfat lodged and bacteria grew—at the stave joints and around the bottom, on the inside, and outside, where the staves join the head. Use a flashlight and your nose to check the inside. If it looks or smells bad, forget it.

New wooden churns of maple, cedar, white pine and sometimes basswood are sold through home dairy supply outlets. These tools will be free from decaying wood but they still need care. New upright and crank churns without glass or plastic liners should be soaked to swell the seams and make the vessel milk/cream tight. Use clean water, and then after each use the churn should be rinsed with cold water, vigorously scrubbed with a cleanser in warm water, rinsed and then scalded. When you are scrubbing, pay particular attention to the seams and where the ends are dadoed to accept the sides. Before using it the next time, it is safest to scald or steam the churn again. Many wooden churn users regularly clean and sanitize their churns with dairy chemicals.

Ceramics and Glassware—Stoneware is another traditional material of the home dairy. Like the coopers, the farmware potters are mostly gone now but examples of their craft are far more abundant than those of the woodjoiners. In the days before refrigeration, and cheap glass and steel, stoneware was best. Its thickness made it both durable and a fair insulator when compared with dishware, and earthen jars were particularly esteemed for the cool storage of butter. Included among stoneware implements are jars, pitchers, bowls, crocks and churns. When purchasing any of these items for dairy use and not as antique art, select those with sound finishes. Cracks and chips lead to bacterial buildup. If you use a stone crock with a button valve or spigot as a gravity cream separator, be sure to remove and clean it after you've drawn off the skim milk and cream.

Most outstanding of several negative stoneware features is weight. A 5-gallon crock, for instance, can weigh 40 pounds. Stoneware also can break when dropped or struck with a solid object, and some glazed surfaces can be toxic. Whereas stoneware is most often glazed with the simple addition of salt at the correct kiln firing point, some white and white-trimmed jars and pitchers were glazed with a mixture of borox and lead. Initially it was held that the fusing which occurs during firing, an action called *fritting*, kept the lead insoluble, but today, with such normally far-from-the-mouth materials as paint, gasoline and birdshot proven dangerous, people might well wonder what effect lactic and other ripening milk acids have on their heirloom white pots.

Glass implements are found everywhere in the home dairy. Graduates for measuring starters and cultures, bowls for mixing them in, and vessels for flavoring curds and collecting whey can be made of plastic, but clearly transparent glass is a better choice. Several popular butter churns have clear glass bases or large canning jars, and while the disadvantage of breakage is great, the advantages of moderate cost and ease and thoroughness of cleaning (with just a measure of care throughout) make glass a good investment. Be sure to get sturdy glass; the heavy oven and dishwasher-safe weights are surest to weather years of sterilizing temperatures.

Enamelware and Tin — Enamelware, both speckled and in solid colors, is low on the dairyware list. Tin, if used with care and cleaned correctly, is good. One might assume that the best grade of enamelware would be a perfectly sound dairy material — the cores fabricated of heavy sheet or cast iron or of steel with all sides protected with several coats of glaze — because the glass-like surface resists milk acids, won't rust and, like glass, is easy to clean. All true. What happens, however, is that before the enameled piece is easily cleaned too many times, it is ruined by scorching or chipping. The speed of heating and the nature of such a glaze as speckled enamel make it easy for foods, especially milk solids, to stick and burn. Scouring the scorched area may remove the burned milk but it also takes away deteriorated enamel, and this hot spot is where milk will scorch again. Further scouring will eventually expose the bare metal core to the milk being processed, giving it an unpleasant metallic flavor. Enamelware is also prone to chipping. A dropped enamel pot is generally a loss on the first fall, and some will chip when rapped against the side of a sink or even set down firmly on a counter.

Tin is an element highly resistant to moist air and, when used as a dip or applied electrostatically to vulnerable iron and steel, can make them safe and inexpensive materials for milk product preparation and storage. Cream separators, milk and cream cans, milk pails and even sealed containers of evaporated milk and cheese are tinned. During the years between the exclusive use of wood and stoneware, on one end, and stainless steel, on the other, virtually all dairy metals coming into contact with milk were tin-plated.

Cleansing tin used in milk processing is similar to cleaning other metals, the exception being the special care required by its softness. Since tin is soft, just a shade harder than lead, steel wool or abrasive cleansers should not be used to scour milky surfaces. Tin cleaning steps are:

1. Flush the utensil with cool water immediately after use.

2. Scrub with a nylon or fiber bristle brush and cleanser in lukewarm water.

3. Flush with warm water.

4. Scald and let the hot tinware air dry.

Some people like to bring out the lustre of the metal by burnishing the warm tin with a soft linen cloth. Unless this cloth is sterilized each day and each tin part is sterile, there is a big danger of spreading bacteria over otherwise clean parts.

Aluminum—Lightweight and reasonably priced, aluminum is a good and durable dairyware material up to the point milk is ripened. Then milk acids react with the metal, creating minute pits of corrosion which are hard to clean and are potential microbial traps. Aluminum dents more easily than steel, and it can be gouged if scoured with a coarse steel pad. However, a big advantage of aluminum is that after initial dulling by air and water, the oxidized surface becomes very resistant to moisture corrosion during normal daily use.

Plastics—Many generic classes of plastics, nylons, acrylics and epoxy are manufactured into utensils which can be used as dairyware. Before deciding on any one, check into its ease of cleansing and durability, and be certain that it is made of a non-toxic material resistant to corrosion. Look for surface smoothness and have the manufacturer or distributor specify the degree to which it will absorb milk

products. The control for smoothness—that condition being a requisite for cleansing effectiveness and ease—used by the U.S. Public Health Service and the Dairy Industry Committee in drawing up standards for dairy plastics acceptability is 18-8 stainless steel sanded to a 120-grit finish. For plastics to qualify they have to be smoother or at least as smooth as the steel.

Since plastics are relatively soft when compared to steel, manual scrubbing should be restricted to nylon and bristle brushes. Steel scrubbing pads are destructive, scratching out breeding places for bacteria and a zone for milk stone build-up. To keep bacteria counts down, users of plastic dairy equipment depend upon chemical cleansers and sanitizers. Therefore, before making the final selection of your plastic dairyware, check the plastic for corrosion and chemical resistance as specified in the manufacturer's or distributor's ratings. Measure the plastic against all possible cleansers and sanitizers you might use, as well as any chemical properties in the milk product. Iodine, for instance, has a severely deleterious effect on epoxy, while a nylon bowl will break down when filled continually with ripening milk which contains lactic acid. Additionally, some plastics flavor milk products and others are toxic. The U.S. Food and Drug Administration recently ruled that polyvinyl chloride materials were not permissible in finished milk product containers.

Stainless Steel—Light, durable and with a smooth, easy-to-clean finish, the seamless stainless steel utensil, while costing sometimes twice as much as other metals, will usually last twice as long. Although resistant to most dairy chemicals when they are mixed to proper strengths, stainless will react unsatisfactorily to strong iodine solutions. When scrubbing stainless steel with a pad make sure it is of the same material and that you scrub with the grain — the sanding striations. Using non-stainless scrub pads can lead to rusting when a splinter breaks off and becomes lodged in a sanding grit track.

CLEANSING MILKING EQUIPMENT

One of the primary causes of high bacteria counts in different home dairy products can be traced to the beginning — dirty milking equipment. You might expect to make tasty cheeses or flavorsome butter from sound milk using cultures over which you have a large measure of control. But if poor cleansing and sanitizing of milking equipment start you off with a raw material teeming with spoilage bacteria, you might just as well skip the whole project because the results will be disappointing. Milk is one of the best bacteria-growing mediums and only by scrupulous cleaning of equipment and prompt chilling can the milk be protected.

These are the steps in cleaning and sanitizing milking machines, pails, strainers, cans and other tools:

1. Rinse all utensils in cool water immediately after milking to remove excess milk. Do not use scalding water.

2. Prepare a bath by filling half of a double sink with hot water to which has been added the correct proportion of dairy detergent. This detergent should not be perfumed but rather an alkaline detergent added at the manufacturer's recommended rate. If you are filling the sink for the first time it's best to measure the detergent-to-water formula exactly by ounces to gallons because the proportion has to be exact to be effective. Commercial detergents sold at farm supply stores can contain iodine and phosphoric acid and serve additional roles as germicides and sanitizers.

3. Still-soak the utensils in the detergent-hot water solution for about 5 minutes. This will loosen any built-up milk residues.

4. Scrub all utensils thoroughly with nylon or natural bristle brushes. Milking machines and cream separators require differently shaped brushes to scrub cups and recesses unique to the machine, while pails and cans are easily scrubbed with a common dairy brush. Try to avoid using steel scrubbing pads as they can scratch finishes or leave splinters which can rust. If you have a problem with calcium deposits (milk stone) and you are milking every day, substitute an acid cleanser every third day instead of using alkaline detergents all week long.

5. Prepare the rinse bath by filling the adjoining deep sink with water just as hot as you can stand it. Dunk the scrubbed pieces into the bath and swirl them around so that all of the detergent is rinsed away.

6. Place the hot utensils on a drying rack and let them air dry. The rack should be made out of wood or a plastic-coated material which will not rust and should be positioned away from such sources of contamination as the floor or a window opening onto the barnyard. All cans and pails must be inverted so that the excess rinse water will drain promptly, allowing water tracks to dry before the metal cools.

7. Pre-milking sanitizing is a worthwhile precaution in the event flies or some other contamination source visited the equipment between milkings. The method is simple — fill one of the sinks with water, add the chemical sanitizing agent and immerse the milking equipment for 5 minutes. Again, the proper ratio of chemical to water is important — too little and the bath won't be effective; too much can be harmful to some types of equipment while not improving the protection. A heavy measure of iodine is corrosive and will even damage stainless steel, while a wetting agent used with some chemicals is harmful to some plastics. The recommended strength of sanitizer/water, figured in parts per million (ppm) are: Iodophor, 15 to 25 ppm; acid-wetting agent complex, 200 ppm; quaternary ammonium, 100 to 200 ppm; chlorine compounds, 100 to 200 ppm.

A popular strip cup manufactured by Leyse Aluminum Company.

CUPS, PAILS AND STRAINERS

Starting with the first step in home dairy production — milk from an animal splashing into a man-made utensil — extreme care must be taken to protect the highly perishable and easily contaminated raw material.

Strip Cup — At each milking the first milk drawn from an animal is examined and discarded as the probability is high that it contains bacteria which collected in the teat orifice. If this is not removed the bacteria will contaminate the bulk of milk that follows. A strip cup is used to collect these first few streams and, most important, it offers the milker an opportunity to examine the milk closely. A popular strip cup is made of aluminum and is available with a stainless steel screen or a black anodized tray with a drain slot for the detection of abnormal milk and mastitis. The cups are equipped with handles and come with or without hooks for hanging on the edge of a milking pail.

Milk Pails — These are made of tinned steel, stainless steel, aluminum, plastic and, if you frequent rural antique shops, wood. They can be small (just over 3 pints) or very large (almost 15 quarts), and some have flared sides while others are straight. Some milk pails are of seamless construction while others are soldered and riveted. Whatever your choice, balance cost against ease and thoroughness of cleaning, durability and the probable life of the utensil. It also makes sense to pick a pail which is comfortable for you and is appropriate for the size of the animal you are milking. A 15-quart steel pail weighing 5 pounds is a bit excessive

A nickel-stainless pail by Terriss-Consolidated Industries.

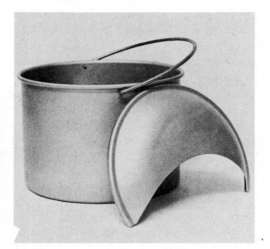

Goat-milking pails of aluminum and stainless, both with 4-quart capacities.

for the average goat, and it would be hard to fit it under the animal. With the exception of several small flared tin pails, which are often used as paint buckets, and aluminum and stainless steel pails made especially for goats, most milk pails commercially available are suited for cows. One tip: If you favor plastic, consider pails made of high-density polyethylene which will withstand corrosive and steam sterilization.

Pails of stainless and aluminum designed for milking goats are a good choice if you have goats. First, the profile is low enough to fit under a dairy goat (less than 6 inches high), yet there is a capacity of 3½ to 4 quarts. Second, the pails are of solid construction with 2 accessories, a bail handle and a half-moon lid which can be disassembled for easy cleaning and sterilization. Third, the half-moon cover keeps hair and dust out, and splashing milk in, during the rigors of hand milking.

Milk Strainer—The secret of milk straining is in the filtering. There are any number of simple tinned milk strainers with woven brass screens which will remove hair and larger pieces of unwanted matter from the milk supply, but only with finely woven cotton filter discs will

Stainless milk strainer with 18-quart bowl and baffle cup.

all of the sediment be removed. Two such strainers are a seamless tinplate with 10-quart capacity and a stainless steel consisting of a baffle cup and 18-quart receiving bowl. Each uses 6½-inch filter discs. These discs are made of interwoven layers of cotton and are available in both 6- and 6½-inch diameters, 100 filters to the box.

Milk Pails and Tote Pails—If you are milking 1 or 2 goats, a 2- to 4-quart milk pail will serve well for carrying the morning or evening's collection from milkroom to dairy. For more or larger animals, stainless tote pails up to 16 and 20 quarts are available. All should have snug-fitting lids or flanged covers. Some tote pails have handles on both the cover and at the base of the pail for easier handling as well as a cover hook for hanging the cover on the pail edge.

Cream Cans—Whether you separate your cream by gravity or machine, there is use for a cream can. For use with separators there are 2-quart tinned cans which fit under the cream spout and 10-quart cans of .0118-gauge tinplate, each with a handle and tight-fitting cover, to use in cool storing cream until you have enough to crank up the churn. For gravity separators there are 12-quart shotgun cans which can also be used for cool storage.

Covered tote pails of stainless (left and center) and an aluminum milk pail (right).

PASTEURIZERS

Telex Automatic Milk Pasteurizer— This utensil will process up to 2 gallons in 25 to 60 minutes. The pasteurizer has no moving parts—you turn it on and a buzzer sounds when the milk is pasteurized. A preset thermostat maintains the correct temperature throughout the pasteurization process and when complete the milk bucket is processed under a cold bath. The Telex consists of a brushed aluminum milk bucket with handle and a white enameled heating element which operates on 110 to 120 AC volts, 60 cycle. It is lightweight (less than 8 pounds) and portable. Extra milk buckets are available.

SafGard Pres-Vac Home Pasteurizer.

SafGard Pres-Vac Home Pasteurizer— Produced in 5-quart and 8-quart sizes, it utilizes the pressure/heat-vacuum/cool system. A thermostat maintains a 155°F pasteurizing temperature under pressure and a buzzer signals when the process is complete. Cold water displaces the hot for fast and even vacuum-sealed cooling. The container is constructed of anodized aluminum with Bakelite panel and handles. The heating element is rated at 1250 watts for 115 AC volts, 60 cycle.

SafGard Milk Pasteurizer— With agitator and thermostat-controlled indirect heat, this machine pasteurizes 2 quarts to 2 gallons of milk or cream automatically. The agitator promotes thorough bacteria kill by keeping the milk in motion during heating and cooling. The entire process— heating, shut-off, cooling and signal buzzer—takes about 40 minutes.

Telex automatic milk pasteurizer and spare bucket for the Telex.

THERMOMETERS

Floating Dairy Thermometer — This Taylor Instrument product is an 8-inch, all-glass instrument graduated to cover a temperature range of 20° to 220°F. The thermometer floats in the milk during the heating process to give instantaneous accurate readings in red spirit. The degree calibrations are recorded in black while important dairy points — freezing, churning, cheese, scalding and boiling — are spelled out.

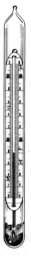

Taylor Instrument's floating dairy thermometer.

Floating Stainless Steel Cheese Thermometer — This gauge has a 9-inch stem capped with a 2-inch, glass-faced dial graduated from 0° to 220°F. The large dial makes it easy to read when you are using large pots of steaming milk and single-piece stainless construction makes it moisture-proof and impossible to sink accidentally.

Stainless Steel Stem Cheese Thermometer — A 12-inch stem is capped with a 2-inch dial scaled from 0° to 220°F. This instrument is watertight and the steel part virtually unbreakable. The thermometer is equipped with a pot clip and its long length makes it ideal for deep cheese pots.

Refrigeration Thermometer — It does double duty in the home dairy. Used to monitor curing cheeses and also to check freeze limits preparatory to hardening ice cream or making still-frozen ice cream, this unit hangs or stands on a shelf. The dial is graduated from −30° to 70°F. The case is aluminum and compact, 2¾ by 3½ inches.

Humidity Gauge or *Hygrometer* — Use this to check humidity in cheese curing chambers.

BUTTER CHURNS

Upright Churn — Made of red cedar staves locked by oak bands, it is less than 2 feet high and weighs under 15 pounds. The plunger/dasher is inserted through a hole in the round cover, which adds a little more than a foot to the overall height.

Crank Churn — Usually made of white pine, it can churn 5 quarts of cream. The paddle/dasher is easily removed for cleaning. The 12-by-15-inch churn weighs a little more than 10 pounds.

Crockery Churns — These include the traditional brown on white, of 9-quart capacity, and 2 sizes of blue and white stoneware churns, 12-quart and 20-quart. Although the stoneware churns are only 9 inches wide, they are heavy — up to 30 pounds. The churns take standard plunger-type dashers 36 inches long.

Glass Churns — They come with 1-, 3- and 5-gallon glass jars and are powered by electric motors; several hand-cranked types are available with glass or plastic jars. Additionally, extra and/or replacement jars are offered for all models. A leader in the field is the Alabama Manufacturing Co., Inc. with its Gem Dandy Line.

The Gem Dandy Standard Model is a 110 AC volt motor mounted on an aluminum jar cover which fits the company's 3- or 5-gallon jars. It also has 4 rubber-tipped support arms which will limit movement and vibration when mounted over containers with mouths larger than jars. The Standard has a detachable and adjustable aluminum shaft and dasher.

The Gem Dandy De Luxe has a vinyl-lined aluminum cover stepped and threaded to fit many container opening widths. The aluminum shaft and dasher are powered by a 115 AC volt motor designed for use with 3- and 5-gallon jars. These jars have handles and lids.

The Gem Dandy New De Luxe Jr. is sold with a 4-quart jar and will churn up to 3 quarts of cream. An aluminum shaft and dasher are detachable and adjustable and the motor is a heavy-duty 115 AC volt housed in chromed steel. Extra jars for this model have lids only, no handles.

YOGURT MAKERS

Yogurt-making tools are uncomplicated and very easy to use. Two of the most basic are the Yogotherm and the Solait Multi-Culture Non-Electric Cooker. One operates on the principle of the vacuum bottle, the other, insulation. The Yogotherm, a single container with a top, has a capacity of up to 2 quarts and is available in a choice of colors—red, white, avocado or gold. Both the Yogotherm and the Solait may be used for incubating other types of cultured foods and starters. The Solait, consisting of a 1-quart glass container which fits snugly into an insulated sleeve,

is usually sold in kit form with a dairy thermometer and freeze-dried yogurt starter culture. Additional Solait jars are available for those who like more than one batch of yogurt on hand. To operate, bring the container and the whole or skim milk to the correct inoculation temperature—this can be up from cold milk or down from pasteurization—pour it into the yogurt maker, add the culture of your choice and close the top. The yogurt will be done in 5 to 12 hours.

Electric yogurt makers are made by Salton in 1- and 2-quart models, both with 5 jars, and take 110 AC volt current. The yogurt makers are equipped with "time out" dials on clear plastic tops which indicate when the yogurt is done. The entire culturing process is controlled by a thermostat. These yogurt makers are sold with thermometer-spoons which test for correct temperature before spooning in the right quantity of culture. A similar yogurt maker made by Hamilton Beach is called The Culture Center. This unit has a "flavor guide" dial and thermometer mea-

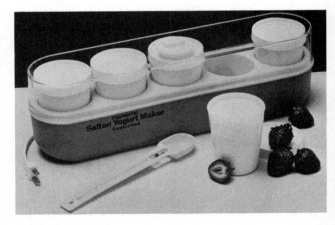

Salton Yogurt Maker.

suring spoon. The Culture Center has a capacity of 6 cups and it, too, can be used for other cultured products.

FARM CREAM SEPARATORS

The Westphalia Cream Separator has a cast iron body coated with oven-baked celluloid green paint. Parts which have direct contact with milk are coated twice with tin by the double-bath tin system. All rotating parts are balanced. This separator is available in 2 models (Model 85 and Model 140), each being able to process 85 and 140 liters per hour, respectively. The bowl capacity for the smaller model is 11 liters, while the larger bowl will hold 15 liters. Crank speeds are 75 and 70 rpm. This machine is shipped FOB from the Janesville, Wisconsin factory.

Very similar to the Westphalia, and also handled by the Schlueter Co., in Janesville, are the imported GAS 85 and GAS 140 hand-cranked separators which process 90 and 148 quarts of milk per hour, respectively.

Electric table models are French-made — the Elecrem No. 1, which processes 132 quarts of milk per hour, and the Elecrem No. 2, which processes 211 quarts per hour.

International Harvester built its last cream separator in 1957, but because of the many models built by the company in earlier years, many turn up at auctions or are sold privately.

Today's commercial "separator" — a giant cream centrifuge manufactured by Alfa-Laval.

MODELS OF INTERNATIONAL HARVESTER SEPARATORS

Courtesy of
International
Harvester

Model	Separating Capacity (pounds per hour)	RPM
Primrose (Built prior to 1939)	...	...
Model "S" Line Operator Manual No. 1004016R4 — $3.50 (Built 1939 to 1951)		
No. 2-S	500	60
No. 3-S	750	60
No. 4-S	1,000	48
No. 5-S	1,250	48
Model "F" Line Operator Manual No. 1009820R5 — $1.40 (Built 1951 to 1956)		
No. 3-F	750	48 to 60
No. 4-F	1,100	48 to 60
Model "G" Line Operator Manual No. 1009826R5 — $1.40 (Built 1955 to 1957)		
No. 3-G	750	48 to 60

International Harvester has never made reconditioned separators available, although some local IH dealerships rebuilt trade-in separators for sale. Some parts, such as bowl seal rings, are available from local IH dealers through the company's Parts Distribution Centers.

Manuals for the above models are available. To obtain the proper ordering form, #GF-39T, write to:

Customer Request
International Harvester Co.
Printing and Distribution Services
807 Blackhawk Drive
Westmont, IL 60559

RETINNING

The Tinning Company, also known as the New England Retinning Co., has long been associated with the New England dairy industry and are specialists in retinning dairy equipment, especially cream separators. Depending upon condition, a separator retinning job will take 3 or 4 weeks to complete. Send inquiries to:

> The Tinning Co.
> 69 Norman St.
> Everett, MA 02149
> Attn. John Correia
> Telephone 617-389-3400

BUTTER MOLDS, PADDLES AND WORKERS

The butter molds in greatest use are the rectangular wooden-plunger types of 1-pound capacity. These molds can make plain or illustrated butter prints by changing the face of the pressure plate. Another 1-pound brick mold is cast of aluminum and can also be used for shaping sausage and scrapple. Wood and aluminum also figure in the construction of round 1-pound molds and in butter paddles. When selecting a paddle for packing a particular mold, be sure the width of the edge is the same as the opening of the mold. If it is wider, you'll wind up smearing butter over the frame of the mold. Butter workers, or *Scotch hands*, are usually made of wood and the best have grooved faces for better grip when kneading freshly churned butter to remove trapped buttermilk.

BASIC CHEESE-MAKING NEEDS

Cheesecloth—Many "cheese" cloths are sold for straining and polishing but after you put the time and effort into making a good cheese, stay away from cloths with synthetic fibers and use proper butter muslin. You will find 2 grades: Coarse, a heavy-duty weave for draining curds, and Fine, a tightly woven cloth for lining cheese molds so that the curds won't drain away when you put on the pressure.

Skimmer—Safest to prevent tainting ripening milk from the moment of stirring in rennet to the moment of scooping out curds is the stainless steel skimmer with a long handle and large perforated skimming disc.

Cheese Kettles—Large pots are needed in cheese making. Ideally they should be made of stainless steel in order to be resistant to ripening milk acids and for ease in cleaning. One pot should fit snugly into another in the manner of a double boiler so that the milk is heated by water and never exposed to direct heat.

Colander—A stainless steel or acid-resistant plastic colander is perfect for draining curds.

Long-bladed Stainless Steel Knife—Select a knife that will reach to the bottom of your cheese kettle on those deep, oblique cuts, one that cuts cleanly and one which won't taint the curds as some carbon steels will.

Rennets—Cheese rennets of both animal and vegetable origin are usually sold in tablet form sealed in strips of 10 or 12. Liquid rennet is available through some home cheese equipment suppliers.

Starter Cultures—Cottage, Cream and Baker's Cheese culture is freeze-dried and packaged in foil envelopes. This culture can also be used for culturing buttermilk and sour cream. The yogurt, acidophilus yogurt and acidophilus cultures that contain the microorganisms needed to make yogurt of milk are sold in 2- and 3-gram envelopes. Specialty cultures include a goat yogurt microorganism developed in Europe especially for goats' milk, and kefir, the cultured milk drink of the Caucasus.

CHEESE PRESSES

French Coulommiers Mold—This type contains 2 3-by-4¼-inch hoops which lock together, a pair of ¾-by-6-inch square cheese boards and 2 cheese draining mats.

Trow Cheese Press—This press operates on the turned-screw principle and consists of a hardwood base and frame, a hardwood screw and a pair of different-size followers with a pair of plastic hoops whose diameters match the followers. The hoops will make cheese from 2 to 4 gal-

The Trow Cheese Press.

lons of milk curd. To operate the press, raise the screw, place a hoop on the base and fill it with curd. (Don't forget the cheesecloth liner.) Cover the curd with the follower and exert pressure by turning the screw.

Weighted-drive Cheese Press—This type of press is constructed of a maple base, pressure arm, dowel frame and driver, and a 3¾-inch follower. The pressure builds as bricks are stacked on the pressure arm. Common bricks weigh just under 5 pounds each so you can figure pressure roughly by simple addition. The follower is designed to pass through tin cans from 3⅞ inches to 4 inches in diameter. Avoid coffee cans and others with indented bands as the cheese under pressure will conform to the shape of the can and will be difficult to remove. Best are smooth-sided fruit and juice cans which have both ends cut out and small drain holes punched from inside out. If the holes are punched in reverse the sharp edges will snag on the cheesecloth. The operating procedure is similar to all presses: Place the can on the base, line with the cheesecloth and fill with the cooked curds. Position the follower on top of the curds, place the driver dowel over the follower and insert it into the pressure arm which has been dropped down over the dowel frame. Add bricks or other objects of known weight until the specified pressure is achieved.

Wheeler Cheese Press—English-made of hardwood and stainless steel, this press design is a bit unusual in that instead of weights, screws, hydraulics and levers, your hand is the source of pressure. The Wheeler includes a stainless steel hoop (large enough to make a 4-pound cheese) and a base drain tray which is crimped to form a whey drip channel. Stainless lock blocks which ride up and down stainless frame shafts lock the pressure bar against the follower at any pressure up to 50 pounds. In the event smaller cheeses are being made, the follower is built up with hardwood blocking. This press is equipped with a pressure gauge.

ICE CRUSHER

Cast of iron and crank-driven, the traditional ice crusher has been dressed up in bright enamel and tin and will deliver about 5 pounds of crushed ice every 4 minutes. The hopper will hold up to 8 average ice cubes or comparable pieces of cracked ice and due to its weight (just under 10 pounds) the crusher will not rock across your table when cranked.

ICE CREAM FREEZERS

Small in numbers, the manufacturers of home ice cream freezers produce a huge assortment of models and sizes. Freezers made by the Richmond Cedar Works and White Mountain Freezer, both churn-type makers, start at 2 quarts and go right up to the White Mountain KD-700, a unit capable of making 20 quarts of commercial "homemade style" ice cream every 20 minutes. Smaller ice cream makers include the Salton Ice Cream Machine and the French SEB, both with 1-gallon capacity and chilled in the freezer, and the Il Gelataio by Simac and the Italian Minigel Ice Cream Machine, both self-contained freezing units.

White Mountain Ice Cream Freezers — Those designed for the home have either cranks or electric motors and wooden or fiberglass tubs. The hand-cranked models feature "triple motion action," which

Nomenclature of Churn Freezers

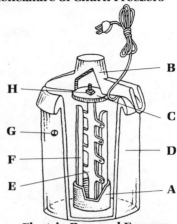

Electric-Powered Freezer

A	freezer can
B	motor
C	freezer-can cover
D	freezer tub
E	dasher
F	dasher paddle
G	drainage hole
H	freezer-can cover hole

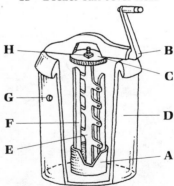

Hand-Cranked Freezer

A	freezer can
B	hand-crank gear
C	freezer-can cover
D	freezer tub
E	dasher
F	dasher paddle
G	drainage hole
H	freezer-can cover hole

means the crank turns one way, the freezing can another and the dashers a third. The gear housing and crank are cadmium-plated to inhibit rusting. The tubs are of maple-finished pine or avocado green fiberglass and the steel freezer can, iron mixer and all metal parts exposed to the ice cream mix are tin-plated. The self-adjusting dashers are of beechwood, which helps control ice crystals but cannot be used for sherbet slushes. Electric models operate on 115 AC or DC volt current. The motor is self-aligning and the motor housing is cream colored.

Richmond Cedar Works — These freezers also have crank and electric, salt and crushed-ice models with tubs made of wood or synthetic materials. The wooden tubs are naturally finished or are stained walnut with the staves held by chromed or brassed hoops. Synthetic tubs are of high-density polyethylene and are colored white or gold. The freezer cans are of

White Mountain ice cream freezers — electric and crank.

tinned steel with freezer can caps and dashers molded of plastic. The frames and motor housings are cast of rustproof thermoplastic and the motor housings mounted on plastic tubs are color-coordinated. The motor is 120 AC volts, 60 cycle, equipped with an automatic reset which guards against the machine running past a timed stop at the end of 20 to 30 minutes.

The Salton Ice Cream Machine— Here is a compact (8-by-8) single-quart-capacity freezer requiring no salt and crushed ice, just a freezer or a good, cold freezing compartment. To operate, fill the tinned steel can with an ice cream mix,

position the plastic dashers and close the plastic lid. The freezer can fits into a round white plastic base, and the top, which contains a 55 watt electric motor with top-mounted cooling fan, is in position over the can to drive the dashers. According to your preference, the top is available in vanilla, chocolate or strawberry coloring. From the point of loading, locking and putting the machine into the freezer, it operates automatically, finally shutting off when the ice cream reaches the correct texture. The power cord has a reinforced sleeve to protect it as it passes through the freezer door and the plug is grounded. Since a cord passes between

Salton Ice Cream Machine.

the door and frame of the freezer, the machine does not carry the UL seal. When you pick a wall outlet be sure it's grounded.

SEB of France — This is another freezing compartment ice cream maker, also with a single quart capacity. The unit is about the same width as the Salton but only half its height. The shallow profile is achieved by housing the motor in the center of the aluminum freezer can. The machine resembles a cake mold — the motor in the center driving the dashers around the edges, finally lifting automatically when the right texture is reached. The cap of the SEB is made of red plastic and, like the Salton, it disassembles for easy cleaning.

Speed of freezing favors the powerful Salton, about 20 minutes against more than an hour for the SEB, but the French machine is the space-saving winner.

Simac's *Il Gelataio* and the *Minigel Ice Cream Machine* — These are 2 other small-capacity ice cream makers. Both are modernistically crafted tabletop units with self-contained freezing systems and exposed chambers so you can watch the mix turn into ice cream. Controlled by switches and timers, both are automatic and do their work in around 20 minutes.

MOLDS AND SCOOPS

Ice cream molds are constructed of aluminum, tinned steel and plastic and come in a variety of sizes and shapes. There are the traditional bricks of Neopolitan fame, squares, melon- and beehive-shaped molds, as well as specialty forms for such things as many-tiered ice cream "cakes" or Spumoni molds for making 1-cup portions of that famous Italian dessert. There are also novelty molds cast as busts of famous men or copied from landmark buildings and terrain features. Salad and dessert gel molds also do extra duty as shapers of ice cream.

The same basic method of use applies to all. Chill the molds first and then fill them with frozen, but still workable, ice cream and return them to the freezer for hardening. Molds with rosetted crowns and novelty molds with etched features are sometimes first coated with a neutral vegetable oil or clarified butter to prevent sticking, but these substances can detract from the frozen art by causing a sticky sensation on the roof of your mouth. Although the art suffers a bit, a better way is to take a tip from the jello makers and dip the mold quickly into hot water, place the serving dish over the bottom and then promptly invert the whole thing. The disadvantage is that just a fraction of a second too long exposure to hot water will soften or erase some mold detail.

Ice cream scoops, dippers and spades are made of polished aluminum, stainless or chrome-plated steel and chrome-plated brass, all designed to reduce sticking. One manufacturer, the *Roll Dipper Co.*, features a line of dippers and spades with the handles filled with a permanently sealed defrosting fluid which keeps handles and dip warmer than the ice cream (and stick-free). While such a dipper, known as the Zeroll, and spade are of solid construction, others, such as the Atlas, have stainless steel bowls fitted with thumb-powered, spring-return scraper blades. The scraper is designed to cleanly slice a perfect ice cream ball or, with a different-shaped scoop, a conical mound, from the metal. Constructed of several stainless moving parts, the handles of the Atlas and other scraper models are of plastic or wood.

The Atlas, Zeroll and other makes are available in many sizes with most determined by the number of scoops it takes to empty a quart of ice cream. The Atlas models have capacities of 8, 10, 12, 16, 20, 24, 30 and 40 scoops per quart with each size color-coded at the butt of the grip, a blessing for the scooper at a busy soda fountain. Zeroll dippers come in 3 sizes, from 12 to 24 (1½-ounce, 2-ounce and 2½-ounce, respectively), according to the number of scoops it takes to finish off a quart. Roll Dipper's spade is almost 9 inches long and is the perfect tool for loading molds and storage containers since the warmed handle conducts heat to the cutting edge to neatly slice through the hardest ice cream.

Possibly the world's most versatile scooper is a West German balled-food server. Starting at 12 scoops per quart, this tool can gather up to 100 minute scoops per quart and at that range is far better suited for melon balls than ice cream. The scoop is brass coated with chrome and has a powerful stainless steel spring. It is different from other scraper scoops in the way it is powered — the handle is squeezed together to operate the scraper rather than a thumb-operated lever.

MILKSHAKE MAKERS AND BLENDERS

A milkshake machine designed for the home kitchen and featuring an enameled and stainless steel base and a 1-quart milkshake cup is manufactured by *Hamilton Beach*. However, more versatile in kitchen affairs than a shaker alone and perhaps a better choice, is the blender. These tools have capacities ranging from a quart up to the gallon of big commercial blenders, such as those made by *Waring*. Speeds accelerate from the fixed-bladed, single-speed blenders to 14-speed machines with a panel of push button controls. All will make good milkshakes.

Homemade Cheese Press

It's not hard to understand why so many home dairy cheeses are dried with home-crafted presses. These presses are simple and inexpensive to make and will work just as well as any of the few that are available commercially. Some, built of such things as scrap lumber, broom handles and stacks of bricks, lack the finesse of a gleaming stainless steel and polished wood English import. Others, adapted from materials and tools easily located—a cider press screw, a wood vise mounted on end or even a car jack—look a bit more professional, but all have one thing in common. They make cheese. Even where farm furnishings are sparse, a 2-by-4-inch lever weighted with a bucket of water to drive a follower (chain-sawed from a round log) into a curd-filled cookie tin will make cheese.

Driven by a pair of threaded rods, this press has a unique slatted hoop which looks more like a wine press basket than a form for cheese. Each slat is drilled through to accept 2 strands of stainless steel wire, and by adding or subtracting the number of slats and varying the diameter of the follower proportionately, you can make cheeses weighing from 2 to 20 pounds. The total cost of the material and hardware to make the press was around $15.

Materials

Note: The sizes listed for lumber are actual, not nominal, sizes.

1¾'' × 1¾'' × 9' hardwood
¾'' × 1½'' × 12' hardwood
¾'' × 12'' × 12'' hardwood
¾'' × 15'' hardwood dowel
2'' × 5'' hardwood round or ¾'' × 5'' × 1' hardwood
2'' × 10'' hardwood round or ¾'' × 10'' × 2' hardwood
6 1'' mushroom caps or 6 plugs

Hardware

1   ⁵⁄₁₆'' × 24'' threaded rod
8   ⁵⁄₁₆'' × 2½'' lag screws with hex heads
12 ⁵⁄₁₆'' flat washers
2   ⁵⁄₁₆'' wing nuts
2   ⁵⁄₁₆'' lock nuts
6' 20-gauge stainless steel wire

Tools

handsaw or circular saw
screwdriver
drill and bits
¾'' spade bit
1'' spade bit
½'' socket with driver
needle nose pliers
hacksaw
rattail file
sandpaper
carving tool

Steps

1. From the 1¾'' × 1¾'' hardwood, cut 2 pieces, each 16'' long, for the driver guide crossbeam and the pressure arm; 4 pieces, each 12'' long, 2 for the uprights and 2 for the base supports; and 2 pieces, each 12½'' long, for the base cross supports. From the ¾'' × 1½'' hardwood, cut 2 pieces, each 4½'' long, for the twisters; and 20 pieces, each 6'' long, for the hoop slats. From the hardwood dowel, cut 1 piece, 10'' long, for the long driver. The remaining 5'' piece of dowel is used as the short driver. The ¾'' × 12'' × 12'' hardwood is used as the base plate, and the hardwood rounds will be used as the followers, or presses. An alternative method of making the followers is given. Label all parts as you cut them.

2. On the driver guide crossbeam, mark positions for mounting holes, ⅞'' from each end and centered. On each end of each base support, make a position mark 3½'' from the end and centered. Turn the base supports a quarter turn, and make a third position mark on each, centered on the pieces. Be sure that, when drilled, this hole will be at a right angle to the other 2 holes, as shown in detail. With the 1'' spade bit, drill counterbore holes to

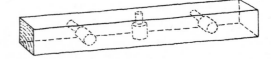

a depth of ½'' at all 8 marks. Complete the mounting holes with a ⁵⁄₁₆ '' bit.

3. Drill a ¾'' guide hole for the drivers in the center of the driver guide crossbeam. In the center of the pressure arm, drill a ¾'' blind driver-gripper hole, ¾'' deep. Be sure both of these holes are parallel to the holes already in the pieces.

4. Drill ⅜'' holes for the threaded rods, 4'' from each end and centered, in both the driver guide crossbeam and the pressure arm, parallel to the holes already in the pieces. These 2 pieces can be stacked and holes drilled through both at one time for more accurate alignment.

5. On both base cross supports and both uprights, mark diagonal lines from corner to corner on each end to find the exact center. Where the lines cross, drill ¼'' pilot holes in all 4 pieces.

6. Mark diagonal lines from corner to corner on one side of each of the twisters and drill a ⁵⁄₁₆ '' hole where the lines cross.

7. Drill 2 ⅛'' holes through each of the hoop slats, 1½'' from each end and centered on the ¾'' side of the slat.

8. If you are making the followers from hardwood rounds (2'' slices cut off hardwood logs), first debark the rounds, then file and sand them to bring them to the correct diameters of

Figure 1 **Homemade Cheese Press**

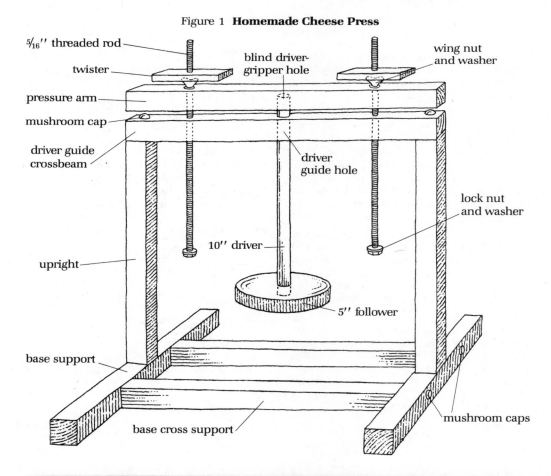

⁵⁄₁₆ '' threaded rod

twister

pressure arm

mushroom cap

driver guide crossbeam

upright

base support

blind driver-gripper hole

driver guide hole

10'' driver

5'' follower

base cross support

wing nut and washer

lock nut and washer

mushroom caps

5″ and 10″. An alternative method is to cut 2 5″-diameter pieces from the ¾″ × 5″ × 1′ hardwood and 2 10″-diameter pieces from the ¾″ × 10″ × 2′ hardwood. Glue the 5″ pieces together with their grains perpendicular to each other, using a water-resistant glue that is safe for contact with food. Repeat with the 10″ pieces. Drill a ¾″ blind hole ¾″ deep in the center of each follower.

9. Assemble the press frame as shown in figure 1, using 2½″ lag screws and flat washers. First, fasten the uprights to the base supports, aligning the pilot holes in the uprights with the mounting holes in the centers of the base supports. Then place the base cross supports between the base support/upright assemblies, again aligning the pilot holes with the mounting holes, and fasten. Next, fasten the driver guide crossbeam on top of the uprights, aligning the pilot and mounting holes. Tighten all 8 lag screws into the counterbored holes with a ½″ socket and driver. Sand the assembly, then cover the 6 exposed lag screw heads with mushroom caps or plugs.

10. Enlarge the guide hole in the driver guide crossbeam slightly with a rattail file and sandpaper, so the drivers can slide through without binding. Pass one of the drivers through the driver guide crossbeam and fit it into the hole in one of the followers. The long driver should be combined with the 5″ follower to make small cheeses and the short driver with the 10″ follower for larger cheeses.

11. Press the blind driver-gripper hole in the center of the pressure arm down onto the free end of the driver, resting the pressure arm on top of the driver guide crossbeam. Friction should hold the driver and follower in place; if not, support them temporarily with scrap wood.

12. Cut the threaded rod into 2 12″ pieces. Put the rods through the holes on the pressure arm and down through the driver guide crossbeam. On the upper end of each rod, place first a washer, then a wing nut. On the lower end, place first a washer, then a lock nut.

13. Thread the twisters down on the rods so that they rest squarely on the wing nuts, with the wing nuts centered lengthwise under the twisters. Tap the twisters lightly so that the wood bears a slight impression of the wings, then remove the twisters from the rods. Using a ⅛″ bit and a carving tool, cut a groove to cradle the wings, ⅛″ wide, ⅜″ long, and ½″ deep, following the impression on either side of the hole. Replace the twisters on the rods with the groove down to fit over the wings. The twisters will make it easier to turn the wing nuts when you want to apply a lot of pressure.

14. To assemble the hoop, cut the stainless steel wire into 2 3′-long pieces. With needle nose pliers, shape a twisted eye in one end of each piece, and string the slats together, using a follower as a form. To fit the 5″ follower, you

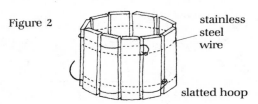

Figure 2   stainless steel wire

slatted hoop

will need 10 slats; when you want to use the 10″ follower, add the other 10 slats. When the hoop is completed, run the ends of the wire through the eyes in the other ends, then back between several slats to lock them in place. Keep the free ends of the wire outside the hoop to prevent tearing the cheesecloth.

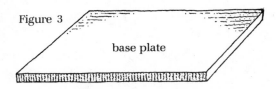

Figure 3   base plate

15. Place the base plate on the base cross supports and the hoop (with a pan beneath it to catch runoff) on top of the base plate, with the follower hanging into it. Your cheese press is now ready to use.

Appendix

SOURCES OF INFORMATION, SUPPLIES AND EQUIPMENT

BOOKS

The Dairy Cookbook, Olga Nickles (Celestial Arts, Millbrae, Calif., 1976).

Fact Book on Yogurt, Kefir and Other Milk Cultures, Beatrice Trum Hunter (Keats Publishing Co., New Canaan, Conn., 1973).

The Yogurt Gourmet, Anne Lanigan (Quick Fox, New York, 1978).

Cheese and Fermented Milk Foods, Frank V. Kosikowski (Box 139, Brooktondale, NY 14817; 1978).

Cheese Making at Home, Don Radke (Doubleday and Co., Garden City, N.Y., 1974).

Cheese Varieties and Descriptions, USDA Agricultural Handbook No. 54.

Kitchen Cheesemaking, Lue Dean Flake, Jr. (Stackpole Books, Harrisburg, Pa., n.d.).

Making Cheeses at Home, Susan Ogilvy (Crown Publishers, New York, 1976).

The Complete Book of Homemade Ice Cream, Milk Sherbert and Sherbert, Carolyn Anderson (Saturday Review Press, New York, 1972).

Frozen Delights, Easy-to-Make in Your Refrigerator-Freezer, Diana Collier and Nancy Goff (T. Y. Crowell, New York, 1976).

The Great American Ice Cream Book, Paul Dickson (Atheneum Press, New York, 1972).

The Old Fashioned Homemade Ice Cream Cookbook, Joyce and Christopher W. Dueker (Bobbs-Merrill Co., Indianapolis, Ind., 1974).

PERIODICALS

The Cheese Press Newsletter, New England Cheesemaking Supply Co., Box 85, Ashfield, MA 01330.

The Dairy Council Digest, National Dairy Council, 6300 N. River Road, Rosemont, IL 60018.

The Dairy Goat Journal, Box 1808, Scottsdale, AZ 85252.

Journal of Dairy Research, National Institute for Research in Dairying, 32 E. 57th Street, New York, NY 10022.

Journal of Dairy Science, American Dairy Science Association, 309 W. Clark Street, Champaign, IL 61820.

COURSES AND WORKSHOPS

Check with your state university and extension service for specialized courses in making dairy products; both Cornell University in New York State and the University of Wisconsin offer courses in various dairy products. The University of Guelph in Ontario, Canada, offers specialized and intensive dairy products courses in cheese making, ice cream, bulk milk handling, and other dairy-related subjects. Write to:

Department of Food Science
University of Guelph
Guelph, Ontario N1G 2W1

In the Northeast, cheese-making workshops are given frequently by Bob and Ricki Carroll. Contact:

New England Cheesemaking Supply Company
Box 85
Ashfield, MA 01330

A correspondence course in dairy goats is offered by Pennsylvania State University, and by the University of Guelph, Ontario. Write to:

Dairy Goats, Course 105
Correspondence Courses
202 Agricultural Education Building
Pennsylvania State University
University Park, PA 16802

University School of Continuing Education
University of Guelph
Guelph, Ontario N1G 2W1

GENERAL HOME DAIRY AND CHEESE-MAKING SUPPLIERS

You are apt to find anything from dairy thermometers to stainless steel goat milk pails through these suppliers. Some are more specialized than others. Study the catalogs carefully and compare prices and quality before you buy.

American Supply House
Box 1114
Columbia, MO 65205
—goat dairy supplies

C. H. Dana Company
Hyde Park, VT 05655
.—farm and ranch supplies

The Coburn Company
Box 147
Whitewater, WI 53190
—dairying equipment

Countryside General Store
103 N. Monroe Street
Waterloo, WI 53594
—home dairy, cheese-making, ice cream supplies; pasteurizers; separators

Cumberland General Store
Rt. #3
Crossville, TN 38555
—home dairy supplies

Hoegger Supply Company
Box 331
Fayetteville, GA 30214
—goat dairy supplies

Homecraft
111 Stratford Center
Winston-Salem, NC 27104
—cheese-making supplies

Nasco Farm and Ranch
901 Janesville Avenue
Fort Atkinson, WI 53538
—dairy supplies and books

New England Cheesemaking Supply Company
Box 85
Ashfield, MA 01330
—cheese-making supplies, presses, books, cultures

The Schlueter Company
112 E. Centerway
Janesville, WI 53545
—home dairy equipment, separators, pasteurizers, pails, tanks, etc.

Top Line Corporation
Box 264
Bradford, PA 16701
—tote pails, strip cups, etc.

CULTURES AND RENNET

The major corporations that produce dairy products starter cultures, such as the Dairy Laboratories, Chris Hansen's, Marschall Dairy Laboratory, and many others, prefer to sell large amounts in bulk rather than fill individual orders. However, general dairy suppliers, cheese-making supply stores and some health food stores usually carry good lines of cultures from the manufacturers. Here are several sources.

American Supply House
Box 1114
Columbia, MO 65205

Countryside General Store
103 N. Monroe
Waterloo, WI 53594

Hamilton R & R Sales
319 S. Broadway
New Ulm, NM 56073

New England Cheesemaking Supply
Company
Box 85
Ashfield, MA 01330

Walnut Acres
Penns Creek, PA 17862

ICE CREAM MAKERS AND MOLDS

Many gourmet food shops carry fancy ice cream molds and imported ice cream machines. There are many listings of ice cream equipment in *The Cooks' Catalog*, ed. James Beard et al., Avon Books, New York, 1975.

Molds, milkshake machines, sherbet makers and much else available from:

Williams-Sonoma, *Catalog for Cooks*
Mail Order Department
Box 3792
San Francisco, CA 94119

Molds in the shapes of presidents' heads, the Eiffel Tower, Mt. Everest and other fascinating shapes are available from:

Fr. Krauss' Sons
Eighth Street
Milford, PA 18337

Special scoops come from:

Bloomfield Industries, Inc.
4586 West 47th Street
Chicago, IL 60632

Roll Dipper Company
207 Conrad Street
Maumee, OH 43537

Ice cream making machines are manufactured by the following:

Richmond Cedar Works Manufacturing Corporation
400 Bridge Street
Danville, VA 24541

Salton, Inc.
1260 Zerega Avenue
Bronx, NY 10462

SEB of France
521 Fifth Avenue
New York, NY 10175

White Mountain Freezer Inc.
Lincoln Avenue
Winchendon, MA 01475

Dairy thermometers are standard items at most dairy supply houses, but you may wish to write for the name of the supplier nearest you from these manufacturers:

H. B. Instrument Company
4303 N. American Street
Philadelphia, PA 19140

Taylor Instrument Company
Consumer Products Division
Arden, NC 28704

Butter churns are carried by many of the general suppliers of home dairy equipment listed above, but a small electric churn is made by:

The Alabama Manufacturing
   Company, Inc.
900-T Alton Parkway
Box 384
Alton, AL 35015

Separators are also carried by the general dairy suppliers listed, usually the Westphalia Cream Separator manufactured in Janesville, Wisconsin.

Dairy cleansers and sterilizing solutions are available from the farm and ranch suppliers listed above. Popular are:

IOSAN, a detergent germicide made
   by:
West Agro Chemical Inc.
Shawnee Mission, KA 66222

and

MON-O-DINE, made by:
H. B. Fuller Monarch
3900 Jackson Street N.E.
Minneapolis, MN 55421

Stainless steel equipment and plastic food-grade tanks and containers are available from the following:

Bel-Art Products
Pequannock, NJ 07440

Industrial Safety & Security
   Company
1390 Neubrecht Road
Lima, OH 45801

Terris Quality Control Equipment
807 Summerfield Avenue
Asbury Park, NJ 07712

United Utensils Company, Inc.
Box 710
Yennicook Avenue
Port Chester, NY 10573

Index

C

E

F

Z